'PAX BRITANNICA'?

STUDIES IN MODERN HISTORY

General editors: *John Morrill and David Cannadine*

This series, intended primarily for students, will tackle significant historical issues in concise volumes which are both stimulating and scholarly. The authors combine a broad approach, explaining the current state of our knowledge in the area, with their own research and judgements; and the topics chosen range widely in subject, period and place.

Titles already published

'PAX BRITANNICA'?
British Foreign Policy
1789–1914

Muriel E. Chamberlain

LONGMAN
London and New York

LONGMAN GROUP UK LIMITED,
Longman House, Burnt Mill, Harlow,
Essex CM20 2JE, England
and Associated Companies throughout the world.

Published in the United States of America
by Longman Inc., New York

© Longman Group UK Limited 1988

First published 1988

BRITISH LIBRARY CATALOGUING IN PUBLICATION DATA
Chamberlain, M. E. 'Pax Britannica'?
  British foreign policy, 1789–1914.—
  (Studies in modern history).
  1. Great Britain——Foreign relations—
  19th century
  I. Title   II. Series
  327.41   DA530
  ISBN 0–582–49442–7

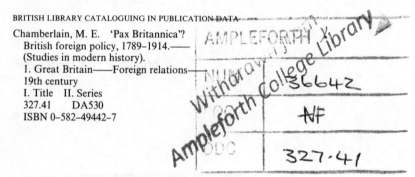

LIBRARY OF CONGRESS CATALOGING-IN-PUBLICATION DATA
Chamberlain, Muriel Evelyn.
  'Pax Britannica'? British foreign policy,
  1789–1914/Muriel Chamberlain.
    p.   cm. —— (Studies in modern history)
  Bibliography: p.
  Includes index.
  ISBN 0–582–03079–X
  ISBN 0–582–49442–7 (pbk.)
  1. Great Britain——Foreign relations——19th century. 2. Great
Britain——Foreign relations——1789–1820. 3. Great Britain——Foreign relations——
1901–1936. I. Title. II. Series: Studies in modern history (Longman (Firm))
DA530.C46 1988
327.41'009——dc 19   87–34182   CIP

ISBN 0-582-03079-X CSD

ISBN 0-582-49442-7 PPR

Set in 10/11pt Times Comp/Edit 6400

Produced by Longman Singapore Publishers (Pte) Ltd.
Printed in Singapore

CONTENTS

LIST OF MAPS

LIST OF ABBREVIATIONS

AP	Aberdeen Papers
BD	*British Documents on the Origins of the War* (eds G. P. Gooch and H. M. V. Temperley), 1926–36
BFSP	*British and Foreign State Papers*
BP	Broadlands (i.e. Palmerston) Papers
CHBFP	*Cambridge History of British Foreign Policy* (eds A. Ward and G. P. Gooch), 3 vols, 1920–23
DP	Disraeli (formerly Hughenden) Papers
GP	Grey Papers
Hansard	Parliamentary Debates; 3 series
HH M3	Hatfield House MSS: 3rd Marquess of Salisbury
LQV	Letters of Queen Victoria
NP	Northbrook Papers
PP	*Parliamentary Papers*
QR	*Quarterly Review*
RP	Rosebery Papers

LIST OF ABBREVIATIONS

Introduction

THE MYTHS OF BRITISH FOREIGN POLICY*

THE IMPORTANCE OF FOREIGN POLICY

Between the two World Wars diplomatic history replaced constitutional history as the flagship of historical investigation, at once the most important, the most exact and the most sophisticated of historical studies. After the Second World War, it looked for a time as if the ship had sunk without trace. New kinds of history, social history in particular, seemed set to replace it. What had caused the wreck?

The study of diplomatic history had not fulfilled its early promise. It had not enabled men to understand the international system so well that they could avert a further catastrophe – and that hope had been a very real spur to the minute investigation which had been undertaken in the 1920s and 1930s. A generation which had endured the horrors of four years' trench warfare and the terrible loss of young lives involved, gave a high priority to trying to prevent a repetition. But, in an age of nuclear deterrence, a proper understanding of foreign policy is still obviously as vital to national survival as ever. It is not the study of foreign policy which is redundant. But it is probably true that the particular type of study which dominated the inter-war period had reached its natural limits.

When war broke out in Europe in the summer of 1914, all the main combatants rushed to publish extracts from their archives to prove that each and every one of them was the innocent victim of other countries' aggression. The Germans published their White Book first, closely followed by the British Blue Book – the names derived simply from the traditional colours of the covers – and later by the yellow, red and orange books of France, Austria and Russia respectively. It was soon clear that they could not all be telling the truth.

---

* Some of this chapter has appeared, in a rather different form, in *History Today* July 1985: 43–8.

The 'battle of the coloured books', as it was called, was only the first skirmish in what was to be a long war of attrition on the question of who was responsible for the catastrophe. This was partly because the First World War became a propaganda war on a scale unknown since the wars of religion. To persuade civilian populations to accept the hardships of total war it was necessary to convince them that they were not fighting simply for national advantages but were waging a righteous war against evil men. The reparations issue prolonged the need to portray Germany not just as the defeated nation, but as the convicted nation which had unscrupulously broken international law. A reaction was inevitable and 'revisionist' historians, both German and American, began to argue that the war had not been due to the perfidy of any one nation but to the whole system – militarism, the arms race, secret diplomacy or the alliance system itself.

When the war ended, the pre-war governments had been overthrown in Germany, Austria and Russia and their archives were open to the critical eyes of their successors. Once again the Germans were the first off the mark. They began the publication of the fifty-four volumes of their *Die Grosse Politik der Europäischen Kabinette*, covering the whole period from the formation of the German Empire in 1871 to 1914. The publication was complete by 1926. The British replied more modestly with the twelve volumes of their *British Documents on the Origins of the War*, covering the period 1898–1914. They showed – as would have been true of most British Blue Books of the period – that the publication of August 1914 was truthful but selective.

Although Britain had not been overtaken by revolution, there had been strenuous criticism of Britain's pre-war policy and there was little inclination to try to conceal the facts. The publication of the *British Documents* was authorised by Ramsay MacDonald's first Labour government but quickly confirmed by the incoming Conservative Foreign Secretary, Austen Chamberlain. The two men to whom the task was entrusted, Professor H. W. V. Temperley, a professional historian, and Dr G. P. Gooch, a radical critic of British policy before 1914, were regarded as a sufficient guarantee of the impartiality of the publication. In fact, since the archives have become available for general study, it has become clear that Gooch and Temperley were both frank and judicious in their selection – but a selection it inevitably remained.

The appearance of these volumes naturally whetted the appetite of scholars for further information from the archives. There were problems. Gooch and Temperley had had a special dispensation to study the recent past but the generality of scholars were still bound by the rule which kept official records closed to the public for fifty years – only amended in the 1960s to thirty years.

One of the attractions of diplomatic archives was that they tended to be fuller and more complete than domestic records. Instructions had to be sent to ambassadors; ambassadors had to report back to their governments; frequently accounts could be checked against each other. Often there would be two accounts of an interview, that of the ambassador and that of the Foreign Secretary of the other power. The chances of getting at the truth seemed to be high and some magisterial work was undoubtedly done between the wars, notably Professor Temperley's studies of George Canning and of the Eastern Question and Professor Webster's studies of Castlereagh and Palmerston. One snag was that historians were so delighted by the riches of the official archives that they were in some danger of becoming obsessed by them. To many readers history from the archives could come to seem a rather inhuman game of chess, fascinating if you liked chess of this kind, very dull if you did not.

History from the archives, what is sometimes now called the 'high politics' approach, still has its distinguished practitioners and strenuous defenders. Some recent writers (e.g. Martel 1986: 252–3) would argue that it is indeed possible to understand all we need to know of British foreign policy by a study at this level. The same approach is adopted by Zara Steiner in her *Britain and the Origins of the First World War* (1977). (For further discussion see below p. 174.) The assumption is that we are dealing with rational men, making free decisions on the basis of the evidence which is set out in the documents. Up to a point this is true and it is preferable to the crude determinism which suggests that all politicians are mere puppets of blind forces, economic or otherwise.

Nevertheless, the present author believes that greater depth can be achieved by asking searching questions about the inter-relationship of domestic and foreign policy. This is a line of enquiry which has gone much further in Germany than it yet has in Britain but it is an area where the new insights of social and economic history, which have advanced so much since the Second World War, can illuminate great tracts of diplomatic history.

So far only some periods have been analysed in any detail from this point of view. One is the period of the French revolutionary and Napoleonic wars. Studies such as J. E. Cookson's *The Friends of Peace: Anti-war Liberalism in England, 1793–1815* (1982), A. Goodwin's *The Friends of Liberty: the English Democratic Movement in the Age of the French Revolution* (1979) and Roger Wells's *Insurrection: the British Experience, 1795–1803* (1983) all probe the complex relationship between events on the continent, the tensions within British society and the government's attempts to fend off what it saw as the enemy both within and without.

The other period where some investigation has been undertaken is that of the so-called 'new imperialism' of the late nineteenth century, which saw a sudden massive increase in the size of the British empire. There is nothing on the scale of H.-U. Wehler's *Bismarck und der Imperialismus* (1969) in which he argued that Germany's imperial activities were all directed towards maintaining stability at home. But there is an outstanding elucidation of the intermeshing of foreign and domestic politics in Marvin Swartz's *The Politics of British Foreign Policy in the Era of Disraeli and Gladstone* (1985). Paul Kennedy also tries to knit together foreign and domestic pressures in his *The Rise of the Anglo-German Antagonism, 1860-1914* (1980). The simplest form of this explanation is that governments under pressure look to foreign successes to unite their countries and distract attention from domestic grievances and this makes its appearance in Freda Harcourt's explanation of Disraeli's intervention in Abyssinia in 1868 (1980). A much more general and far-reaching attempt to relate developments at home to foreign policy and more especially British expansion overseas is that of Peter Cain and A. G. Hopkins (1980, 1986, 1987) who argue that overseas expansion between 1750 and 1914 can best be explained by 'linking it with the process of modernisation in Britain' (1980: 489) and that 'explanations of imperialism ought to begin with a close study of economic structure and change in Britain' (1987: 17).

THE MYTHS OF BRITISH FOREIGN POLICY

The genesis of modern British diplomatic history meant that there was a natural tendency to see all studies leading up to the great climax of the First World War. The end of the Napoleonic wars had a particular attraction for students, not least because comparisons could be made with the Versailles Settlement of 1919. It chanced that one of the most influential diplomatic historians of the inter-war period, Professor (later Sir) Charles Webster, had been seconded as an adviser to the Paris Peace Conference of 1918-19 and specifically charged with the task of looking up the precedents of the earlier conference at Vienna in 1814-15. His researches were subsequently published as *The Congress of Vienna, 1814-1815* (1934). All this helped to create an impression of a self-contained period running from 1815-1914.

As a result it is still customary to begin a study of this kind in 1815 with an analysis of the Vienna Settlement. The nineteenth century then becomes the story of the undoing of the Vienna Settlement. One fallacy implicit in this was apparent to Lord Salisbury in 1862, although it has been less so to later historians. Vienna was not a new beginning. It was a staging post along the way. As Salisbury put it, 'Its [the Congress's] proceedings were only one stage in a great work, by the past of which it was already pledged, and to whose future permanence it was bound to look.' (*QR* 1862: vol. III, 215.) Salisbury was referring particularly to the engagements entered into during the Napoleonic wars – an important and often forgotten point – but his argument can be understood in a wider context as well.

Most of the great issues which determined British foreign policy in the nineteenth century began in the eighteenth. The loss of the American Colonies encouraged British trading and strategic interests to turn to Asia, and especially to India (see below pp. 22–3). The defence of India was omnipresent in nineteenth-century British foreign policy. Russia, under Catherine the Great, began a new advance against the Turks and so confronted Europe with the Eastern Question – the problem of what was to replace the Ottoman empire when it finally collapsed. The Eastern Question not only dominated much of nineteenth-century diplomacy but was also, arguably, the immediate cause of the First World War. The French Revolution and the wars which followed it reshaped not only the geography of Europe but also its political and intellectual framework. Even more fundamental from Britain's point of view were those momentous economic changes taking place at home, which are still most conveniently, if rather loosely, called the industrial and agricultural revolutions, which altered not only the structure of British society but her relations with the rest of the world. It was with these changes and the challenges which they implied that nineteenth-century British Foreign Secretaries were wrestling, sometimes consciously, sometimes rather blindly.

Many myths grew up about the Vienna Settlement. It is remarkable that, although the Whig interpretation of history has been minutely examined and drastically modified in our understanding of British domestic history, whole chunks of it survive, virtually unexamined, in our understanding of British foreign policy. It is true that most serious studies would not today regard the Vienna Settlement as simply an attempt to set the clock back, still less as an ideological attempt to restore 'legitimacy' in every case. But it is still seen as a reaffirmation of the old order by men who were very limited in their perceptions (*cf.* Webster 1934: 164–6). It therefore followed not only that the history of the nineteenth century was the undoing of that settlement but its necessary and inevitable undoing by the new forces of liberalism and nationalism. Those British Foreign Secretaries, such as George Canning or Lord Palmerston, who most clearly perceived those forces and consistently sided with them, are the natural heroes. Their opponents, Lord Castlereagh, the Duke of Wellington or Lord Aberdeen, who had doubts about this simple scenario, were at best blind and, at worst, malevolent.

It is not intended to argue in this book that there is no truth in the Whig interpretation of British foreign policy. Cautiously used, it may still be a useful tool. But, once a detailed examination is undertaken, problems appear. It presupposes that there were clearly identifiable liberal and constitutional causes in Europe from Poland to Portugal, which were bound to triumph in the end. It did not look like that to British politicians at the time. It was often as hard to tell the 'goodies' from the 'baddies', or even to identify those who really had the support of the majority of their countrymen, as it is in Central America today. Even Canning at first thought the radicals in Portugal, whom he eventually supported, 'fierce, rascally, thieving, ignorant ragamuffins', who hated England (Hinde 1973: 376). It was perfectly possible for honest men of goodwill to hold different opinions on whether the kings of Piedmont–Sardinia were national heroes, trying to unite Italy (which the ordinary Italians may or not have wanted) or ambitious petty princelings, trying to acquire other people's territory a sliver at a time. Nor did even the most 'liberal' British Foreign Secretaries support such movements, if they seemed contrary to British national interests.

The Whig belief in the existence of 'good' liberal causes, which enjoyed British patronage, is the starting point for a whole range of myths. The century from 1815 to 1914 is seen as a self-contained unit, which was at once unique and the norm, in Britain's relations with the outside world. The underlying belief was that Britain was indeed in the immortal words of Sellar and Yeatman (1930), 'top nation', at least until 1918 when the title passed to the United States and history, as the British understood it, came to a full stop. 1066 and All That was a satire but, like all successful satires, it was based on astringent truth. The British public did believe that Britain held a unique position in the world and when the gap between the myth and the reality became all too apparent in the twentieth century, a period of disillusionment and bewilderment set in. Whereas most early twentieth century studies of British foreign (and imperial) policy centred on the rise of Britain to the status of a world power, the books now being published are more likely to ask such questions as – when did Britain's decline begin? – or – could it have been avoided?

Some of these questions are based on false premises. The term 'world power' is itself ambiguous. Britain was a world power, in the sense of having world-wide interests, from the eighteenth century onwards, while some of the other European Great Powers were much more purely continental powers, but the term 'world power' easily slides into the modern meaning of 'super power'. Britain was never that in her relations with the other Great Powers.

The half-conscious belief that she was is itself part of the Whig belief that other Powers deferred to Britain. There were, of course, always Anglophiles from Montesquieu onwards, who admired British institutions and commended them to their countrymen, but the feeling was nothing like so universal as complacent Englishmen liked to suppose. When Palmerston preached to the Austrians in 1848–49 on their conduct in Italy, there were Austrians who were not slow to remind him that British actions in Ireland or the Ionian Islands had been scarcely better – or different. The belief in the benevolence of British influence was transferred towards the end of the period under discussion from Europe to the empire. There were many who sought the moral justification for Britain's imperial policy in the belief that British rule spread liberal, constitutional government throughout the world. One of imperialism's severest critics, J. A. Hobson, made short work of this in 1902 when he argued, 'Not five per cent of the population of our Empire are possessed of any appreciable portion of the political and civil liberties which are the basis of British civilisation.' (1938 edn: 116.) He went further and believed that the need to govern the empire in an authoritarian manner would, in the end, destroy British liberty at home.

But, despite dissenting voices, the British public liked to believe both in British benevolence and in British power. The very characteristic image that the British had of themselves began to take shape in the eighteenth century but it received considerable reinforcement during the Napoleonic Wars. British public opinion believed at the time, and nineteenth-century historians continued to tell their countrymen, that it was Britain who defeated Napoleon. The virtual omission of the role of Blücher and the Prussian army at the battle of Waterloo from many text books was only one example – although a striking one – of the kind of distortion which was common. Britain played her part. Her financial subsidies to her allies were important – although the strain they imposed on the British economy has only become a subject of study in recent times. Her navy swept the French from the seas but her insistence on her own interpretation of 'maritime rights' offended her allies almost as much as the French, and Napoleon's Continental System and the British blockade had such dire effects on the British economy that they brought Britain herself close to revolution in 1812. Wellington's campaigns in the Iberian Peninsula, on which British eyes were fixed, did pin down large numbers of French troops but the crucial battles of 1813–14 were fought in Central Europe by the armies of Russia, Prussia and Austria, and Britain took no part. It was the diplomatic skills of Castlereagh, rather than any military strength, which allowed Britain's voice to be heard to some effect in Vienna.

From 1815 to 1871 Britain's role in the settlement of European affairs was often peripheral. Only occasionally, as over Belgium or Portugal, when immediate British interests were considered to be at risk, did Britain become deeply involved. Her voice was not decisive in the settlement of Greece, or of Italy, or of Germany. Equally she played little real part in the great revolutionary upheavals of 1848–49. This was not the image which Englishmen cherished of their role in the world. They believed, as they had in 1815, that Britain could give the law to the world both materially and morally. The man who told them so repeatedly and frequently was Henry John Temple, third Viscount Palmerston. As a young man, Palmerston was an indifferent speaker and publicist but in the 1840s he seems to have stumbled on the secret of how to rouse his countrymen to patriotic fervour and, incidentally, win public support for himself. Sometimes, of course, he paid the price of his success, as when he lost office in 1858 because he was judged to have been too subservient in agreeing to Napoleon III's demands that he should change British law to prevent what would today be called terrorists from finding asylum in Britain.

The heirs of the Palmerstonian tradition were, in their different ways, Benjamin Disraeli and Joseph Chamberlain. Palmerstonian bluster passed easily into imperialist fervour in the late nineteenth century. The idea that British policy dominated Europe began to look a little unconvincing even to the most patriotic after the unification of Italy and Germany and the rise of Otto von Bismarck. The transition of attitude was easily made. British power was now turned outwards towards her empire and her chosen stance in Europe was that of 'splendid isolation'. Scholars today would not accept that isolation was ever Britain's preferred position (see Howard 1967). If it had been, there could be no greater irony than the fact that Britain's decline can realistically be dated – although this is more apparent with hindsight than it was at the time – from the First World War which, despite its name, was essentially a great war about the balance of power in Europe.

THE FACTORS IN FOREIGN POLICY

One problem about writing a history of British foreign policy in the nineteenth century is that the basic assumptions upon which it was based are almost never discussed by those who made it. They seldom spelled them out in Parliament and very, very rarely analysed them in letters or despatches. A comparison between the British and French records is revealing. Because French governments changed so frequently under the Third Republic, it is not uncommon to find analyses of the principles upon which policy was being conducted, usually drawn up by permanent officials for the information of the incoming ministers. There is nothing comparable in the British records. British ministries were comparatively long-lasting and the most that would happen was that the outgoing Foreign Secretary would give his successor a verbal briefing on the matters immediately under discussion.

In any case everyone assumed that everyone else knew the underlying principles. Some things were, of course, fixed, notably Britain's geopolitical position. The Age of Discovery had shifted the balance of power in Europe from the centre to the Atlantic littoral. Trade, and with it economic power, came to be dominated by shipping and shipping routes rather than, as formerly, by land routes. Britain, which already had a fishing and maritime trading tradition, was ideally suited to take advantage of this shift (see Kennedy 1983: 13–35).

The importance of the Royal Navy to British policy throughout the nineteenth century can hardly be over-stressed. It has been well analysed by Paul Kennedy in his *The Rise and Fall of British Naval Mastery* (1983) and by Bernard Semmel in his *Liberalism and Naval Strategy* (1986).

Both British governments and the British public were well aware how dependent their security was upon a strong navy. Hence their concern at the beginning of the century for 'maritime rights' and their hostility at the end of the century to German naval development. The British navy, they argued, could never threaten a land power like Germany but the German navy, backed by a strong army, could not but be a threat to Britain.

The British always distrusted armies. A large standing army was unBritish. It could be used to bolster up despotism and threaten civil liberties in a way in which the navy never could. In 1882 the Liberal government of William Gladstone found it psychologically quite impossible to believe that the rebellious Egyptian army might represent a genuine nationalist movement (see below pp. 141–2). In some ways the British deceived themselves. They did have a large standing army on call in India and occasionally they used it – as in the Egyptian campaign of 1882, or as they were to do in the First World War. But most British wars in the nineteenth century were of the remote colonial kind which Byron Farwell (1973) accurately describes as 'Queen Victoria's little wars'. During the long period of the so-called 'Pax Britannica', there was scarcely a year when the British army was not fighting somewhere. But these wars represented no real threat to the homeland.

When Britain did become involved in a major European war, as in the Crimean War of 1854–56, the years of neglect became all too apparent. The British showed plenty of gallantry in the Crimea but most of the efficient fighting was done by their allies, the French. Naturally, the government of the day got the blame but the chaotic and rundown condition of the army was the result of the actions – or inaction – of every government since the close of the Napoleonic Wars. Britain was only saved from a similar fate in 1914 because the mounting tensions in Europe had finally compelled her to reform and professionalise her army. Ironically, those reforms had been carried through largely by Liberal governments, beginning with Cardwell's reforms under Gladstone's first government of 1868–74 and completed by Haldane after 1906, as Britain tried to assimilate the lessons of the Franco-Prussian war of 1870–71 and the Boer War of 1899–1902. But, however much of an élite force the British army was now becoming, it remained small. If the Kaiser ever made use of the phrase which gave rise to the proud nickname of the 'Old Contemptibles', it seems likely that what he really referred to was 'Britain's contemptibly little army', i.e. it was its size, not its fighting qualities, which made him judge it safe to ignore it while the great issues were settled – as it was expected they would be – in a matter of weeks by the great conscript armies of the continental powers.

British complacency about her land forces sprang directly from her confidence in her naval superiority. The industrial revolution actually made Britain more dependent on sea-power than ever. In the 1780s

Britain finally ceased to be a net exporter of wheat. For the next sixty years the Corn Laws – essentially a mechanism for regulating domestic supplies as well as protecting the agricultural interest – were to be a major factor in British politics. With a rapidly rising population, Britain could no longer feed herself without food imports although some contemporary analysts believed that, if Britain ever lost control of the seas, she would be forced into surrender by the lack of raw materials for industry and war purposes before she was actually starved into submission. The chaos caused by the interruption of cotton supplies during the American Civil War illustrates just how many hostages Britain had given to fortune.

It might have been expected that Britain's industrial lead would have given her technological advantages in maintaining her naval superiority. In fact, except in some aspects of gunnery (Kennedy 1983: 124–8), Britain was slow to adopt new technology for naval requirements. This caution became a positive liability later in the century when belief in Britain's superiority in sail held back the use of steam. When technology did become important in the years before 1914, it was to prove very damaging to British security. The revolutionary design of the *Dreadnought*, although a British invention, by rendering previous battleships obsolescent, showed that Britain's long lead in naval construction could be wiped out almost overnight. The invention of the submarine – which British naval officers, not surprisingly, considered 'unsporting' – put all Britain's communication routes in jeopardy.

The battle of Trafalgar of October 1805 is rightly remembered as one of the decisive battles of history. Britain's dominance at sea was not seriously challenged for nearly a century but, by the late nineteenth century, Britain was in the position of having to defend every ocean in the world. The British began to realise that they were over-extended. The Anglo-Japanese alliance of 1902 was a conscious attempt to find a partner who would provide some security in the Pacific Ocean so that Britain could concentrate more of her forces in home waters against the new threat from Germany. But the ultimate reasons for the decline in the British position were more fundamental. With the coming of the railways, and later air power, the balance of advantage began to swing away from shipping and so from the coastal states back to the great continental powers. Britain's naval mastery from Trafalgar to the eve of the First World War was not a myth but it was a unique and unrepeatable phase in British history not, as the Victorians so often assumed, the natural order of things.

The basic physical facts, that Britain was an island off the north-west coast of Europe, essentially a trading nation, well-endowed with the most important raw materials of the first industrial revolution, coal and iron ore (although the latter eventually had to be supplemented by imports) and with a steadily increasing population, remained constant throughout the period. Almost everything else changed.

In the 1780s Britain was already a parliamentary state but the king, George III, still had considerable powers. Cabinet government was not yet established. When he came to the throne George III may well only have wished, as Namier expressed it, to take his rightful place as the foremost among 'the electioneering, borough-mongering gentlemen of England' and not, as his enemies suspected, to resume the prerogatives of the Stuarts, but it would have been unthinkable to either George or his ministers that he should not have the right to be consulted about foreign affairs. The fact that he was also the Elector of Hanover helped to give him an independent interest in the affairs of Europe. Only the débâcle of the loss of the American colonies and, more importantly, George's later bouts of insanity, began to erode the traditional royal power.

Both George IV and William IV took what their ministers often regarded as a wilful and over-personal interest in foreign affairs, especially when people they liked or disliked were involved. But the balance of power really swung during the reign of Victoria. Victoria believed, and was encouraged in that belief by her husband, Prince Albert, and Albert's favourite adviser, Baron Stockmar, that she had a special rôle to play in foreign policy. She exchanged sharp words, not only with the masterful Palmerston, but even with the much more tactful Aberdeen, when the despatches were sent off without her seeing them or her wishes were not followed as to diplomatic appointments. In terms of historical precedents, Victoria may well have been right but the constitutional tide was running too strongly in the opposite direction. Sheer longevity and experience – and the fact that she was almost literally 'the grandmother' of European royalty – restored a little, but only a little, of her influence towards the end of her life. She had deliberately excluded her son, the future Edward VII, from any influence in her lifetime. He did not gain a great deal after her death. He was a popular figure, who could sometimes make the wheels of diplomacy turn more smoothly, as he did in improving the atmosphere between Britain and France in 1903 but the idea that he played an independent rôle has not survived the opening of the archives.

As the monarch lost influence, the Cabinet gained it. The Cabinet evolved slowly in the first fifty years of this period from being a group of ministers, who each owed his office directly to the king and did not necessarily agree with his colleagues even on basic questions like Catholic emancipation, to a corporate body which would normally stand or fall together. Cabinets expected to be consulted about questions of foreign policy and both incoming and outgoing despatches were normally made available to all members. Some Foreign Secretaries had great difficulty in fighting their policies through Cabinet meetings. They evolved various techniques for combating that, including the deliberate withholding of information (see below pp. 73–4, 80, 166, 169–70, for some examples). But a Foreign Secretary who remained in office for a long time, like Palmerston, acquired a considerable advantage because critical colleagues could no longer match his knowledge or expertise.

One colleague no Foreign Secretary could afford to ignore was the Prime Minister. In fact which of them had the dominant voice on foreign affairs depended a great deal on personality. The public seldom had much doubt. They spoke confidently of the policy of the Younger Pitt, of Gladstone or of Disraeli – all Prime Ministers – or of the policy of Castlereagh, Canning, Palmerston or Sir Edward Grey – all Foreign Secretaries. Historians have generally followed the contemporary impression, although with some interesting exceptions, such as the relative influence of Grey and Palmerston in the early 1830s.

Neither contemporaries nor historians have doubted that the dominant figure at the beginning of this period was the Younger Pitt. He laid down what Professors Temperley and Penson rightly called the 'foundations' of British foreign policy for the next century (1938). John Derry in his biography of Castlereagh (1976) equally rightly calls attention to the pervasive legacy of Pitt. During what may for convenience be called the 'classical age' of British diplomacy, from Castlereagh's assumption of office in 1812 to the death of Palmerston in 1865, all the major figures who played a role in British foreign policy, Canning, Wellington and Aberdeen, as much as Castlereagh and Palmerston, declared themselves to be Pitt's disciples and the heirs and custodians of his policy. All had links with him. Castlereagh had been his friend and colleague, associated with him in important initiatives like the formation of the Third Coalition. Canning found his first political patron in Pitt. Aberdeen, orphaned as a child, became Pitt's ward and lived in his household. Palmerston's connection was less close but his first mentor in diplomacy was Pitt's friend, Lord Malmesbury, and by proclaiming himself a disciple of Canning, Palmerston consciously placed himself in the same tradition.

All undoubtedly inherited some part of the Pittite legacy. It is often forgotten, especially in the case of Palmerston, how much men of the eighteenth century they all were. Longevity meant that Palmerston was still Prime Minister in the middle of Victoria's reign and he is often thought of as the archetype of Victorian foreign policy. In fact, he was already in his fifties when Victoria came to the throne. When Aberdeen became Prime Minister in December 1852 he startled many by telling the House of Lords, 'The truth is ... that though there may have been differences in the execution, according to the different hands entrusted with the direction of affairs, the principles of foreign policy of the country have, for the last thirty years, been the same.' (3 *Hansard* 1852: cxxiii 1724; cf. McKnight 1855: 1–2.)

Some agreed with that pronouncement. Others violently disagreed. But one thing is clear. There was not the simple division between conservatives and liberals which a later generation was to assume. It was not only their attachment to the memory of Pitt. All the leading statesmen concerned with foreign policy in this period believed in the very eighteenth-century values of balance and stability. The Glorious Revolution of 1688 was the usual point of reference for Britons. The supposedly ultra-conservative Castlereagh told the continental statesmen that he could not condemn all revolutions since his own country owed its liberties to one. In fact, after 1815 Castlereagh was a much less committed conservative in domestic affairs than was Canning. Similarly, by 1852, Aberdeen wanted further parliamentary reform; Palmerston was violently opposed to it (see below pp. 42, 62, 69, 104).

In what then did those differences which were apparent to contemporaries consist? In part it was a matter of temperament. It has been suggested (Southgate 1966: 266) that the real difference between nineteenth-century Foreign Secretaries was whether they were 'active' or 'passive' characters. On this analysis, Canning, Palmerston and Russell would be 'activists', Aberdeen, Granville and Malmesbury 'passivists'. Similarly, C. J. Lowe, analysing a slightly later period suggested that the temperamental distinction was between 'Consolidationist' and 'Forward', which again he carefully distinguishes from conservative and liberal (Lowe 1967: vol. 1, 1-2). Temperament and general cast of mind can explain something but not everything.

At least as important as natural character was previous experience. A very plausible case can be made for suggesting that the essential difference sprang from their different introductions to diplomacy. Attitudes to Europe were vital. Castlereagh, Wellington and Aberdeen had all been closely involved with the diplomacy at the end of the Napoleonic wars. They had come to know their continental opposite numbers well and were used to conference diplomacy. Canning and Palmerston had no such contacts. Canning made no attempts and Palmerston only very limited ones, to cultivate them. Instead they played to their own strengths. Canning was from the beginning a good speaker and effective propagandist. Palmerston was not so originally but he learnt the art in middle age. Castlereagh and Aberdeen, although skilful and patient negotiators, were both ineffective public performers.

These differences of style might have counted for very little. Canning and Palmerston in fact shared their opponents' belief that diplomacy was a highly skilled matter, best left to the experts, and did not welcome even the intervention of their Cabinet colleagues. What made the differences important were the other fundamental changes which were taking place in British society. In the eighteenth century, a statesman had to retain the confidence of the king and the respect of parliament. By the end of the nineteenth he had to appeal to a wide electorate.

Canning found it convenient to tell the continental powers that he could not join in certain courses of action because British 'public opinion' would not agree to it and he was certainly more open in the communication of diplomatic documents to parliament, and therefore

'Pax Britannica'? British Foreign Policy 1789–1914

in practice to the public, than any of his predecessors (Temperley and Penson 1966: 30–7). Palmerston followed Canning in this. There is no question but that the Canning–Palmerston approach was better adapted to a modern society than the remoteness of an Aberdeen or a Castlereagh. But it brought its own dangers. Palmerston increasingly presented to the British public the image they wanted to accept and, in the end, became the prisoner of it (see below pp. 94–5, 98–9, 112–3).

But the intervention of public opinion in foreign affairs was by no means necessarily a benevolent force. It nearly caused war with France over the Tahiti incident in 1844. It played a major rôle in bringing about the Crimean War in 1854 (cf. Kingsley Martin (rev. edn) 1963). Not for nothing did the nineteenth century believe that democracies could be more dangerous mavericks in foreign affairs even than absolute monarchies.

But the lines of descent of different traditions in British foreign policy are more complex than they appear at first. William Gladstone achieved greater success in communicating with a wider public even than Palmerston. As Hammond puts it, 'It is safe to say that for one portrait of anybody else in working-class houses in the eighties of the last century there were ten of Gladstone.' (Hammond 1938: 698.) Yet Gladstone regarded himself as the pupil of Aberdeen in foreign affairs. Despite their one serious disagreement over Italy, Gladstone shared Aberdeen's concept of the unity of European civilisation and totally repudiated the insularity of Canning and Palmerston.

The mere mention of the phrase 'public opinion' raises a forest of problems. It is not easy to establish what the public really thinks about anything today, even with the aid of frequent and sophisticated opinion polls. In considering the nineteenth century, the historian is at the mercy of accidents of recording and survival. It is all too easy to equate public opinion with press opinion. The press is a better guide in the nineteenth century than it would be today because there were far more independent newspapers, covering the whole spectrum of political opinion. The press was influential – particularly The Times in its great days of genuine political independence in the middle of the century. Ironically press influence on government was probably less towards the end of the period, when it was spoken of with awe as the 'Fourth Estate', than it had been earlier. But the rise of the popular press about 1900 had an incalculable effect in exciting public opinion. Politicians certainly learnt to be wary of the press and to feed it with information for their own purposes. The mechanisms by which this was done are minutely analysed by Stephen Koss in The Rise and Fall of the Political Press in Britain (1981). The technique of the controlled 'leak' was very well understood.

By late Victorian times pressure groups, or even 'lobbies' as the term is used today, were well established. Their great prototypes had been the campaigns for the suppression of the slave trade and the Anti-Corn Law

League, both of which themselves had implications for foreign policy. Later in the century one of the most famous was the Bulgarian agitation analysed by Richard Shannon (2nd edn 1975). Some imperial questions led to organised campaigns, for example for the cancelling of the Anglo-Portuguese Congo treaty in 1884 or for the retention of Uganda in 1892. There was an element of organisation in the anti-German propaganda of the pre-1914 period (Kennedy 1982).

Any study of British foreign policy must also take account of those whom A. J. P. Taylor (1957) called 'the trouble-makers', those who criticised and condemned official policy, either for its immorality or its ineffectiveness. (Their activities overlapped with but are not synonymous with the 'single issue' pressure groups.) Some of the trouble-makers, like the Manchester School with their great leaders, Richard Cobden and John Bright, came in time to have a powerful influence on policy. The dissent of one generation could be the orthodoxy of the next. Even those who never won mass support or converted the political establishment, the Peace Societies for example, kept up an informed chorus of comment on foreign policy.

Sometimes attitudes formed in response to foreign questions created allies or enemies in domestic politics. Sometimes the opposite happened. Foreign and domestic questions became intermeshed in complicated ways – which brings one back to the question – who actually made foreign policy? For the determinist this is a non-question. For some schools of thought, notably although not exclusively the Marxist school, the explanations for foreign policy decisions cannot be found in the idiosyncratic decisions of individuals, or even in the equally idiosyncratic movements of pressure groups, or in irrational public opinion. The explanations must be rational ones, rooted in social and political forces, which are themselves ultimately rooted in economic change.

For those who do not subscribe to those views, the problem is infinitely more complicated. The reasons for individual decisions must be teased out from all the available evidence. For Britain the process is helped – sometimes, indeed, only made possible – by the fact that an unusually rich vein of the private papers of the most important Prime Ministers and Foreign Secretaries from William Pitt to Lord Salisbury survive and are available for scholarly study. In the early twentieth century the picture becomes slightly less rich. The papers of the Prime Ministers, those of A. J. Balfour and Henry Campbell-Bannerman in the British Library and those of H. H. Asquith in the Bodleian Library in Oxford are not essentially different from (although sometimes rather less voluminous than) those of earlier Prime Ministers. But the papers of the Foreign Secretaries, Lord Lansdowne and Sir Edward Grey, in the Public Record Office do differ from those of, say, Palmerston and Aberdeen. They are much more the working papers of the office, containing a mixture of trivialities and 'sensitive' material, such as embarrassing imbroglios with foreign royalty, but not normally including the wide-ranging discussions with colleagues which are such an important feature of earlier collections. For the period as whole it is the private papers of leading Cabinet ministers, rather than the formal Cabinet papers, which allow the historian to trace out the evolution of policy.

There is also the problem of the role of the permanent officials and of the diplomats themselves. In the earlier part of the period under discussion, communication even with European capitals was still slow. There were no telegraphs or railways. The fastest means of communication was the messenger on horse-back. Beyond Europe the time lag was even greater. It took three weeks to get a message to or from Constantinople, two months or more to get one to China. Ambassadors were often left without instructions and had to make their own decisions in rapidly changing situations. The key part played by a few great ambassadors, such as Stratford Canning at Constantinople, has always been recognised. When communications became faster in the 1860s there was, predictably, a move on the part of the Treasury to reduce ambassadors' salaries on the grounds that they no longer carried the weight of responsibility which had been theirs in the past but could always receive up-to-the-minute instructions from home. It failed partly because the government was still heavily dependent on the quality of the information it received from its ambassadors and on their prestige and influence in foreign capitals. Men like Lord Lyons or Sir Francis Bertie in Paris, Edward Malet or Frank Lascelles in Berlin, or Arthur Nicolson in St Petersburg still had key rôles to play.

The position of the permanent officials at home was rather different. Robinson and Gallagher in their important book, *Africa and the Victorians: the Official Mind of Imperialism* (2nd edn 1981) attribute a crucial role to the independent life of Foreign Office tradition, although in this case involving politicians as much as officials. Only in recent years has the Foreign Office itself received much attention in books such as Ray Jones's *The Nineteenth-Century Foreign Office* (1971) and C. R. Middleton's *The Administration of British Foreign Policy, 1782–1846* (1977). Until late in the century the Office was incredibly primitive by modern standards, with a small staff, organised generally as the result of historical accidents, rather than rational decisions, and entirely lacking any specialist bureaux to provide technical information. Since it was still assumed that French was the language of diplomacy, it was rare to find a Foreign Office official who could speak German.

Everything of importance came, or was assumed to come, to the Foreign Secretary in person. The burden was enormous and, although most of them were very tough men, it killed or helped to kill several of them, Castlereagh, Canning and Clarendon among them. Ironically, it was the strength of its political chiefs which held back the development of the Office itself. Virtually all of them were major politicians, with an authority second only to that of the Prime Minister. Most of them were also very strong personalities. Up to, and including, Lord Salisbury, they tended to treat even senior officials as their clerks. As a result the Foreign Office evolved into an expert advice-giving body comparatively late. The Colonial Office, which had a succession of strong permanent under-secretaries, like Sir James Stephen and, until 1895, usually second-rank politicians at its head, evolved much faster.

The balance began to change in the early twentieth century. In fact the Office started to acquire more influence as Salisbury's health declined in his last years. Lansdowne did not arrest the process and, under Grey, it accelerated. This critical change and its implications for British policy are carefully analysed by Zara Steiner (1963, 1965, 1969). Grey certainly did not become 'a puppet of his permanent officials' as E. D. Morel supposed (quoted Taylor 1957: 97), but Steiner concludes that 'the relationship between Grey and [Charles] Hardinge was more one of peers than any previous partnership between a foreign secretary and his permanent under-secretary' (1969: 93).

Many attitudes have changed in the twentieth century and it is worth pausing to consider what might be called the underside of diplomacy, the connection between foreign policy and intelligence-gathering or espionage. Today no one finds it strange that GCHQ Cheltenham eavesdrops on any available information. In this we have reverted to the attitudes of the eighteenth century. As might be expected, espionage played a large part during the Napoleonic wars and no one then felt any reason to be ashamed of it. Later the Victorians persuaded themselves that only despotic régimes, like Metternich's Austria, would stoop to such practices as intercepting letters. Nothing could have been further from the truth. Until 1844 when embarrassing light was shed on the matter by the radicals' discovery that the government was intercepting the letters of the Italian nationalist hero, Mazzini, the British intercepted 'under general warrant' any diplomatic correspondence which passed through their hands. The full ramifications of the network were kept from the public in 1844 but the government found the system too dangerous to continue. It has even been suggested (Ellis 1958) that British diplomacy never recovered from this blow, but this judgment seems exaggerated in view of the fact that all governments assumed that interception occurred and took appropriate precautions.

Victorian refusal to acknowledge the existence of a 'dirty tricks' department in the conduct of foreign policy was not entirely either naïvety or hypocrisy. There was a very genuine attempt during Victoria's reign to raise standards of public morality. Nepotism and the casual mixing of public and private interests which would have raised no eyebrows a century earlier, were now increasingly regarded as unacceptable. Similarly, in international affairs there was a move towards the acknowledgement of international law, of the existence of standards which should be observed by all nations, in the settlement of disputes or the treatment of prisoners of war for example, and of the desirability of international co-operation over a whole range of practical questions.

Against that stood ranged the apparently increasing conviction that nationalism had priority over all other claims and interests. To a non-European too it would probably seem strange to speak of a growing sense of international morality at the very time when Europe was becoming most ruthless in the assertion of its claims against the rest of the world and seizing other people's territory either on the grounds of superior civilisation or Social Darwinian arguments of the survival of the fittest.

Britain played a key rôle in this expansion of Europe and emerged with the largest empire of all. Recent historians have generally argued that this was the defensive reaction of an economy already severely under challenge rather than, as it often seemed at the time, the final triumph of a strong and secure nation. Even at the time a minority, such as J. A. Hobson, argued that the remedy was worse than the malady. Resources badly needed at home were being diverted overseas for little advantage, and the tensions created only aggravated the growing militarism of the period which was to end in the First World War, which began the process that culminated in not only Britain, but Europe as a whole, losing their dominant position in the world.

This is a small book on a large topic. It is intended as an interpretive essay rather than a text book on British foreign policy. Subjects have not been covered in uniform depth nor has chronology always been adhered to. The classical diplomatic studies of the 1930s must still provide the basic skeleton of knowledge and it would be impossible to deal with the subject coherently without some framework of negotiations, treaties and even battles. But a conscious attempt has been made to look at the subject through the eyes of the 1980s, to concentrate on incidents and developments which need re-interpretation and more particularly to suggest (it would be premature to do more) relationships between domestic and foreign policy and to try and bring at least some insights from social and economic history to bear on the understanding of foreign policy.

I. THE STAGE IS SET: THE AGE OF PITT

Chapter 1

THE CONSEQUENCES OF THE AMERICAN WAR, 1783–1792

The eighteenth century was an age of contrasts. On the one hand it was a time of rationality and noble aspirations. Men believed that, by the exercise of reason, they could discover the laws which should govern human society, just as they were discovering the laws which governed the natural universe. On the other hand, it was an age of violence in both national and international affairs. Crimes were savagely punished because governments felt that the skin of civilisation was thin and demonic forces could easily break through. In international affairs the eighteenth century – much more than the post-Bismarckian era – was the age of *realpolitik*, when national or dynastic interests were everything and no sovereign state recognised any authority superior to itself. As A. J. P. Taylor puts it, nations ran up and down the scale 'with dizzy rapidity' (Taylor 1954: xxii). Poland and Spain, which would have been accounted Great Powers at the beginning of the century, were both the prey of ambitious neighbours by the end. Russia, and more doubtfully, Prussia, were coming to be recognised as the Great Powers of the future. In such a world it was even more true than when Palmerston said it in the following century, that Britain had no eternal allies, only eternal interests (3 *Hansard* xcvii 122; 1 March 1848). But, if Britain appeared to have a constant enemy, it was France.

Britain and France fought each other four times in the eighteenth century. During the war of the Spanish Succession at the beginning of the century, Britain joined with Austria, Prussia, Holland, Denmark and Portugal to curb the power of Louis XIV, and the Treaty of Utrecht at the end of the war was one of the key treaties of European history, still appealed to even after the Vienna Settlement at the end of the Napoleonic wars. The War of the Austrian Succession some thirty years later confirmed Britain as a permanent part of the balance of power in Europe. The Seven Years War (1756–63) brought Britain glory, previously undreamed of, even though the final stages of the war were marked by serious strains with her principal continental ally, Prussia, which may in the long run have weakened Britain's position in Europe (Horn 1967: 162).

But, in 1763, the British public were much more impressed by their almost unqualified success overseas. The French had surrendered Quebec to Britain and the long-standing threat to Britain's thirteen colonies on the eastern seaboard of North America seemed to be over. The French had also, for all practical purposes, given up their claims in India and the English East India Company was left unchallenged as the most important European influence in the sub-continent. In an age dominated by mercantilist theories of economic rivalry and the desirability of economic self-sufficiency, colonies were the objects of fierce competition among the European powers. Britain could now claim to be recognised, not only as a first-class European power, but also as a world power.

Within twenty years the dream crashed in ruins. In 1776 the Thirteen Colonies rebelled and France, Spain and even Holland came to their aid. Irritated by Britain's interpretation of her 'maritime rights', in particular her right to seize enemy goods on neutral ships, Prussia, Russia, Austria, Sweden, Denmark and Portugal all joined in the 'Armed Neutrality' of 1780 to resist the British claims. (For a clear exposition of the different points of view see Semmel 1986: 13–18.) Some belated naval successes saved Britain from the worst consequences of this almost total isolation, but America was a lost cause. In September 1783, by the Treaty of Versailles, Britain had to recognise the independence of the United States.

Britain's humiliation appeared complete. Lord Shelburne, who as First Lord of the Treasury from July 1782 to April 1783 played an important role in the final settlement, had believed only a little earlier that, if American independence were granted, 'the sun of Great Britain is set, and we shall no longer be a powerful or respectable people'. The novelist Horace Walpole wrote to the childless Lord Stafford, 'You must be happy now not to have a son, who would live to grovel in the dregs of England', and prophesied that England would become virtually a province of France (quoted Coupland 1930: 12–14). Europeans agreed. Joseph II of Austria thought that England had descended for ever to 'the rank of a second rate power like Sweden and Denmark' (quoted Ehrman 1969: 476). On good mercantilist principles sober-minded Englishmen feared not only disgrace and loss of international prestige, but also trade depression and national bankruptcy.

None of this came to pass. It was left to a later generation to analyse why not. Professor Vincent Harlow argued convincingly in the 1950s (Harlow 1952; but see also Marshall 1964, Hyam 1967 and Mackesy 1984: 11) that the loss of the American colonies only confirmed and accelerated changes in British development which were already under way. Colonies of settlement in the west were becoming less important than trading opportunities in the east. India and Asia now mattered more to the British economy than North America. The agricultural and industrial revolutions were fundamentally altering Britain's relations with the rest of the world. Mercantilist theories of controlled and restricted trade were on their way out. Free trade theories were on their way in. One early sign of this was the steady increase in trade between Britain and South America, where she had no political control.

At home Britain settled down to a decade of practical administrative reforms during the 'peace ministry' of the youthful William Pitt. More far-reaching reforms, even parliamentary reforms, were discussed. Humanitarian ideas which swept through the whole of western Europe (Cobban 1960), not just Britain, led to the questioning of evils like the Atlantic slave trade. In general the 1780s were a decade of hope, rather than despair.

The government soon roused itself to defend Britain's remaining world-wide interests. In 1784 Pitt's India Act established the dual system of crown and company government, by which the British Crown and the East India Company were to co-operate to govern large tracts of the Indian sub-continent until after the Mutiny in 1857. In 1791 Pitt's Canada Act regulated the government of the former French Canada which, surprisingly, had not taken advantage of the events of 1776–83 to throw off British rule.

The British were ready to reassert themselves in both North America and the Pacific. They manoeuvred to try to retain control of the lucrative fur trade in the interior of North America. The distant prize was trade with China. Captain James Cook's three great exploratory voyages, carried out between 1768 and 1781, suggested glittering possibilities to his fellow countrymen. One of the problems was that there were few western goods that the Chinese wanted in return for the tea, silks and porcelain which the West desired from them. Furs were one of the few exceptions.

In 1778 Cook identified a site, Nootka Sound on what became Vancouver Island, which seemed to have excellent potential as a station from which furs could be shipped to China. Ten years later a group of Britons established themselves there with the blessings of their government. A triangular trade was envisaged, which would also have drawn in the Pacific whalers and seal-trappers.

The objections came, not from the Americans, but from the Spanish. Although Spain was already a declining power in Europe, she clung fiercely to her claims to trading monopolies in both the Pacific and the South Atlantic. In 1770 Spain had expelled a number of Britons from the Falkland Islands. A European war nearly ensued but a compromise was reached by which the Britons were sent back, although apparently with a promise, fulfilled in 1774, that they would leave voluntarily. (Palmerston subsequently denied that there had ever been such a deal, *BFSP* 1833–34: 1386, 1393–4; but Harlow accepts it as probable, 1952: 22–32.)

In April 1789 the Spaniards similarly expelled a group of British whalers from Patagonia. They resented, but could not prevent, the new British settlement at Botany Bay on the eastern coast of Australia, which they saw as a threat to their principal Pacific base in the Philippines.

Spain still claimed the whole west coast of America up to the boundary of what is now Alaska, which had been in Russian hands since the 1740s. The British, on the other hand, had never accepted the validity of Spanish claims north of the modern American state of California, then part of the Spanish province of Mexico.

In May 1789 two Spanish warships sailed into Nootka Sound, hauled down the British flag, and later arrested the British traders and seized their ships. News of this confrontation did not reach London until the following January. Public opinion would not have allowed Pitt to back down even if he had been disposed to do so; as a contemporary said, 'The din of war ran through the country like wild-fire.' (Quoted Ehrman 1969: 558.) But in fact Pitt saw the opportunity for a comprehensive settlement by which the Spaniards would be compelled to withdraw their far-reaching claims over unoccupied American territory. In May 1789 Britain began to equip a naval squadron and Parliament voted over £1 million credit.

Both sides looked for allies. Spain found both France and the United States unresponsive but Britain succeeded in engaging the support of Prussia and Holland, who also disliked the Spanish claims to monopoly. In October Pitt presented an ultimatum to the Spaniards who had no alternative but to accept it. The British ships were released and compensation agreed. The Spaniards withdrew their claims to the coast north of California and recognised British trading and fishing rights in the Pacific as long as they did not encroach upon established Spanish territories.

It seemed a fairly comprehensive victory. It opened the way for the establishment of British Columbia and the creation of a British North America which stretched from the Atlantic to the Pacific and became the modern state of Canada. But what was mainly at issue in the 1790s was the Pacific trade. Within less than a decade of the apparently disastrous Treaty of Versailles, Britain had re-asserted herself as a maritime power and as a world trading power.

Her interventions in European politics, where decisions of crucial importance for the future were also being made, were less successful. In Eastern Europe both Poland and Turkey, important components in the eighteenth-century balance, were beginning to crumble. Their weakness presented a continual temptation to their neighbours, particularly Russia. British interests in Poland arose mainly from the fact that it represented an alternative source of timber and other naval stores after the loss of the American colonies (Anderson 1966: 18). The question of what would replace the Turkish (Ottoman) empire, if it collapsed altogether, was one of the most disturbing problems of nineteenth-century diplomacy.

In 1774 Catherine the Great compelled the Turks to sign the Treaty of Kuchuk Kainardji, which gave Russia a firm footing on the Black Sea, the right to pass through the Bosphorus and the Dardanelles into the Mediterranean and an ill-defined right to 'protect' the Christian subjects of the Sultan. In 1783 the Russians annexed the Crimea and began the construction of the great naval base of Sebastopol.

A new war four years later alarmed Europe but this time Russia was less successful and, by 1791, Catherine was willing to sign a compromise peace but she was anxious to retain the fortress of Ochakov on the Black Sea. The Ochakov incident, as it became known, marked Britain's first active participation in the Eastern Question. The defence of India, which was such an important motive for British involvement later, was not in the forefront of the government's mind in 1791. They felt some concern for eastern European trade routes – Ochakov was supposed to command the mouths of the rivers Bug and Dniester and so important routes into the Black Sea. But Pitt seems to have been persuaded to act by the young British envoy in Berlin, Joseph Ewart, who argued the need to give Prussia a *quid pro quo* for her support over Nootka Sound (Ehrman 1983: 8–12, 15–16, 29).

Pitt took unusually precipitate action. In March 1791 he sent an ultimatum to St Petersburg and asked the House of Commons for an increase in the fleet with a view to possible action against Russia. For once he had badly miscalculated. His cabinet was divided and both Parliament and the public hostile. They were unconvinced as to the value of Ochakov and there was a powerful lobby, which objected to the disruption of Britain's considerable trade with Russia. A special envoy, William Fawkener, was sent to St Petersburg for talks and, in the end, Britain acquiesced in the Treaty of Jassy of 1792, which made the Dniester the frontier between Russia and the Ottoman empire and so ceded Ochakov to Russia, although minor commercial safeguards were written into the treaty.

Britain's lack of success over Ochakov may have persuaded the British government that there was little they could do in the Polish question, which was to have such a destabilising effect on eastern Europe in the eighteenth century and to prepare the way for the perpetual conflicts of the nineteenth. By the First Partition in 1772 Russia, Prussia and Austria deprived Poland of half her population and a third of her territory. They were hungry for more. In particular, Prussia wanted the Vistula port of Thorn (Torun) and the great Baltic port of Danzig (Gdansk). Events in France and the distraction they provided enabled Russia and Prussia to carry out a further partition in 1793 and all three Eastern powers joined in the final partition in 1795.

In such a world of *realpolitik* it was inevitable that the outbreak of serious political troubles in France in 1789 should at first have been assessed by diplomats and politicians mainly in terms of its likely effect on the international equilibrium. Charles James Fox might write to a friend of the fall of the Bastille on 14 July, 'How much the greatest event it is that ever happened in the world! and how much the best!' (Russell

1863: vol. 2, 361) but he was untypical. On the other side of the question, Edmund Burke was almost alone in warning his countrymen that 1789 was not in the least like their own revered revolution of 1688, which had been concerned to preserve the constitution. This revolution would unleash forces which the French would not be able to control and its most probable outcome would be a military dictatorship.

Chapter 2
THE FRENCH WARS, 1792–1812

The British, on the whole, eyed the early stages of the French revolution benevolently enough. Anything which distracted and embarrassed the French king was likely to be to their advantage. The British Foreign Secretary, the Duke of Leeds, even wrote to the British ambassador in Paris, a fortnight after the fall of the Bastille, 'I defy the ablest Heads in England to have planned, or its whole Wealth to have purchased, a Situation so fatal to its Rival, as that to which France is now reduced by her own Intestine Commotions.' (quoted Ehrman 1983: 4) The fact that involvement in the American War of Independence had helped to administer the *coup de grâce* to the over-strained French finances could not but add relish to their satisfaction. Most English observers expected some form of limited monarchy to emerge from the troubles in France, undoing the absolutist work of Louis XIV. That too would be a gain. Absolutist monarchies were believed to be more aggressive and ambitious than constitutional ones. On 17 February 1792, Pitt made his famous prophecy that he expected fifteen years of peace in Europe.

Pitt was devastatingly wrong but his speech illustrates his pragmatic approach to events in France. Holland Rose's verdict on Pitt's attitude to the Revolution still stands; 'It was not that of a doctrinaire but of a practical statesman', which 'changed with changing events' (Holland Rose 1911: vol. 1, 537; cf. Ehrman 1983: 47–9, 79–81). Unless and until British interests were directly threatened, there was no need for British intervention. Such a threat could only come from a challenge to British obligations in Europe or an open appeal to sedition beyond the borders of France. Neither seemed likely in the early years of the revolution. But both came in 1792.

The direct threat to British interests came in the Low Countries, in the Austrian Netherlands (modern Belgium), which Austria had acquired from Spain in 1714. In November 1792 the French revolutionary armies drove the Austrians out of Belgium and, on the 16th of that month, the new French National Convention issued a proclamation promising that the River Scheldt would be open to navigation.

The fate of the Low Countries had always been regarded as a vital British strategic interest, but Britain's attitude to the Scheldt question had not always been consistent. By the Treaty of Münster of 1648, at the end of the Thirty Years War, the Dutch had secured the sole right of navigation of the Scheldt estuary, thus effectually stifling the trade of the great Belgian port of Antwerp, which lay further up river. As recently as 1780, when she was at war with Holland during the American War of Independence, Britain had used the threat of opening up the Scheldt against the Dutch. But the circumstances of 1792 were very different. Now France was in control of Belgium and looked likely to invade Holland. No rival Great Power, and certainly not France, must control the Low Countries. Pitt's government took their stand on the sanctity of treaties, in this case the Treaty of Münster.

Two months earlier, in September 1792, the French king, Louis XVI, had been deposed and on 19 November the National Convention issued another proclamation offering to help all people who were struggling to free themselves from their kings. This was to throw down the gauntlet with a vengeance and the British government could not but take it seriously.

The forces of 'law and order' were very thin in an age when there was no regular police force but only the Commission of the Peace, the magistrates, with powers to enrol special constables and, if the worst came to the worst, to call out the troops. Riots were endemic, often occasioned by 'shortages' and the resulting high prices for food. But food riots, serious though they could be, were not a deliberate challenge to the political system. When a more overtly political element crept in, as in the very dangerous Gordon riots of 1780, when London was out of official control for three days, the movement was often, in a perverse way, conservative. The Gordon rioters regarded themselves as defending the Protestant constitution against concessions to the Catholics. (See the very good discussion in Ehrman 1983: Chs IV and V.)

The 1790s saw the emergence of a quite different danger. The challenge was no longer contained within the constitution but was an actual challenge to it, basing itself upon new and different principles. In February 1792 the second part of Thomas Paine's *Rights of Man* was published. It was produced very cheaply and immediately had an enormous sale. Drawing upon both the American and the French revolutions, it was rightly seen as a call to action and not merely a political analysis. Passages such as 'I do not believe that monarchy and aristocracy will continue seven years longer' caused shudders in comfortable, propertied circles. The foundation of political reform societies, like the London Corresponding Society and similar organisations in provincial cities such as Sheffield, reinforced their fears, particularly when such societies had low subscription rates which brought in tradesmen, shopkeepers, clerks and artisans. In May 1792 Pitt's government resorted to a Royal Proclamation to forbid seditious meetings and the spread of seditious writings.

English conservatives watched the course of events across the Channel with growing horror. The arrest of the king in August 1792 was followed by the September massacres. France seemed to be collapsing into anarchy. The trial and subsequent execution of the king also genuinely shocked large sectors of British opinion. The British royal house had no personal ties such as those which bound the Austrian Hapsburgs to the French queen, Marie Antionette, the daughter of the Empress Maria Theresa, and neither the British government nor the British public would have contemplated war, either to save or to avenge Louis XVI. But a climate of opinion was created in which war began to seem both acceptable and unavoidable.

Nevertheless, the war with France came about in the confused and slow-motion way, in which Britain has so often gone to war. Poor communications played some part in this. So did the uncertain position of the French ambassador, the Marquis de Chauvelin, a young and inexperienced man, who bore little resemblance to the ruthless intriguer immortalised in the Scarlet Pimpernel saga. He was frequently by-passed in unofficial negotiations through secret agents (Ehrman 1983: 199–202, 210–11). After the deposition of Louis in September 1792, the British government was undecided whether to accept that Chauvelin still had any accreditation.

Throughout the winter of 1792–93 the government began to believe that the London Corresponding Society was the centre of a spider's web of sedition. They feared that various riots and strikes, including an important seamen's strike on the Tyne, were inspired by foreign agents. Ireland was always recognised as a danger point but the government was completely taken by surprise by an upsurge of violence in Scotland, not only in cities like Edinburgh and Aberdeen, but even in rural Berwickshire. In most cases the grievances were local ones but the government saw them as part of an international conspiracy and responded by moving regular troops to potential trouble spots, embodying the militia, and passing an Aliens Act, which provided for both the registration and deportation of foreigners.

In December 1792 the French asked for formal recognition of Chauvelin's status, which would have implied recognition of the French Republic. The British government was in no mood to respond. In turn the French were misled by reports from their own spies in England, who reported that revolution was imminent. Even so negotiations about the Scheldt question went on through both official and unofficial channels all through December and most of January until, on 23 January, the British government learnt of the execution of the king two days earlier. Chauvelin was ordered to leave. He arrived in Paris on 29 January, where the news of his expulsion was greeted with anger. On 31 January the French government decided to attack Holland and on 1 February, the Convention voted for war with both Holland and Britain and, in accordance with the decree of 19 November, extended an invitation to the British people to rise.

Once war was declared, winning, or at least avoiding defeat, naturally became the government's priority, to which all other considerations were subordinated. Englishmen were fond of saying, then as later, that the hour would bring forth the man and this time it seemed to have done so spectacularly. William Pitt, who remained Prime Minister, with one break from 1801 to 1804, until his premature death in 1806, was the son of Lord Chatham, the revered war leader of the Seven Years War, and he was very willing to assume his father's mantle. In Parliament, most politicians rallied to him. Only a small group of Whigs, associated at first with Charles James Fox and later with the second Earl Grey, who put more emphasis on the need for domestic reform, especially parliamentary reform, than on the quarrel with France, stood out. Pitt called himself a Whig to the end of his days but the government he led was now a coalition, in which the Tories eventually predominated.

Pitt seemed to personify the national effort. His death was greeted with horror and men looked back to him as the great exemplar. There is commonly a gap between legend and reality. Historians have examined Pitt's conduct of the French wars more critically than contemporaries generally did. The questions which must be asked about the revolutionary and Napoleonic period foreshadow those which must also be asked about later periods. What rôle could Britain, predominantly a naval and trading power, play in a great continental struggle? How did foreign and domestic policy interact? What were the effects of the war on the British economy? What image of themselves did the British acquire as a result of the war?

Britain had won her overseas successes in the Seven Years War by frequently turning her back on the continent. In the French wars too she often gave priority to her world-wide interests. She experienced no serious difficulty in capturing French colonies like Martinique and Guadeloupe, or the colonies of France's allies and clients, notably the Cape of Good Hope and Ceylon from the Dutch after the French had defeated the Dutch and set up the Batavian Republic. Britain's reaction to Bonaparte's Egyptian expedition of 1798 was determined by the realisation that its ultimate aim was probably to re-establish the French position in India. In India itself Arthur Wellesley, later the Duke of Wellington, acted swiftly to eliminate potential French allies, such as Tippoo Sultan of Mysore. One side effect of the Napoleonic wars was a considerable extension of British control in India.

Fear of a renewal of French colonial ambitions in the West Indies and even in continental America, following the French acquisition of the Spanish claims in North America, was an important factor in the breakdown of the Peace of Amiens in 1803, which ended the only brief interlude of peace between Britain and France between 1793 and 1814. The French admitted defeat in the colonial sphere and sold their

American claims to the United States, by what was known as the Louisiana Purchase later in 1803. Britain entered the peace negotiations of 1814 with the colonial possessions of most of the other European powers in her hands as potential bargaining counters.

This was possible because of Britain's supremacy at sea. Her strength during the Napoleonic wars sprang from her position as a world trading nation. She had the ships and she had the trained men. The navy also had good leaders and surprisingly high morale in view of the harsh conditions of service. The priority to be given to naval operations was clear to the British cabinet. Henry Dundas, the Secretary of State for War, wrote to Lord Spencer, the First Lord of the Admiralty, in 1799, '[France] will always be the enemy of this [country], and if it is within our power we ought to use our best exertions to annihilate their naval power ... We are a small spot in the ocean without territorial consequences, and our own power and dignity as well as the safety of Europe, rests on our being the paramount commercial and naval power in the world.' (quoted Mackesy 1984: 13)

The fact that Britain's strength lay at sea meant that she continued to maintain a doctrine of 'maritime rights', which was now unacceptable to virtually every other power. In particular, she claimed extensive rights to intercept neutral ships on the high seas. Behind this lay a complex legal argument. Britain still accepted the 'old rule', endorsed by Grotius and other jurists, that international law allowed the seizure of enemy goods even on neutral vessels but various treaties, including the Treaty of Utrecht, had reversed this, and while now allowing the seizure of neutral goods on enemy vessels, declared neutral vessels sacrosanct (Semmel 1986: 13–30.) It was these claims which led to the formation of various 'Armed Neutralities' against Britain and they also played a critical part in bringing about war between Britain and the United States in 1812.

There was a further aggravation here in Britain's claim to the 'right of impressment'. Since the mercantile marine was the source from which the navy was recruited in time of war, the government claimed the right to 'press' men into service. This was the basis upon which the press gangs operated in British coastal towns. (In theory they pressed only sailors into service.) But Britain went further and claimed the right to repossess her sailors from the merchant ships of other nations. This caused particular problems with the United States because ideas of 'naturalisation', of changing one's nationality, were still in their infancy. The British took a very rigid view that anyone born a British subject remained one, wherever they were domiciled. Consequently they pressed even men who, in their own view, had emigrated and acquired American nationality.

Britain's successes at sea and actions such as the 'Glorious First of June' in 1794 concealed from the public the fact that British influence on the course of events on the continent of Europe during the First Coalition was minimal. The British briefly held Toulon in 1793 in an abortive attempt to aid the French royalists and a small army under the Duke of York was despatched to help the Dutch. (His unproductive marching and counter-marching gave rise to the song, 'The Grand Old Duke of York'.) The French over-ran the Low Countries and established a client state in Holland, the Batavian Republic. The remnants of the British army left from Bremen in March 1795. By then the First Coalition was collapsing. Prussia withdrew from the war to concentrate on the Third Partition of Poland. Spain and Naples made peace with France. The French seemed to have secured what henceforth they would call their 'natural frontiers', the Rhine, the Pyrenees and the Alps. The Austrians fought on for a time but, following Bonaparte's spectacularly successful Italian campaign of 1796–97, they made peace with the French at Campo Formio in 1797. In 1796 Pitt too tried to make peace with the French, using the Earl of Malmesbury as his intermediary.

The period after the failure of the First Coalition was one of great danger for Britain, and more especially for the established order in Britain. Foreign and domestic policy became thoroughly intermeshed. It began to look as if revolutionary ideas were indeed spreading from the continent (see in particular Wells 1983). Even the navy seemed at risk. The Channel fleet at Spithead mutinied in April 1797 and this was followed by a mutiny at the Nore in May. The Nore mutiny was more overtly political and collapsed from its own internal divisions but that at Spithead was well-disciplined and confined its demands to practical questions of conditions – indeed, the mutineers said they would put to sea if the enemy came in sight. The government felt compelled to give in to their demands. There was a bad harvest in 1799 which led to high prices and food riots. Despite the British command of the seas, Bonaparte was able to prevent the export of grain from many continental ports.

In Britain more and more repressive legislation seemed necessary. Thirteen leading members of London reform societies, including Horne Took, Thomas Hardy and John Thelwall, were arrested and charged with high treason. To the government's dismay they were acquitted. A comparable group in Scotland, including Thomas Muir and the Rev. T. F. Palmer, were less lucky. They were sentenced to transportation. In May 1794 the Habeas Corpus Act, that traditional bastion of English liberties, was suspended. Over the next few years, the law of treason was extended, public meetings forbidden, newspapers subjected to high stamp duties and registration, and both political reform societies and workers' combinations (in effect, trade unions) banned.

But the greatest danger came from Ireland (Elliott 1982). An attempted French invasion in the winter of 1796–97 was prevented by the weather, not by British action. In August 1798 a French force under General Humbert landed in County Mayo but the Irish rebellion it had come to support was already virtually crushed. The rebellion had begun in Presbyterian Ulster. The United Irishmen and their leader, Wolfe Tone, were Protestants and radicals. Catholic, conservative Ireland was as yet scarcely mobilised against the English. But Tone and those who sympathised with him resented English domination of Irish politics and did not hesitate to seek French support against their stronger neighbour.

Severe repression in Ireland and stern action against dissidents in both Scotland and England bought time for the government but other forces also worked strongly in their favour. The British working classes had their own traditions of radicalism, sometimes perhaps manipulated from above, as in the Priestley riots in Birmingham in 1791, but deeply rooted. As E. P. Thompson put it, 'The stance of the common Englishman was not so much democratic, in any positive sense, as anti-absolutist. He felt ... protected by the laws against the intrusion of arbitrary power.' (Thompson 1968: 79–80, 87–8). This was linked with his perception of the 'Glorious Revolution' of 1688 which does not always command instant sympathy today, when some would condemn it for its inherent discrimination against Roman Catholics, but this is to misunderstand its hold on the loyalty of both upper and lower classes. It was what differentiated England from the absolutist monarchies of the continent. It did afford protection. In the last resort, Horne Took and his associates had been acquitted. In comparison, the freedom offered by Jacobinical theories could look uncertain and anarchic, and anarchy was no more popular with the majority of the working class than with any other class. Moreover, no one had forgotten that France was the traditional enemy. The priorities of the mutineers at Spithead were very revealing. There was in the mid-1790s what today would be called a backlash. The middle-class reformers drew back. In 1798 the London Corresponding Society debated a motion that it would form a loyal corps to resist a French invasion. When agitation resumed at the end of the century, it was centred on the industrial towns and was a response to the unprecedented problems of the industrial revolution, rather than to the ideas coming across the Channel (Watson 1960: 360–3; cf. Thompson 1968: 193–203). Nevertheless, the defeat of revolutionary France still seemed to the government a necessary prelude to a return to tranquillity in Europe and, more particularly, an end of the threat in Ireland.

The ill success of Bonaparte's Egyptian expedition and the ambitious policy of the Directory encouraged Austria and Prussia, together with Naples and Portugal, to join Britain in a new coalition against France. But the Second Coalition fell apart as the First had done. The military situation was transformed by the return of Bonaparte. The Peace of Lunéville of February 1801 left France in virtual control of Italy. Further, Bonaparte persuaded Russia, Sweden and Denmark to renew the Armed Neutrality of 1780 against Britain's exercise of maritime rights. In response, in April 1801, Nelson destroyed the Danish fleet at Copenhagen.

But, by the autumn of 1801, Britain was ready to consider peace with France. Domestic considerations played a part. The National Debt was rising alarmingly. Bread prices were high and general outbreaks of disorder were anticipated. Pitt himself had resigned on a domestic issue in March 1801. In his attempt to settle Ireland after the rebellion of 1798, he had put through the Act of Union by which Ireland lost her independent Parliament but, in return, he had promised to lift the disabilities which prevented Catholics from becoming MPs. When George III refused to consent to this saying that it would violate his Coronation oath, Pitt felt compelled to resign. It was therefore Pitt's successor, Henry Addington, later Viscount Sidmouth, who concluded the Peace of Amiens with the French in March 1802 but, although he had hoped for slightly better terms, there is no reason to suppose that Pitt would have done otherwise.

It was not a glorious conclusion to the war. The playwright, Richard Sheridan, called it 'A peace which every man ought to be glad of but no man can be proud of' and 'this necessary but disgraceful treaty of peace' (1 *Hansard* xxxvi 17, 817). Of her colonial conquests Britain retained only Ceylon and Trinidad. The Cape of Good Hope was returned to the Dutch and various West Indian islands to France and Spain. Britain promised to return Malta to the Knights of St John. Technically, it was Britain's refusal to carry out this clause which led to the renewal of the war in May 1803 but behind the British attitude lay a wealth of suspicion about Bonaparte's intentions.

At this time Britain had no allies. A new rebellion, that of Robert Emmett, broke out in Ireland. The rebellion itself was a fiasco but it was alarming for the government and Emmett had in fact obtained a promise of assistance from Napoleon Bonaparte. The following year, 1804, Napoleon himself assembled an army of 150,000 men, the 'Army of England', at Boulogne, ready to mount an invasion.

In May 1804 Pitt returned to power. He lost no time in trying to form a new alliance and the Third Coalition between Britain, Russia, Austria and Sweden took shape in the spring and summer of 1805. Its lasting importance for British policy lay in the fact that it led to the clear formulation of allied war aims and even foreshadowed post-war policy. It was now becoming apparent that Napoleon was redrawing the map of Europe. All the familiar landmarks were disappearing and revolutionary France seemed to pose a threat to the whole structure of Europe much greater than Louis XIV had ever done.

Pitt, in collaboration with his Secretary of State for War, Lord Castlereagh, took the lead. In January 1805 the new Tsar, Alexander I, enquired as to the British position. Pitt's reply of 19 January 1805 laid the foundation of British nineteenth-century foreign policy. He first set out the three objectives which he believed that Britain and Russia shared:

1st To rescue from the Dominion of France those Countries which it has subjugated since the beginning of the Revolution, and to reduce France within its former limits, as they stood before that time. –

2ndly To make such arrangements with respect to the territories recovered from France, as may provide for their Security and Happiness, and may at the same time constitute a more effectual barrier in future against encroachment on the part of France. –

3rdly To form, at the Restoration of Peace, a general System of Public Law in Europe.

Pitt spelt out in some detail the settlement he would like to see. The French should evacuate Germany and Italy. Piedmont and Savoy should be returned to the King of Sardinia and the security of Naples guaranteed. The independence of the United Provinces (Holland) and of Switzerland should be guaranteed. At the same time he was well aware that any settlement would depend upon military fortunes and, more particularly, whether Prussia could be persuaded to join the Coalition. If she could not, he doubted whether they could recover the Netherlands or the left bank of the Rhine.

He showed his statesmanship in seeking to reassure the French people that the Allies did not wish 'either to dictate to them by Force any particular Form of Government, or to attempt to dismember the ancient Territories of France.'

Even more importantly, he sought to give a more definite form to the ideas of post-war co-operation, which had been vaguely suggested over the previous decade. He wrote,

It seems necessary at the period of a general Pacification, to form a treaty to which all the Principal Powers of Europe should be Parties, by which their respective Rights and Possessions, as they then have been established, shall be fixed and recognised, and they should all bind themselves mutually to protect and support each other, against any attempt to infringe them. (Document given in full in Temperley and Penson 1938: 10–21.)

Pitt himself did not live to see any of his aims achieved. In September 1805 Napoleon, having failed to gain control of the Channel, abandoned any idea of invading England and marched against Austria. In November he was in Vienna and, on 2 December, he won his greatest victory against the armies of both Austria and Russia at Austerlitz. If it was not strictly true that 'Austerlitz killed Pitt', the strain of twenty-two years almost continuously in office, half of them during a great war, probably did. Napoleon was now undisputed master of Europe. The Holy Roman Empire, which still gave Germany some kind of unity under the Austrian emperor, was abolished. The smaller German states were dissolved and the French-dominated Confederation of the Rhine established.

In July 1807 Napoleon concluded the Treaty of Tilsit with the Tsar Alexander. The treaty was signed in the greatest secrecy but its terms quickly became known to the British and it was immediately recognised as a major new threat. France and Russia divided the hegemony of Europe between themselves and Britain believed that the French were encouraging the Russians to move against British India. Certainly, Alexander was to mediate between France and her one remaining enemy, England, and if England refused to accept the mediation, it was agreed that Denmark, Sweden and Portugal should be compelled to come into the war against her.

It was knowledge of the Tilsit terms which forced Britain into one of the most legally dubious acts of the Napoleonic Wars – the attack upon the Danish fleet at Copenhagen in August 1807. Countering Tilsit also began British involvement in the Iberian Peninsula and led to her only major continental campaign of the Napoleonic Wars. Warned of French intentions, the Portuguese royal family escaped to Brazil. In November 1807 the French General Junot sailed into Lisbon and, in the winter of 1807–8, French armies entered Spain. Despite Portuguese requests for assistance and a rising in Spain, the British hesitated to embark on a continental operation after their ill success in the Low Countries in the 1790s but, in August 1808, a small force under Sir Arthur Wellesley was sent to Portugal. Later that month Wellesley defeated Junot at Vimiero but the advantage was thrown away when the overall commander General Dalrymple, signed the Convention of Cintra, allowing Junot to sail away with his force intact.

In November 1808 Napoleon himself arrived to take command of the campaign in the Peninsula. The Spaniards were defeated and the British army driven back to Corunna. It was the beginning of a long period of fluctuating fortunes. Wellesley returned in April 1809 but, after some initial success, he was forced back on Lisbon, which he protected by the defensive lines of Torres Vedras – a name which became known to every Victorian schoolboy.

In May 1811 the French were finally driven from Portugal but it took two more years of hard, and not always successful, fighting before Viscount Wellington (as he now was) defeated the French at the battle of Vitoria on 21 June 1813 and compelled them to evacuate Spain. The eyes of the British public were firmly fixed on the Peninsula. Wellington was their hero. For them it was the main theatre of operations against Napoleon, paralleling the naval victories which had culminated at Trafalgar.

From the perspective of continental Europe, it looked rather different. In the spring of 1809 Austria had again gone to war with Napoleon only to suffer further disastrous defeats culminating, after the battle of Wagram, in the humiliating Peace of Schönbrunn, which cost her much territory. The British had tried to aid the Austrians by a diversionary attack on the Scheldt. Forty thousand troops were despatched under Lord Chatham, Pitt's elder brother, but they were trapped on the island of Walcheren and suffered heavy casualties,

The French wars, 1792-1812

although more from disease than from enemy action. The failure of the Walcheren expedition led to bitter recriminations within the British cabinet and so to the notorious duel between Lord Castlereagh, the Secretary of State for War, and George Canning, the Foreign Secretary, which compelled both men to resign from the government.

From 1809 until 1812 and the beginning of Napoleon's Russian campaign, Britain was virtually banished from the continent of Europe, apart from her toehold in the Iberian Peninsula. She was isolated diplomatically and was almost entirely in the dark about the policies of the other European powers. She was excluded economically by Napoleon's Continental System, which forbade trade with Britain, although it is true that this was widely evaded by smuggling. Even Napoleon had to grant exemptions and it was said that the Grande Armée wore overcoats made in Leeds and shoes made in Northampton. In retaliation Britain proclaimed what was in effect a counter-blockade and enforced her maritime rights even more strenuously against neutrals who traded with the ports from which she was excluded. An older generation of historians had no doubt that the continent suffered more than Britain from this severing of trade relations. Modern opinion is less sure. It certainly played some part in turning continental opinion against Napoleon and it may have done something to stimulate British industry and agriculture to try to satisfy all home needs but it also created an economic crisis in Britain which led to serious disturbances in many parts of the United Kingdom in 1812. This is one point where investigations by social historians in general and labour historians in particular have suggested a very different perspective on the Napoleonic Wars (Watson 1960: 466–70; Emsley 1979: 134–61).

When the war was resumed after the breakdown of the Peace of Amiens, the British people had seemed more united than before. The imminent threat of invasion made radicalism, with its French associations, suspect and unpopular even among those Englishmen who might otherwise have been attracted to it. But the combination of a poor harvest in 1810 and the slump, particularly severe in the textile districts of Lancashire and Yorkshire and among the hosiers of Leicestershire and Nottinghamshire, tried working people's patience past bearing. This was the time of 'King Ludd'. Contemporaries certainly believed the situation to be very dangerous. Some modern historians have agreed with them. E. P. Thompson believed, 'Sheer insurrectionary fury has rarely been more widespread in English history.' Emsley on the other hand answered the question 'Was Luddism a revolutionary threat?' doubtfully on the grounds that the Luddite disorders united the government and the propertied classes. There was certainly a growing movement in favour of peace although Cookson sees the relationship between the peace movement and the distress which led to Luddism, as a very complex one (Thompson 1968: 624; Emsley 1979: 158–9; Cookson 1982: 238–41).

On 24 June 1812 Napoleon crossed the River Niemen with an army of 600,000 men. The Russian campaign had begun. It came at a very opportune moment for the British government. It again opened up the possibility of finding continental allies and ending the economic stalemate. It would at once distract public opinion and offer a real hope of an improvement in conditions. By chance a new government was formed in London the same month that Napoleon invaded Russia. The new Prime Minister was Lord Liverpool, who was to remain in office until 1827. His Foreign Secretary was Lord Castlereagh, to whom was to fall the task of forming the final coalition against Napoleon and all the problems of the post-war era.

II. THE CLASSICAL PERIOD OF NINETEENTH-CENTURY DIPLOMACY

Chapter 3

CASTLEREAGH: VILLAIN OR STATESMAN?

Castlereagh stayed at the Foreign Office for ten years until his suicide in August 1822. During his lifetime he was the subject of an extraordinary smear campaign and he remained out of public favour during most of the nineteenth century – although significantly a future Foreign Secretary, whose merits were much more quickly recognised, the third Marquess of Salisbury, wrote vigorously in his defence in the 1860s (*QR* 1862: vol. 3, 201–38). Only in the twentieth century has he come to be regarded as one of England's greatest Foreign Secretaries.

The serious rehabilitation began during the flowering of diplomatic studies between the two World Wars. Sir Charles Webster's two massive volumes, *The Foreign Policy of Castlereagh, 1812–1815* (1931) and *The Foreign Policy of Castlereagh, 1815–1822* (1925) revealed Castlereagh's sheer technical skill and also showed that the tag of 'ultra-conservative' was misconceived. But the very detail of Webster's work meant that it remained inaccessible to all but those with a quasi-professional interest in diplomacy. In more recent years Castlereagh has been the subject of two fair and balanced biographies by C. J. Bartlett (1966) and Wendy Hinde (1981) and a penetrating biographical study by John Derry (1976). It has become more and more apparent that the virulent public opposition to Castlereagh owed more to his rôle in Irish politics and to his supposed rôle in English domestic politics after 1815 than to any considered criticism of his foreign policy.

Robert Stewart, later Viscount Castlereagh, was born in Dublin in 1769. Although he was related to the English aristocracy on his mother's side, his father's family were descended from Scottish Presbyterians, who had settled in Donegal early in the seventeenth century. They were, as Derry describes them, 'tough, hard-working, unromantic Ulstermen' (1976: 27), who had prospered moderately and were still establishing themselves even in Castlereagh's own lifetime. His father became a member of the Dublin Parliament and was ennobled as Lord Londonderry in 1789. Although Castlereagh went up to St John's College, Cambridge, in 1786, his early life was spent in Ireland and he was educated, not at one of the great English public schools, but at the Royal School in Armagh.

When he entered the Dublin Parliament himself, which he did as a matter of course in 1790, it was as a Whig, tenacious of Irish rights and hostile to the corrupt establishment at Dublin Castle. As a boy he sympathised with the American rebels and, as a young man, he had a radical reputation. But visits he paid to France and Belgium in 1791 and 1792 left him with mixed feelings about the French Revolution; it is worth remembering that first-hand experience of this kind influenced the thinking of many of those responsible for British foreign policy in the next generation. Castlereagh still believed the *ancien régime* to have been corrupt and overdue for change but he saw that the moderates were losing control and was emphatic that he did not wish to see the new French principles exported to other countries. When he entered the Westminster Parliament in 1794, it was as a supporter of William Pitt.

It was the chance illness of Thomas Pelham which catapulted Castlereagh into the Irish Secretaryship in 1797 and so left him with the opprobrium of the suppression of the Irish rebellion of 1798. Castlereagh had no illusions about the matter. He once said, 'With respect to Ireland, I know I shall never be forgiven. I have with many others incurred the inexpiable guilt of preserving that main branch of the British Empire from that separation which the traitors of Ireland in conjunction with a foreign power had meditated.' (Quoted Bartlett 1966: 6.) He did not believe that the status quo could ever be restored and was prepared to support Pitt on the Act of Union, including the provision for Catholic emancipation. To his former Whig associates in Ulster, this was a further betrayal.

Castlereagh resigned with Pitt in 1801 but returned to office the following year as President of the Board of Control for India, which in Pitt's last administration he combined with the Secretaryship for War and the Colonies. He retired to the back benches after his duel with Canning but went back to the Foreign Office under Spencer Perceval.

He not only retained that office under Liverpool but also became Leader of the House of Commons. As a result he had to take formal responsibility for the introduction of the many repressive acts deemed necessary during the economic depression and political unrest of the post-war period and defend actions such as Peterloo. The evidence suggests that Castlereagh was never a hard-liner – much less so than Canning – and preferred moderation whenever possible, although he shared the prevailing parliamentary conviction that the existing order must be protected. But he was in an exceptionally exposed position and became the favourite target of radical critics. Denunciation of his foreign policy was fused with condemnation of his domestic and Irish policies.

It was his particular misfortune that his enemies included some of the most eminent and eloquent literary men of the day, whose attacks would be remembered long after the details of the policies had been forgotten. Shelley, in the *Masque of Anarchy*, portrayed him tossing human hearts to his attendant bloodhounds. In *Don Juan*, Byron, with a savagery of which only he was capable, brought all the charges against Castlereagh together, accusing him of 'dabbling sleek young hands in Erin's gore', before transferring his homicidal mania to 'a sister shore', and then 'cobbling at manacles for all mankind.' This became the nineteenth-century stereotype. Harriet Martineau represented the conventional liberal view when she called him 'an enemy to his race', who had been the 'screw by which England had riveted the chains of nations' (quoted Derry 1976: 2–5). But, as Derry points out, Castlereagh was doubly unfortunate. He was the obvious villain for the liberals but his 'clear-sighted and sober realism' meant that he was not a natural hero for the romantic conservatives either. His indifference to empire prevented him from being taken up by later imperialists and his close involvement with European affairs became steadily less fashionable as the century wore on. He was left singularly friendless among historians, as well as contemporaries.

Up to a point Castlereagh was his own worst enemy. He could not project himself to the public and, only to a limited extent, to the House of Commons. He was a competent but not an eloquent speaker. He radiated no warmth or geniality. His immediate associates respected him but even they sometimes distrusted him. Castlereagh felt no obligation to try to explain his policy to a wider public. International diplomacy he saw as a highly-skilled, very technical, entirely confidential profession. In this, as in much else, Castlereagh was a man of the eighteenth century. He paid the price in reputation but public lack of approbation is a poor measure of Castlereagh's real success. Only a detailed analysis of the diplomatic transactions of 1812 to 1815 can reveal how Castlereagh, starting with very few cards in his hands, held the fragile coalition together, safeguarded Britain's vital interests and secured a settlement which, although he did not regard it as ideal in all aspects, achieved its main purpose of establishing a stable and lasting peace after twenty-five years of war.

Napoleon's invasion of Russia gave Castlereagh the opportunity to re-establish relations with the continental powers. He sent Lord Cathcart to Russia. Cathcart must have seemed a suitable choice. He was a military man, a veteran of the American War of Independence, who had lived in Russia as a boy, when his father had been Ambassador there. When Sweden (now effectively ruled by one of Napoleon's own marshals, Bernadotte) and Prussia also broke with France, Castlereagh sent his own half-brother, Sir Charles Stewart. Unfortunately, Cathcart proved to be excessively slow and cautious while Stewart was a gallant but impetuous cavalry officer, more interested in fighting than in diplomacy. For the post of British Ambassador to Austria, when she too joined the coalition, Castlereagh chose Pitt's former ward, the Earl of

Aberdeen. His choice has often been criticised on the grounds of Aberdeen's youth and inexperience. In fact, at twenty-nine, Aberdeen was neither particularly young nor inexperienced and he made a better impression on the continental professionals than either Cathcart or Stewart.* But the strained relations which developed between the three men complicated British diplomacy.

In 1813 Castlereagh had more fundamental problems to overcome. Among them was Britain's almost total ignorance of continental diplomatic arrangements, resulting from her exclusion from the continent since 1809. Aberdeen's first task, which he performed successfully, was to gain the confidence of the Austrian emperor, Francis I, and his Chancellor, Metternich, and to find out what treaties existed between Austria and other Powers. Although Britain already had a subsidy treaty with Sweden and was shipping substantial quantities of arms to Prussia and Russia through the Baltic, Cathcart and Stewart had not been consulted about the treaty signed at Reichenbach in June 1813 between Russia, Prussia and Austria, by which the three Powers had agreed on a proposed peace settlement. Napoleon's rejection of these terms had finally brought Austria into the war against him, despite the dynastic tie created by Napoleon's marriage to Francis' daughter, Marie Louise.

The British government had two great fears in the summer of 1813; first that the new combination against Napoleon would fall apart, as all previous coalitions had done; and secondly, that the other European Powers would strike a bargain with Napoleon about central Europe, the so-called 'continental peace', which would entirely neglect British interests and objectives. The danger was real. Until Wellington was able to bring an army over the Pyrenees into France – which did not happen until November 1813, five months after the battle of Vitoria – his campaigns were a side-show, as far as the continental allies were concerned; useful for pinning down a French army but nothing more. The real issues would be settled by the armies of the Great Powers in Germany, where Britain had no troops.

Castlereagh had undertaken a major review of British policy in April 1813. It was still based very closely upon Pitt's plans of 1805 and, like Pitt, Castlereagh was well aware that what could be achieved would depend, in the last resort, on the military situation. He divided Britain's objectives into three categories. First, there were those points upon which Britain's honour was pledged – the restoration of Spain, Portugal and Sicily to their rightful sovereigns, and the cession of Norway by Denmark to Sweden. Castlereagh has misgivings on the last point but it had been a necessary bribe to persuade Bernadotte to make common

* For further discussion of Aberdeen, the future Foreign Secretary and Prime Minister, see Chapter Four below.

cause with Russia. In the second category he put those objectives which, while desirable, would depend upon the success and aims of Britain's allies, namely, the restoration of the power of Prussia and Austria to counter-balance that of France, the liberation of Hanover and the re-establishment of Holland as an independent power. The third category was much vaguer. It included the settlement of the rest of Germany and of Italy and Switzerland. On the details, Castlereagh still had an open mind. He was aware that the Austrians did not want to resume control of Belgium but instead to consolidate their power in northern Italy. Castlereagh was not displeased by the idea of an Austrian barrier to future French aggression in Italy. He did not regard British pledges on Sicily as necessarily extending to Naples which was at this time ruled by another of Napoleon's marshals, Murat. If Murat, like Bernadotte, could be induced to change sides, Castlereagh was prepared to offer the Sicilian Bourbons compensation elsewhere for the loss of their mainland territories.

During the late summer and autumn of 1813 Cathcart and Aberdeen negotiated subsidy treaties with Russia and Austria and tried to persuade them to enter into a binding new coalition. Money was the strongest argument they had. Sherwig has exposed the many legends which have grown up about Britain's rôle as the 'paymaster of coalitions' and, more particularly, about 'Pitt's gold' (1969: 356–6). In fact Pitt spent very sparingly during the early days of the war, unwilling to throw away ten years of careful financial management during the 'Peace Ministry' for doubtful gains, although money was spent on mercenaries and on (generally unsuccessful) attempts to persuade the continental powers to accept British priorities, particularly the liberation of Holland. Substantial loans were made to Austria in 1795 and 1797. (The attempt to get them repaid caused endless difficulties between the two countries after the war.) In Britain the anti-war party blamed the Austrian loan, only partly correctly, for the great financial crisis of 1797, when the government had to suspend cash payments.

The opening of the Peninsular campaign in 1808 meant a new and continuing drain on British finances which led to a second financial crisis in 1810. Despite new taxes, the National Debt more than doubled as a result of the war. Only the continued growth of the British economy, despite periodic crises, enabled the government to continue to finance the war and the collapse of the Continental System over a large part of Europe in 1812 gave Castlereagh the extra reserves he needed to offer much larger subsidies to his allies (Sherwig 1969: 352). Arms shipments were now as important as money. In 1813 Britain shipped a million muskets to her allies, as well as supplying £7.5 million in subsidies.

Massive injections of cash helped but, in the last resort, everything depended on the armies. In October 1813 Napoleon was defeated at Leipzig by the combined armies of Austria, Russia, Prussia and Sweden. The slaughter of the great battles of the Napoleonic Wars shocked even the hardened professionals and Leipzig made a deep impression on Aberdeen, seeing warfare for the first time. He wrote to his sister-in-law,

> For three or four miles the ground is covered with the bodies of men and horses, many not dead. Wretches wounded unable to crawl, crying for water amid heaps of putrefying bodies. Their screams are heard at an immense distance, and still ring in my ears. The living as well as the dead are stripped by a barbarous peasantry, who have not sufficient charity to put the miserable wretches out of their pain. Our victory is most complete. It must be owned that victory is a fine thing, but one should be at a distance. (AP, BL. Add. MSS 43225, 22 Oct 1813)

The British public quickly jumped to the conclusion that Napoleon had been finally defeated at Leipzig. Nothing could have been further from the truth. It took many months before he was even driven back to the Rhine and the allied generals were far from convinced that he ever would be completely defeated.

It is in this context that one of the most misunderstood diplomatic transactions of the Napoleonic Wars, the Frankfort proposals, must be interpreted. During a lull in the battle of Leipzig Napoleon paroled a captured Austrian general, Merfeldt, to return to Napoleon's father-in-law, the Emperor Francis, with peace proposals. The offer was addressed specifically to Francis and was a clear attempt to divide the allies. Napoleon offered concessions in Germany and elsewhere but wished to insist on the return of the French colonies captured by Britain and British recognition of the freedom of the seas. London received early warning of what was afoot through Sir Robert Wilson, an eccentric British general, nominally the military attaché in Constantinople, who had accompanied the Russian army to Leipzig. (For details of the whole extraordinary transaction see Chamberlain 1983: 135–6.)

When the allies reached Frankfort-on-Main early in November the Austrian Chancellor, Metternich, decided to take advantage of the presence of Baron St Aignan, the brother-in-law of Caulaincourt, the French Foreign Minister, to reply to Napoleon's overtures. Nesselrode, the Russian Chancellor, and Aberdeen were admitted to the secret. Cathcart and Stewart were not.

There were, from the British point of view, two highly controversial points in the proposals St Aignan took to Napoleon. They offered France her 'natural frontiers' of the Rhine, Alps and Pyrenees, and they suggested that Britain would be prepared to agree 'à reconnaître la liberté du commerce et de la navigation à laquelle la France a droit de prétendre'. French is rarely an ambiguous language but St Aignan had shown himself a worthy countryman of the great Talleyrand in this phrase in his *aide-mémoire*. It could mean either that Britain would recognise those rights which she admitted France was entitled to claim, or that she would recognise *only* those rights which she admitted France was entitled to claim – two very different propositions. Aberdeen was in an awkward position. He was not officially present at the talks at all and he feared that, if he insisted on changes of wording, it would alter the status of the *aide-mémoire* from St Aignan's private notes to that of an agreed document. Castlereagh subsequently upheld him on this. In any case, Aberdeen knew that the offer was a mere gambit. Metternich had no intention of agreeing to the 'natural frontiers' but he wanted to force Napoleon to the negotiating table or if, as seemed more probable, he would not come, to be able to tell the now war-weary French people and French generals that only Napoleon's obstinacy stood between them and a magnificent peace.

For Britain the question of maritime rights was crucial. Count Lieven, the Russian ambassador in London, had raised the question with Castlereagh. Castlereagh had replied, and told Cathcart, that the point was totally non-negotiable. Unfortunately, the same message had not been passed to Aberdeen. Napoleon subsequently made the St Aignan proposals public and there was a great outcry in the English press. *The Times* suggested that for France to ask England to give up her maritime rights was like the burglar asking the householder to draw the teeth of his guard dog (*The Times*, 3 Jan. 1813).

These embarrassments played some part in Castlereagh's decision to go to the continent himself. Negotiations for the final coalition had not advanced smoothly. Some of the fault undoubtedly lay with the three British envoys. They did not work well together. But they were hampered by being in an extraordinary situation. Instead of being accredited to courts hundreds of miles apart, they had to accompany the Tsar of Russia, the Emperor of Austria and the King of Prussia, along with the dozens of minor kings, princes, generals and assorted dignitaries on a tough, and at times very dangerous, campaign across half Europe. Decisions continually had to be taken on the spot and communications with London were very bad, especially after Napoleon regained control of Hamburg in the summer of 1813. The presence of so many crowned heads in one place meant that something like a standing summit conference was convened among the allies. Even if Aberdeen, Stewart and Cathcart had worked together with the utmost harmony, they would have lacked the necessary authority to negotiate successfully.

Even when Castlereagh himself arrived at allied headquarters in January 1814, Britain was in a sense seriously under-represented in the councils of Europe. Castlereagh was not a head of state, or even a head of government. His first triumph was to persuade the British cabinet to give him what amounted to *carte blanche* in the negotiations and to furnish him with instructions which were drawn up by Castlereagh himself.

These instructions still faithfully followed the main points of Pitt's programme of 1805, although as the war situation became clearer, they had become more specific. Although Bernadotte, who, the allies suspected, was keeping his army intact for his own purposes, had not begun his projected campaign in the Low Countries, the Dutch had risen against the French on 15 November. It was now possible to take a stronger line on the settlement of the Low Countries than had been realistic when Napoleon was still in full control there. Castlereagh was therefore to try to secure,

> 1st the Absolute Exclusion of France from any Naval Establishment on the Scheldt, and Especially at Antwerp and 2ndly The Security of Holland being adequately provided for under the House of Orange by a Barrier, which shall at least include Juliers and Antwerp.

If this could be secured, along with satisfactory settlements in Italy and the Iberian Peninsula, Britain was prepared to return the majority of the captured colonies to France and her former allies (document in full in Temperley and Penson 1938: 29–34).

There were exceptions to this offer. Apart from Guadeloupe (where there were further embarrassing promises to Sweden to take into account), Britain was determined to retain Malta, the Cape of Good Hope, Ceylon, Mauritius and the Île de Bourbon (Kerguelen). She was prepared to strike a bargain with the Dutch, by which in return for the cession of the Cape she would give the Dutch £2 million to improve the 'barrier' against the French. Britain's willingness to use colonial territory as a bargaining counter reveals the country's growing indifference to the indiscriminate acquisition of empire, characteristic of the so-called 'separatist' period of the nineteenth century, but also the importance she attached to her stake in Asia, which accords with Harlow's arguments (see above, p. 22). The places she wished to retain were almost all important for the security of the route to India.

When Castlereagh arrived at allied headquarters at Basle, near the Franco-Swiss border, on 18 January 1814, the war was still far from won. Allied troops had begun to penetrate into France but there was considerable fear that the French would rally now they were fighting on their own soil. Aberdeen wrote to Lord Harrowby, 'We are now waging a *Spanish war* with the difference of having to deal with a more intelligent and active population.' (Harrowby MSS, XIV 29–30, 1 March 1814.) The French royalists tried to persuade the British that there was a widespread movement in France in favour of deposing Napoleon and restoring the king but British intelligence reports consistently discounted this. A compromise peace with Napoleon still seemed the most likely outcome. Negotiations were undertaken at Chatillon which lasted from 5 February to 19 March 1814. Castlereagh had no illusions either that a compromise must be accepted, if it could be obtained, or that it would be intensely unpopular with the British public who still believed Napoleon to be entirely defeated. He wrote to Aberdeen, who was his principal assistant at Chatillon, 'My dear Aberdeen, we must sign. Certainly we must sign. We shall be stoned when we get back to England, but we must sign.' Harrowby agreed. He wrote on 11 March, 'We shall all swing together whenever your signature at Chatillon, or elsewhere, brings us to the gallows, for nothing but "no peace with Bonaparte" is to be heard from Land's End to Berwick.' (Chamberlain 1983: 169)

One reason for Castlereagh's conviction that they must make peace, if it was on offer, was the very real possibility that the coalition would once again fall apart. Many Russians had lost interest in the campaign, once the French were expelled from Russian soil. The Tsar Alexander was currently in favour of pressing on to Paris but he was notoriously unpredictable. Other rulers besides Bernadotte might begin to weigh up the relative advantages of defeating Napoleon or doing a deal with him.

It was in these very difficult circumstances that Castlereagh achieved his greatest diplomatic victory. At Chaumont in March 1814 he persuaded Austria, Prussia and Russia to sign a treaty which, not only bound the four Powers not to make any separate peace with France, but also committed them to co-operate together to defend any settlement finally arrived at, against any future French attacks. This was very close to what Pitt had envisaged in his plan of January 1805.

The French rejected the terms offered at Chatillon and on 31 March 1814, the allied troops entered Paris. On 5 April Napoleon abdicated and was allowed to retire to the minute kingdom of Elba. Louis XVI's brother ascended to the throne of France, choosing to be known as Louis XVIII, thereby acknowledging his young nephew, the Dauphin, who had died in prison, to have been Louis XVII. The succession could thus be held to be unbroken. The unfortunate episodes of the republic and the Napoleonic empire were to be wiped out of constitutional memory.

In playing along with this fiction, the allied leaders showed more worldly wisdom than did their successors at Versailles in 1919. With France restored to its rightful ruler, an honourable peace could be made. Here, although not in many other aspects of the general settlement, the concept of legitimacy was important. The First Treaty of Paris, that of 30 May 1814, was deliberately lenient. France was not asked to pay an indemnity. She was to retain (with a few modifications) the gains of the early revolutionary years. Even more surprisingly, the art treasures looted from all over Europe and now in the Louvre were to remain there. But the most important decision of all was that France was to be invited to the negotiations to be undertaken in Vienna to redraw the whole map of Europe.

The Vienna Congress was not to meet until the autumn. During the summer of 1814 Englishmen flocked to Paris, which they had been unable to visit since 1803, while the principal allied dignitaries came to London. The London visit was suggested by the Tsar but Castlereagh encouraged it because he hoped it would provide an opportunity for preliminary discussions of the points to be settled at Vienna. The Austrian Emperor declined but the Tsar and King Frederick William III of Prussia came with their respective ministers, Nesselrode and Hardenberg, as did the Austrian chancellor, Metternich. The principal generals, Wellington, Blücher and Platoff also came. There were great celebrations, including fireworks and illuminations. Perhaps it all helped to fix in the minds of the British public the conviction that they had defeated Napoleon and that the statesmen of Europe were coming to congratulate them. Diplomatically, it was less successful. The Tsar and the Prince Regent took a dislike to each other. Castlereagh, who had previously preferred the Russians to the Austrians, also cooled towards the Russians and began to swing towards the Austrian point of view (Hinde 1981: 218; Nicolson 1961: 108–17). The negotiations were not much advanced, although an important exception to this was the settlement of the Low Countries, in which Britain still felt a special interest.

The great international Congress finally met in Vienna on 1 November 1814. It did not complete its deliberations until 8 June 1815. Although it was also a glittering social occasion, most of the time was spent in hard bargaining and it could be argued that, given the magnitude of the problems and the lack of precedents even about basic organisation, the settlement was reached surprisingly quickly.

Every European power, ally, former enemy and neutral was represented there but by a secret article of the First Treaty of Paris, Britain, Russia, Austria and Prussia kept the most important decisions in their own hands. France had reluctantly agreed to this but other powers, such as Spain, Portugal and Sweden, who had also signed the Treaty of Paris, were not even aware of it. The working distinction between the 'Great Powers' and the rest – it never had any legal basis – was created by the Congress of Vienna (Webster 1934: 79–88; Nicolson 1961: 137).

Once the immediate threat from France was removed, the allies were free to play the old game of power politics, although the French threat dramatically reappeared when Napoleon returned from Elba in March 1815. The Congress completed its deliberations ten days before the battle of Waterloo.

The Congress was not much influenced by ideology. Europe had just emerged from a quarter century of unusually destructive warfare. Almost all the old landmarks had disappeared. Two objectives dominated the minds of the statesmen at Vienna, and of Castlereagh in particular – to prevent any further French aggression and to establish such balance and equilibrium in Europe that stability could be guaranteed for the indefinite future. Balance and equilibrium were two words very close to the heart of the eighteenth century. The Vienna settlement was a settlement of eighteenth-century *realpolitik*. All the Great Powers would watch one another.

Sometimes the restoration of the *status quo ante bellum* did seem the best way to achieve this stability. Spain and Portugal were returned to their former rulers. Both Naples and Sicily were restored to Ferdinand IV, after Murat was so unwisely caught on the wrong side during Napoleon's Hundred Days. The independence and neutrality of Switzerland was recognised and guaranteed. But it was impossible to restore the status quo in Germany, where the three hundred or so states which had existed before the Revolution had gone for ever, or in Italy.

Castlereagh was quite prepared to see Austria assume responsibility for Italy, directly or indirectly, in order to keep the French out. The Austrians regained Lombardy, which they had ruled since 1714, and acquired Venetia (so lamented by Wordsworth when the ancient republic fell to the French in 1797), while minor Hapsburgs were installed in Tuscany and the Central Duchies of Parma and Piacenza. The Austrians were also prepared to constitute themselves the protectors of the Neapolitan Bourbons and of the Pope, now restored to his territories. The task of guarding the French border on the Alps was entrusted to the House of Savoy, in the person of the King of Piedmont and Sardinia, and the kingdom was strengthened by the addition of Genoa. This had been envisaged by Pitt in his 1805 plans where he had classified Genoa among those states 'where either the ancient Relations of the Country are so completely destroyed that they cannot be restored, or where independence would be merely nominal and alike inconsistent with the Security for the Country itself or for Europe' (Temperley and Penson 1938: 13–14). But in April 1814 Lord William Bentinck, the British minister in Sicily, had, in more or less direct defiance of this instruction, promised the Genoese their independence. Bentinck was a prominent Whig (later to be Governor-General of India) and he communicated with his friends at home. As a result Castlereagh was fiercely attacked in Parliament.

On the Rhine, as in Italy, Castlereagh gave priority to establishing effective barriers against future French aggression. The most controversial decision was that Belgium, the former Austrian Netherlands, should be united with Holland under the House of Orange. But in 1814 this seemed a reasonable solution. Belgium, which was comparatively industrialised, would, it was believed, benefit by a union with the Dutch trading empire. The negotiators were not unaware of the linguistic and religious differences which divided the Low Countries but these frontiers did not (and do not) coincide with the political frontier between Holland and Belgium. It could also be argued that similar objections could have been urged against the recognition of the Swiss confederation, which has always been held to be one of the successes of the Vienna Settlement. Most of the problems in the Low Countries arose subsequent to the settlement.

Austria had surrendered Belgium to concentrate on her position in central Europe. Similarly she was prepared to see the Rhineland go to Prussia. This may well have been a cardinal error on Austria's part because she thus allowed the key role of defending Germany from

France to pass from her to her potential rival, Prussia. But in 1814 Prussia, so comprehensively defeated by Napoleon in 1806, did not look like a real threat. It was well into the nineteenth century before Prussia again firmly re-established her claim to be regarded as one of the Great Powers of Europe. In any case Metternich believed that he had secured the initiative for Austria by her Presidency of the German Confederation. Again this settlement was acceptable to Castlereagh since it seemed to promise stability and he had from the beginning declined to express a view on the details of the German settlement.

One crisis, however, could not be avoided. Alexander wished to secure the whole of Poland, although he was still sufficiently influenced by the liberal ideas of his former tutor, the Swiss La Harpe, to promise the Poles a constitution and a personal union with Russia, such as that which existed between England and Hanover. But the Austrians and the Prussians were disinclined to surrender those parts of Poland which they had gained under the three Partitions. The Prussians were, however, prepared to consider a deal. The King of Saxony had continued to support Napoleon a little too long and had been caught on the wrong side at the battle of Leipzig. If Russia would back their claims to the whole of Saxony, the Prussians would accept the Russian claim to Poland. Talleyrand saw the chance to re-assert French influence. Neither Austria nor Britain liked the bargain being struck between Russia and Prussia. On 3 January 1815, Britain, France and Austria signed an alliance, later adhered to by a number of the smaller powers, to resist Russia and Prussia, by force if necessary. In the end Prussia gained only part of Saxony. Poland remained partitioned between Russia, Austria and Prussia, although Russia retained the largest part. Cracow became a free city.

Castlereagh's attitude over the Polish question was a good deal criticised at home. The Whig, Samuel Whitbread, complained on 28 November 1814, 'The rumours were that the emperor Alexander had strenuously contended for the independence of Poland and that he had been opposed in his benevolent views by the British ministers ... We now live in an age when free nations are not to be sold and transferred like beasts of burden; and if any attempt of the kind was made the result would be a bloody and revengeful war.' (2 *Hansard* xxiv 554.) Castlereagh's own defence was that Britain could not decisively influence events in central Europe. He could have preferred a genuinely independent Poland but, if that was not attainable, he wished to prevent too great a westward extension of Russian influence.

Whitbread's criticisms foreshadowed the later charges against Castlereagh that he totally ignored the claims of nationality and was perhaps unaware of them. In fact Castlereagh, as an Irishman, was well aware of the explosive force of nationalism. He had certainly been prepared to mobilise it against Napoleon. In September 1813 he urged Aberdeen to persuade Metternich to make full use of German nationalism. 'Work Metternich up', he wrote, 'to embark *the Nation* in the contest – an armed People is a better security, than a Family Connection with an ambitious Neighbour ... Why not imitate Prussia in rousing their whole Population?' (AP, BL, Add. Mss. 43074, 29 September 1813.) He was equally prepared to use it in Spain and the Tyrol.

But, with a partial exception in the case of Poland, Castlereagh did not see any necessary contradiction between his concept of nationalism and the settlement arrived at, at Vienna. The explanation was that he did not make the automatic connection, which appeared so obvious to later Liberals, between liberalism and nationalism. The national resistance to the French in Spain had been conservative and Catholic; there seemed no contradiction there in the restoration of the monarchy. With the abolition of the Holy Roman Empire, Germany had been provided with some national machinery in the Germanic Confederation and Austria seemed the natural and acceptable President in 1815 – certainly more so than Prussia. Italian nationalism was ignored but Castlereagh was not alone in doubting whether it existed except on a very local scale. Northern and southern Italy seemed to have very little in common.

On the charge of illiberalism, Castlereagh would no doubt have answered that he regarded stability as more important but that there was in fact nothing in the Vienna Settlement to preclude orderly change and reform. Although Castlereagh was no longer the radical of his youth, he still regarded himself, as was to become apparent during the controversies over the Congress System, as a man of 1688. Despotism was alien to the English system and had little to commend it anywhere. The ideal in constitutional matters, as in international diplomacy, was balance in which all interests were properly represented.

On one matter Castlereagh was prepared to throw his weight on the reforming side and that was the abolition of the slave trade. This was a simpler question than slavery itself, which raised awkward problems of property rights. The horrors of the 'middle passage' had been well publicised. William Wilberforce had waged his great campaign in England and gained the ear of his friend, William Pitt. The one real achievement of the 'Ministry of all the Talents' had been to declare the trade illegal in 1807. Now Castlereagh, under considerable pressure from abolitionists at home, persuaded all the nations assembled at Vienna to outlaw it.

Castlereagh reluctantly left Vienna for London towards the end of February 1815, urgently summoned home to lead the House of Commons in what promised to be a stormy session. His place was taken by the Duke of Wellington. But Wellington too was to be summoned from Vienna late in March to confront Napoleon who had landed in the south of France on 1 March. Wellington and Blücher defeated Napoleon finally at Waterloo on 18 June. Louis XVIII was once more restored and a new treaty, the Second Treaty of Paris, was concluded with France on 20 November 1815.

Its terms were somewhat harsher than those of the First Treaty of Paris. France was now reduced, with a few minor exceptions, to the limits of 1789. The French were to pay an indemnity of 700 million francs and also the cost of maintaining allied troops in her frontier fortresses for five years to ensure the payment of the indemnity. The looted art treasures were to be restored to their previous owners. Prussia would have liked harsher terms, including the cession of Alsace and Lorraine to make the Rhine frontier more secure, but Britain objected to that on the grounds that it would make the restored Bourbons so unpopular that France would become unstable (CHBFP 1922: vol. 1, 509). Wellington would have favoured replacing Louis XVIII with his cousin, the Duke of Orleans, later King Louis Philippe, but Castlereagh felt that they were committed to the senior line of the Bourbons.

Whoever governed France, it seemed certain that it was from France that further disruption of the peace of Europe might come. The same day that the Second Treaty of Paris was concluded, Britain, Russia, Austria and Prussia signed an alliance treaty by which they re-affirmed the Treaties of Chaumont of March 1814 and of Vienna of March 1815 (when Napoleon's return was known) and further agreed that the sovereigns, or their ministers, would meet at regular intervals for the consideration 'of such measures as . . . shall be judged most salutary for the peace and prosperity of the nations and for the maintenance of the peace of Europe' (Hertslet 1875: vol. 1, 375). This clause was the beginning of the Congress System. Its context makes its original purpose clear. It was to curb potential French aggression and to provide the guarantee of the peace settlements envisaged at Chaumont. It was entirely in line with Pitt's proposals of 1805. Castlereagh never deviated from this interpretation of its purpose.

Other European statesmen had more expansive concepts of its meaning, notably the Tsar Alexander. Alexander wished to superimpose upon it the idea of the Holy Alliance, by which the Christian sovereigns of Europe would pledge themselves to support one another 'to protect Religion, Peace, and Justice' (Hertslet 1875: vol. 1, 318). Castlereagh managed to avoid the embarrassment of the Prince Regent signing this document by pleading that he was not a reigning sovereign. He found it more difficult to avoid the gradual perversion of the Congress System from its original purpose.

The first meeting under the terms of the Quadruple Alliance Treaty of November 1815 took place at Aix-la-Chapelle in the autumn of 1818. The sovereigns of Austria, Prussia and Russia attended in person. Britain was represented by Castlereagh and Wellington. The main business related to France. The French had requested a normalisation of relations by the withdrawal of the allied army of occupation and the admission of France on equal terms to the councils of Europe. The allies, anxious to ensure the continued stability of the government of Louis XVIII, were prepared to agree. The French were to be admitted to the conference at Aix-la-Chapelle and subsequent meetings but, not altogether reassured, the allies also renewed the Quadruple Alliance. The troops were, however, withdrawn.

Other problems proved more intractable. Alexander I, whose opinions were rapidly becoming more conservative, wished to use the Alliance to enforce the existing status quo, domestic as well as territorial. Castlereagh sharply rejected this idea. He wrote,

> The problem of an universal Alliance for the peace and happiness of the world has always been one of speculation and hope, but it has never yet been reduced to practice, and if an opinion may be hazarded from its difficulty, it never can ... The idea of an 'Alliance Solidaire', by which each State shall be found to support the state of succession, government, and possession within all other States from violence and attack, upon condition of receiving for itself a similar guarantee, must be understood as morally implying the previous establishment of such a system of general government as may secure and enforce upon all kings and nations an internal system of peace and justice. (Webster 1963: 192.)

The British were equally disinclined to countenance a suggestion from Prussia that a European army might be stationed in the Low Countries, under the command of the Duke of Wellington, to deal with any breaches of the peace. The Tsar was fobbed off with a vague declaration.

Of even more immediate interest to Britain was the situation which had arisen in Latin America. The Spanish colonies had taken advantage of the Napoleonic Wars to throw off the rule of Madrid. This had embarrassed the British government as early as 1811, when they found themselves at the same time the ally and potential saviour of Spain in Europe and yet having an obvious vested interest in the independence of her colonies, which would open them up to British trade as the British had so long wished. Castlereagh's policy in 1818 was to play a waiting game and certainly to prevent the imposition of any sanctions, economic or military, by the other powers of Europe. He expected the colonial revolts to succeed and he asked the Russian ambassador, 'By what right could she [England] force a population, which had freed itself because its government was oppressive, to place itself once more under the domination of that same government?' (Webster 1925: 415.) At the same time Castlereagh's own preferred solution would have been for the former colonies to become self-governing but still associated with Spain, perhaps by a dynastic connection.

Aix-la-Chapelle was to be the last such meeting which Castlereagh attended in person. His now well-established contacts with the continental leaders had again facilitated the solution of a number of problems but they were becoming a matter of some suspicion to his Cabinet colleagues, who once again included Canning (as President of the Board of Control for India), as well as to the general public. In fact his memoranda to the cabinet, as well as his communications to the other allied leaders, make plain his own concept of the alliance, and, above all, of its limited functions.

The divergence between Castlereagh and the continental statesmen became even clearer during his remaining four years in office. After a temporary respite, partly as a consequence of the good harvest of 1817 and the apparent return of prosperity, life seemed to be becoming ever more dangerous for European conservatives. In March 1819 a Russian secret agent, Alexander Kotzebue, who also happened to be a well-known playwright, was assassinated in Mannheim by a German student, Karl Sand. In February 1820 the duc de Berri, who was in direct line of succession to the French throne, was murdered and, the same month, the Cato Street conspiracy to assassinate the whole British cabinet was discovered. These events were not directly connected. The deaths of both Kotzebue and de Berri were the work of individual fanatics but it was understandable that nervous conservatives concluded that they were facing a widespread terrorist conspiracy.

Metternich took advantage of Kotzebue's murder to persuade other German states to agree to the Carlsbad Decrees, which severely limited the freedom of the press and of the universities. Castlereagh felt under no obligation to take any line on the Carlsbad Decrees, which he regarded as an internal German matter. It was more difficult to ignore events in Spain and Italy. Ineffective attempts by Ferdinand VII to re-assert Spanish control in the colonies led to disaffection in the army and opened the way for a coup in March 1820 as a result of which Ferdinand was compelled to re-establish the liberal constitution of 1812. The liberal success in Spain encouraged a similar combination of army officers and reformers to compel Ferdinand I* of Naples to accept what was now called 'the Spanish constitution' in Naples and Sicily, although the situation here was complicated by the outbreak of a movement in favour of home rule for Sicily. Austria had treaty rights to intervene in Naples and Metternich was prepared to do so but the Tsar wished to convene a conference to deal much more generally with European unrest. The conference duly met at Troppau in October 1820 and later adjourned to Laibach (the modern Ljubljana).

The powers at Troppau agreed to the Troppau Protocol, which embodied the declaration the Tsar had been seeking. It read, in part,

> States, forming part of the European Alliance, which have undergone change, due to revolution, in the form of their constitution and the results of which menace other states, *ipso facto* cease to be part of the Alliance …
> When states where such changes have been made, cause by their proximity other countries to fear immediate danger, and when the Allied Powers can exercise effective and beneficial action towards them, they will employ, in order to bring them back to the bosom of the Alliance, first friendly representation, secondly measures of coercion … (Webster 1925: 295.)

* The former Ferdinand IV, who had assumed a new title on the union of Naples and Sicily in 1815.

Britain was not represented at Troppau or Laibach. Castlereagh had made his views plain in a State Paper, that of 20 May 1820, which has always been recognised as one of the fundamental statements of British foreign policy. In it he set out his understanding of the nature of the Quadruple Alliance and firmly rejected the right of the powers of Europe to interfere in the internal affairs of their neighbours. The key paragraph read,

> In this Alliance as in all other human Arrangements, nothing is more likely to impair or even to destroy its real utility, than any attempt to push its duties and obligations beyond the Sphere which its original conception and understood Principles will warrant: It was an union for the Reconquest and liberation of a great proportion of the Continent of Europe from the Military Dominion of France, and having subdued the Conqueror it took the State of Possession, as established by the Peace under the Protection of the Alliance: – It never was however intended as an Union for the Government of the World, or for the Superintendence of the Internal Affairs of other States. (Temperley and Penson 1938: 54.)

Unusually for Castlereagh he also brought public opinion into play. He assured his allies,

> We shall be found in our place when actual danger menaces the System of Europe, but this Country cannot and will not, act upon abstract and speculative Principles of Precaution: – The Alliance which exists had no such purpose in view in its original formation: – It was never so explained to Parliament; and if it had, most assuredly the sanction of Parliament would never have been given to it. (*Ibid.*: 63.)

It would therefore be a breach of faith for Ministers to act on such principles now.

He did not consider that events in Spain constituted any threat to the Vienna Settlement, although he conceded that Britain might view an upheaval in the Low Countries differently. He did admit, 'There can be no doubt of the general Danger which menaces more or less the stability of all existing Governments from the Principles which are afloat' (*ibid.*: 53) and he dropped a broad hint that he considered that it was for Germany to settle her own internal problems in her own way.

It was entirely consistent with this policy that Castlereagh did not feel that he could object when Austria agreed to come to the assistance of Ferdinand of Naples under the terms of the Austro-Neapolitan Treaty of June 1815. His objections were to the perversion of the Quadruple Alliance and to any British commitments to acting upon 'speculative' principles, not to the pursuit of conservative policies by the other European powers if they so chose.

Nevertheless, the Alliance was very near to being split before the outbreak of the Greek revolt in March 1821 reminded Britain and Austria that they had many interests in common. Although the Tsar had firmly set his face against those who tried to overthrow established authority, it was difficult to predict what he would do when the authority in question was the infidel Turk and the rebels were Orthodox Christians, whose patron the Tsar considered himself to be. Metternich did not wish to see any further extension of Russian influence in the Balkans.

Castlereagh's attitude was entirely determined, as the Duke of Wellington's was to be later, by considerations of the balance of power in the Eastern Mediterranean. He was determined to see no increase in Russian influence there. He wrote to ask the advice of Aberdeen, who was regarded as an expert on the area as a result of his travels in 1803–04, but Aberdeen's sympathies were with the Greeks. He told Castlereagh, 'I can have no hesitation in thinking them fully justified in using every possible means to shake off the horrible yoke under which they groan.' Since it was undesirable that the Greeks should owe their freedom to Russia alone and so add to the 'aggrandisement of this already colossal power', Britain should help them (Chamberlain 1983: 201). This was by no means what Castlereagh wished to hear. The only one of Aberdeen's suggestions that he adopted was to warn the Tsar that, if he became embroiled in the Levant, it might encourage revolutionary outbreaks in western Europe. Castlereagh himself went to meet Metternich in Hanover in October 1821. They were agreed that the best thing would be if the Greek crisis burned itself out beyond the pale of European civilisation.

It was, however, becoming difficult for Castlereagh to resist the pressures for a new conference to discuss all the impending questions. The conference was intended to meet in Vienna in the autumn of 1822. Castlereagh planned to go himself and, as in 1813, drew up instructions to be approved by the Cabinet for his own guidance. He hoped to prevent France, where the ultra-royalists were now in control, from intervening in Spain but the two questions which interested him most were Greece and the Spanish colonies. In both instances Castlereagh was quite prepared to accept the pragmatic success of the revolutionaries. In Greece he was considering recognising the Greeks as belligerents, and not mere rebels, which would have substantially altered their status in international law. He was also prepared to offer Britain's good offices in negotiations between the Greeks and the Turks. So far as the newly emerging South American states were concerned, the British government had already granted them virtual commercial recognition and he warned Madrid that legal recognition could only be a matter of time and urged the Spaniards to come to a settlement.

On 12 August Castlereagh committed suicide. His friends had noticed that he had been behaving strangely for some time. London was reverberating with the scandal of the Bishop of Clodagh who had fled after being charged with a homosexual offence – which then carried the death penalty. Castlereagh seems to have believed that his political enemies were conspiring to fabricate a similar charge against him. It is unclear whether there was such a plot – although Castlereagh, a happily married man, had been publicly taunted because he had no children. It is more likely that the double burden of the Foreign Office and the Leadership of the Commons brought him to a mental breakdown.

Hatred pursued him to the end. His enemies organised a demonstration at his funeral in Westminster Abbey. Byron bade him farewell with what Derry rightly calls 'vituperative doggerel',

> Posterity will ne'er survey
> A nobler grave than this:
> Here lie the bones of Castlereagh:
> Stop, traveller, and —!   (Derry, 1976: 5.)

The nineteenth century liked its controversy robust.

Chapter 4

FROM CANNING TO PALMERSTON

George Canning was a much more immediately attractive character than Castlereagh. He too was descended from a family which had settled in Ireland, although his more distant forebears came from the West of England. He was born in London in 1770. Family quarrels forced his impecunious widowed mother on to the stage – a source of later taunts against her son – but his father's family was eventually shamed into doing something for the boy and he had a conventional upper-class education at Eton and Christ Church, Oxford.

Canning acquired a reputation for exceptional talent very early. At Eton he edited a journal called the *Microcosm*, which became something of a vogue and was read by George III, who remembered it when Canning became a junior minister. At an uncle's house he met many of the leading men of the day, including Edmund Burke, Charles James Fox and Richard Sheridan, and at Oxford he became a close friend of the future Prime Minister, Lord Liverpool. Politics were beginning to have an irresistible attraction for Canning and he approached Pitt for help in 1792. Like Castlereagh, Canning had at first sympathised with the French Revolution but gradually became more impressed by the dangers it represented.

Pitt helped him to find a parliamentary seat, the rotten borough of Newtown in the Isle of Wight. His maiden speech was a success, despite some over-exuberant gestures which made Pitt himself duck, and significantly Canning himself said that he knew 'no pleasure (*sensual* pleasure I had almost said) equal to that which I experienced' (Hinde 1973: 34). His obvious talents were put to good use when he defended government policies in the *Anti-Jacobin* in 1797–8.

He had already taken his first government post in 1795 as under secretary at the Foreign Office, under Lord Grenville. Canning had wanted an Irish appointment but he soon found foreign affairs absorbing. He witnessed at close quarters the failure of the first Coalition and of Lord Malmesbury's peace negotiations. He also found himself drawn into a web of political intrigue at home, although nothing shook his personal loyalty to Pitt. In 1799 he transferred to the Board of Control for India and the following year became Paymaster General but his career received a check when Pitt resigned in 1801. According to the conventions of the time it was not necessary for Canning to resign with him but he felt himself too much Pitt's man to do otherwise.

Canning returned to the Foreign Office, as Foreign Secretary, when the Duke of Portland formed his administration in 1807. Canning enjoyed the job and consolidated his reputation for eloquence in the Commons but the European situation was bleak. The Third Coalition had collapsed and France and Russia come together in the Tilsit Agreement. It was Canning who had to defend the bombardment of Copenhagen in the Commons.

The most momentous decision for the future and the one which began to establish Canning, rather misleadingly, as the champion of nationalism, was the decision to commit British forces to Spain in 1808. A French army had entered Spain in 1807 and, in May 1808, Napoleon displaced the Bourbons and made his brother, Joseph, king of Spain. Sporadic risings took place all over the country and provincial governments or juntas were set up in Asturias, Galicia and Andalusia. Some Britons opposed intervention on the grounds that it would be yet another unsuccessful continental expedition like the Low Countries in 1794 but there was also an ideological problem. Joseph's accession had been made to comply, at least nominally, with legal forms. Should they help a people to rise against their king, as the French revolutionaries offered to do in 1792? Canning had no doubt. His attitude was similar to that of Winston Churchill offering help to the Russians against the Germans in 1941. In 1808 Canning declared that any nation fighting the French was an ally of England (Temperley and Penson 1938: 23). Only much later did he link this with the recognition of Spanish nationalism as such. He told the Commons in 1823, 'When the bold spirit of Spain burst forth indignant against the spirit of Buonparte I discharged the glorious duty ... of recognizing without delay the rights of the Spanish nation.' (2 *Hansard* viii 1509, 30 April 1823.)

Spain led to the first serious disagreement between Canning and Castlereagh. Both men deplored the Convention of Cintra but, whereas Canning held Dalrymple and Arthur Wellesley equally to blame, Castlereagh acquitted Wellesley on the grounds that he had to obey his superior. But it was the disastrous Walcheren expedition which led to the notorious duel and Canning's resignation from the Foreign Office.

Castlereagh returned to office in 1812 but it began to look as if Canning never would. His debating skills made him an asset in the Commons but his ambitions were deeply distrusted. When Liverpool formed his administration Castlereagh offered to relinquish the Foreign Office to him, which Canning later acknowledged as 'perhaps the handsomest offer that was ever made to an individual' (Hinde 1973: 253). But Castlereagh was not also prepared to yield the Leadership in the Commons and Canning felt that he could not serve under him.

He was less uncompromising later and, after a spell as British ambassador in Lisbon, he became President of the India Board in 1816. The accession of the Prince Regent as George IV in 1820 brought matters to a head. The two men were open enemies and Canning was glad to accept the Governor-Generalship of India. He was about to sail when Castlereagh died so unexpectedly.

In this crisis· Liverpool turned to Canning, despite the king's reluctance. If his own account is to be believed, Canning took the Foreign Office without enthusiasm. He felt that he should have taken it in 1812 when there was still 'fame' to be won. His relations with Castlereagh had improved over the years. It is possible that he was consulted about the famous State Paper of May 1820 and he certainly found no difficulty in accepting Castlereagh's draft instructions for the new Congress, although he decided that he would not go himself as Castlereagh had intended to do, but instead would send the Duke of Wellington. His decision not to go in person is symptomatic of his much more isolationist attitude to European politics. He had none of the personal contacts with continental statesmen, which had made it possible for Castlereagh to be accepted as one of themselves since 1814. Canning was soon to make a virtue of that.

The contrast between Castlereagh and Canning was certainly not really that between the conservative and the liberal – those were labels which later historians pinned on them. When he took office in September 1822, *The Times* predicted that Canning would be 'a fit agent or associate for the Holy Alliance' because he had opposed 'every reform in church and state' (Hinde 1973: 232). Although more extreme than most, such a comment was less startling to contemporaries than it would seem to later generations. Between 1816 and 1820 Canning had played his full part in defending the government's repressive measures and, although his rôle was less conspicuous than that of Castlereagh as Leader of the House, Canning's wit was more memorable. He had been no friend to the idea of parliamentary reform. As early as 1810 he had used language not unlike that of Wellington in 1830. He appealed to the Commons to 'let the venerable fabric, which has sheltered us for so many ages, and stood unshaken through so many storms, still remain unimpaired and holy'. Like Castlereagh he was a man of the eighteenth century who believed that the real safeguard was 'balance', in this case the balance between king, lords and commons. To upset that balance would 'end in national destruction' (Hinde 1973: 282, 284). A man who held such views was clearly, in Harold Nicolson's words, 'not a Jacobin in disguise' but 'a philosophical Tory of the school of Burke' (Nicolson 1961: 274; cf. Temperley 1966: 35–6).

How then did Canning become such a frightening figure to Metternich and the other European conservatives? From 1817 onwards Canning had spoken both in the Cabinet and in public against the Holy

Alliance and even against the idea of periodic meetings of the Great Powers, which he called a 'new and very questionable policy'. His objections arose partly from his belief that they would involve Britain 'deeply in all the politics of the Continent, whereas our true policy has always been not to interfere except in great emergencies, and then with commanding force'. He saw equal dangers arising from the two extremes of 'simple democracy' and 'simple Despotism' (Temperley 1966: 43–4). He made a similar point publicly in 1823 when he asked, 'Can it be either our interest or our duty to ally ourselves with revolution? ... Our station ... is essentially neutral: neutral not only between contending nations, but between conflicting principles.' Even more startlingly he briefed his cousin, Stratford Canning, on the latter's departure for St Petersburg in 1824, that it was 'not ... a British interest to have free States established on the Continent'. It was better for Britain to have neighbours 'whose Institutions cannot compare with ours in point of freedom' and his conclusion once again was that Britain must steer a middle course 'between *Jacobinism* and *altruism*' (Temperley and Penson 1938: 86–7). Canning felt that the only safe policy for Britain was to distance herself from any continental discussions. So began what Metternich called '*la grande déviation*' between Britain and her former allies.

In the event the Congress was transferred from Vienna to Verona and, when it met in October 1822, the only issue raised was that of Spain. The continental powers were themselves divided. Alexander still hankered after a joint European intervention and was prepared to send 15,000 troops. He opposed the idea of an intervention by France alone because he feared that, win or lose, the French army might turn against the king. The Austrians and the French were not prepared to see a Russian army marching into western Europe but Austria and Prussia were willing to give moral support to a French intervention. The *canard* that Wellington secretly conspired with the French and Austrians against Canning's policy is fully examined and rejected by Irby Nichols (1971: 277–85). At the end of November Wellington formally withdrew from the discussions, went to Paris and, on Canning's instructions, offered British mediation between France and Spain. It was rejected and in April 1823 a French army, with the blessing but without the active assistance of the other continental powers, marched into Spain. It easily defeated the Spanish radicals and restored Ferdinand VII to his absolutist position. The contrast with the prolonged Spanish resistance to the Napoleonic armies suggests that the 1812 constitution commanded little real support among the Spaniards.

The question now was whether French intervention might be extended to Spain's former colonies, even though the United States had already recognised the independence of Colombia, Mexico, Chile and the United Provinces of La Plata, as Argentina was then called. Britain's considerable and growing trading interests in South America made

Canning determined that, if France was to control Spain, she should not also control the Spanish colonies. He persuaded the French to sign a document which became known as the Polignac memorandum (Polignac, later Prime Minister of France, was at this time the French Ambassador in London), in which France renounced any intention of intervening by force in any contest between Spain and her former colonies, while Britain agreed to remain neutral so long as there was no outside intervention. Canning took the precaution of making the agreement public almost immediately.

He was less successful in concerting his policy with the United States. The United States was as opposed as Britain to the resumption of European control in South America but sore memories of the war of 1812 lingered and the United States resented the continued presence of a British colony, Canada, on their borders – a grievance which was kept alive by boundary disputes. The Americans refused to co-operate with the British and instead President Monroe issued his celebrated declaration that the time for European colonies on the American continent had passed. The British were irritated by the fact that Monroe had spoken safe in the knowledge that it would be the British navy which in practice would prevent any European intervention in South or Central America.

Whether, or at least when, Britain should recognise the new states was a difficult question, although Castlereagh had already contemplated it. Much turned on the form of government. Both George IV and Wellington would have preferred to see constitutional monarchies and were reluctant to recognise republics. Canning sent out special missions to assess their stability before, in 1824, he resolved to recognise Colombia, Mexico and La Plata.

Canning presented his whole Spanish policy to the public with the flair that Castlereagh had so conspicuously lacked and successfully disguised the fact that it was a failure. He had tried to dissuade the French from intervening and when the French army entered Spain Canning told the Commons he 'earnestly hoped and trusted that she [Spain] would come triumphantly out of this struggle' (2 *Hansard* viii 872; 14 April 1823) – a remark which caused a sensation both at home and abroad. Motions of censure were proposed in both Lords and Commons. Canning realised that he was, as he told a friend, 'upon my trial tonight' (Hinde 1973: 330). He took his stand upon Castlereagh's State Paper of May 1820 in defence of non-intervention and argued that the internal affairs of Spain were not worth a European war. Either Canning's eloquence or realism won the day. He had a comfortable majority in the Lords and an overwhelming one (372 : 20) in the Commons. The opposition returned to the attack when Canning proposed intervention in Portugal in 1826. Canning rose to the occasion with what was to become his best-remembered, if opaque, speech. He admitted that the French victory in Spain was 'an affront' to the pride of

England but, he contended, it was no longer a matter of great practical moment. The balance of power in Europe had changed. Spain was no longer a great imperial power. 'Contemplating Spain such as our ancestors had known her', he said, 'I resolved that if France had Spain, it should not be Spain "with the Indies". I called the New World into existence to redress the balance of the Old.' (2 *Hansard* xvi 397; 13 December 1826.)

Canning was much more willing to intervene in Portugal than in Spain. This was partly because, as he reminded the Commons in December 1826, Britain had ancient treaty obligations, re-affirmed at Vienna, to defend Portuguese territory, and partly because Portugal was easily accessible to sea power. Britain had maintained her influence in Portugal after 1815. The army was commanded by an Englishman, Marshal Beresford, and in fact the Portuguese blamed the English for the depression and heavy taxation of the post-war period. It was while Beresford was absent trying to persuade the Portuguese king, John VI, to return from Brazil that a revolution broke out in Portugal. When John finally returned in 1821 he accepted the new liberal constitution. In 1823 a counter-revolution, led by the army, began which found its champion in John's younger son, Miguel.

Ironically Canning's sympathies at first lay with Miguel and the counter-revolutionaries. The rebels had been violently anti-British and Canning even described them to Charles Bagot as 'fierce, rascally, thieving, ignorant ragamuffins' (Hinde 1973: 376). But the French action in Spain made him change his mind. If France was not to have 'Spain with the Indies', neither was she to have Portugal. In the summer of 1823 he sent a naval squadron to the Tagus with a watching brief. The following spring John took refuge on the British flagship. Miguel lost his nerve, surrendered and was banished to Vienna.

Meanwhile the Brazilians had become restive at Lisbon's attempts to re-assert control over them. John had left his elder son, Pedro, as Regent, and he was now asked to become the emperor of an independent Brazil. Canning was very willing to act as mediator. A British admiral, Lord Cochrane, took command of the Brazilian fleet and a British diplomat, Sir Charles Stuart (later Lord Stuart de Rothesay) played the crucial rôle in working out a settlement between Lisbon and Rio de Janeiro. Canning had been convinced from the beginning that Brazil, like the Spanish colonies, would make good her independence and welcomed what he regarded as the more stable and monarchical form of government adopted in Brazil.

The initial success of Canning's Portuguese policy became clouded after the death of John VI in March 1826. The Portuguese constitution was still unsettled – the liberal constitution had been abrogated in 1823 and never re-instated. Pedro succeeded as heir apparent and granted a constitution which, if Lord Ponsonby is to be believed, Pedro, who was proud of his grasp of political science, compiled with the aid of his secretary between breakfast and dinner – Ponsonby added 'they dine early too in Rio' (Temperley 1966: 366). But Pedro had no intention of returning himself from Brazil. Instead he abdicated in favour of his seven-year-old daughter, Donna Maria Gloria.

This was too much for the Portuguese conservatives. If Pedro was to abdicate, they argued, it must be for his line and not just for himself. They proclaimed Miguel as king. Canning himself was annoyed by Pedro's actions but once again he was mainly concerned to prevent foreign intervention in Portugal. Spain was harbouring army deserters, who were Miguel's supporters, and in November 1826 they began to advance into Portugal. On 9 December the British Cabinet decided to send troops. Presenting the government's case to the Commons on 12 December Canning marshalled his arguments very carefully. He made it clear that he was taking no stand on the question of the Portuguese constitution but responding to a formal request from the Portuguese ambassador for Britain to honour ancient treaties to defend Portuguese territory. But he put it in his usual ringing terms and added an oblique reference to the glories of the peninsular campaign.

> Let us fly to the aid of Portugal, by whomsoever attacked, because it is our duty to do so; and let us cease our interference where that duty ends. We go to Portugal not to rule, not to dictate, not to prescribe constitutions, but to defend and preserve the independence of an ally. We go to plant the standard of England on the well known heights of Lisbon. Where that standard is planted, foreign dominion shall not come.
> (2 *Hansard* xvi 369.)

However carefully Canning worded it at the time, the impression left upon the minds of later liberals was that Canning had inaugurated the defence of constitutional Portugal against despotic attacks.

His attitude to the Greek war of independence was equally pragmatic. The war was widely misunderstood in the West. Classically-educated men persuaded themselves that the spiritual descendants of Homer and Pericles were at last re-asserting Hellenic traditions against the Turks. Western nationalists saw it as a struggle for a national Greek state. In fact the binding force was that of religion, membership of the Greek Orthodox Church, and initially the 'Greeks', defined in this sense, were not primarily concerned with territorial claims in what is now the modern state of Greece, but with overthrowing the increasingly moribund Ottoman empire and reclaiming the ancient Byzantine capital of Constantinople. The first rising in fact occurred, not in Greece, but in the Danubian Principalities (the modern Roumania). The rising in southern Greece, the Morea, was actually a reaction to an attempted pre-emptive strike by the Turks, aimed at disarming the population. The Turks of the Morea were massacred and the Turks wreaked a terrible revenge on Greek communities elsewhere, notably in Smyrna and Chios and, most notoriously of all, they hanged the Patriarch of Constantinople on Easter Sunday.

There was a horrified reaction in the West and volunteers, of whom the best known was Lord Byron, did go out to fight for the Greeks but there was by no means the universal sympathy for the Greek cause which is often assumed. Governments at least were more concerned to ensure that the whole Near East did not explode like a barrel of gunpowder. The honesty and motives of the Greek leaders were doubted and conservative Europe was equally suspicious of the motives of many of those who went to fight for them. A significant proportion had been involved in the risings in Italy and Spain in 1820 and they were regarded either as dangerous radicals or mere mercenaries, soldiers out of a job since the Napoleonic Wars, who would go wherever there was a fight (cf. St Clair 1972). The romanticisation of the struggle came later.

Canning felt some sympathy for the Greeks but his over-riding aim was to maintain stability and balance in the region. Events, however, ensured that his name would become associated with the Greek cause, as it had with the Portuguese. The Greeks naturally regarded him as a friend when he recognised them as belligerents in 1823, although his reasons were as pragmatic as Castlereagh's had been when he contemplated the step. He declined the Tsar Alexander's request for a joint Anglo-Russian mediation and withdrew from a proposed European conference, mainly on the grounds that mediation was unlikely to succeed without a resort to force and in no circumstances would he commit Britain to the use of force. Temperley believed that he was playing for very high stakes and hoped that in the end both the Greeks and the Turks would turn to Britain as the most obviously neutral power to mediate (Temperley 1966: 335–6). If this was so, he was foiled by the unexpected military success of the Turks after the Sultan Mahmud requested assistance from his powerful vassal, Mehemet Ali of Egypt. Mehemet Ali sent his adopted son, Ibrahim, one of the outstanding soldiers of the time. Ibrahim established a base in Crete and conquered the Morea without much difficulty. The Greeks appealed to the British for protection but Canning would not move from his position of neutrality. The Greeks then turned to the Russians.

In December 1825 Alexander died. The Duke of Wellington was despatched to St Petersburg, nominally to congratulate the new Tsar, Nicholas, on his accession but in reality to concert British and Russian policy on the Near East. The choice of Wellington as the envoy did not augur well for the Greek cause. Wellington had never made any secret of his view that stability must come first and that meant upholding the Turkish empire.

Nevertheless, Wellington concluded the Protocol of St Petersburg with the Russians in April 1826, by which the two powers agreed to offer their mediation to the Turks. They proposed that Greece would remain a tributary state of the Ottoman empire but with internal autonomy.

The French were prepared to join with Britain and Russia and the new three power agreement was incorporated in the Treaty of London of July 1827. The Treaty of London was stronger than the Protocol of St Petersburg, mainly because Ibrahim's continued victories had made a solution urgent if the Greeks were not to be completely defeated. The Treaty demanded an immediate armistice and the deadline was set for 7 September 1826. It was agreed that, if either combatant refused to adhere to the armistice, the allies would prevent further 'collisions'. How they would do this was left ambiguous. The British admiral, Admiral Codrington, asked the advice of the British ambassador in Constantinople, George Canning's cousin, Stratford Canning, on how he was to interpret his confusing instructions. Stratford Canning told him that, although he should avoid force if possible, in the last resort he must enforce the armistice 'with cannon shot' (Lane-Poole 1888: vol. 1, 449). Ibrahim refused to co-operate and, after a series of misunder-standings, shots were exchanged between the allied fleet and a Turco-Egyptian fleet in Navarino Bay on 26 October 1827. Within two hours the Ottoman fleet had been destroyed. By this time George Canning was dead.

In April 1827, only three months before his death, Canning had become Prime Minister. Canning had every intention of continuing to run British foreign policy and even considered holding both the Foreign Office and the premiership but, in the end, he appointed a personal friend, Lord Dudley, as Foreign Secretary. Dudley was a nonentity and his own comment on his accession to office was rather extraordinary even for the time. He told Aberdeen he knew the office was beyond his capabilities but he had 'a curiosity ... to have a peep at official life' and he did not think he could 'do *much* harm to the publick, or to myself' (Chamberlain 1983: 193).

When Canning died early in August 1827, British politics were thrown into fresh confusion. Canning had formed his ministry with difficulty, losing many of the Tories who had supported Liverpool, mainly because of his known sympathy for Catholic emancipation. In January 1828 the king asked the Duke of Wellington to form a government. Instead of forming a High Tory government, as many people expected, Wellington set out to bring the Liverpool coalition together again. This meant bringing in the group who were already known as the Canningites. In particular it meant leaving Dudley at the Foreign Office.

The Canningites, Dudley, Palmerston, William Huskisson and Charles Grant only remained in Wellington's cabinet until May 1828.* The break came over a domestic issue but there had been strains over foreign affairs too. Of the four, two played little further part in politics. Huskisson died dramatically as the result of an accident with Stevenson's *Rocket*. Dudley became ill. Grant went on to play an

---

*For a discussion of the policy of the Wellington government see Chapter 4.

important rôle in Indian and colonial affairs. But the significant figure was Palmerston and his resignation from Wellington's cabinet was to be of crucial importance because it left him free to join Lord Grey's Whig cabinet in November 1830. Grey did not originally intend to appoint Palmerston as his Foreign Secretary. His first choice would have been Lord Holland. There was very little in Palmerston's previous career to make him look an obvious choice for the Foreign Office.

The office for which Palmerston seemed naturally destined, and which was in fact repeatedly offered to him, was that of Chancellor of the Exchequer. Although he bore an Irish title (derived from a small town near Dublin) and had estates in the west of Ireland, his family were essentially English country gentry, originating from the Midlands but, by Palmerston's own day, having their main seat at Broadlands in Hampshire. At the same time the family had strong connections with the City of London. Palmerston's maternal grandfather and great-grandfather were both Governors of the Bank of England and his grandfather was also Lord Mayor of London. Palmerston's branch of the Temple family had not previously been prominent in politics. Palmerston's father had sat in parliament for many years for a succession of rotten boroughs but had preferred an active social life and a dilettante interest in the arts to the fatigues of office. He seems to have thought that his two sons might find careers in the diplomatic service and Palmerston and his brother, William (who did become a diplomat), were carefully trained in French and Italian. He sent his elder son to the University of Edinburgh to complete his academic education before tasting the more purely social delights of Cambridge. In Edinburgh Palmerston came under the influence of Dugald Stewart, the disciple of the famous Adam Smith, and from him he acquired a firm faith in the virtues of free trade, about which he was inclined to lecture foreign statesmen to the end of his life. The other crucial event of his boyhood may well have been the journey through France which he made with his parents in 1792, when some of the party were nearly arrested in revolutionary Paris and Lady Palmerston and her children were badly frightened by the rough citizen army they met on their way to the Swiss border. Later in life, for all his liberal reputation, Palmerston had an almost pathological distrust of the lower orders.

Palmerston entered parliament in 1807 for the rotten borough of Newport in the Isle of Wight. The patrons, the Holmes family who had also controlled Canning's old seat of Newtown, allowed him to have the seat on condition that he did not disturb their interests there by ever setting foot in the constituency. He made his maiden speech in 1808 in defence of the Copenhagen expedition but this was a rare early manifestation of an interest in foreign affairs. In 1809 he turned down the first offer of the Chancellorship of the Exchequer. Although it was still a much more junior office than it later became, it was a surprising offer to an untried man. Palmerston refused it partly because he feared making a fool of himself in the Commons. As a young man, Palmerston, unlike Canning, was not a fluent or successful speaker. His friends were disappointed. Surprisingly, in view of his later reputation, his main problem seems to have been diffidence.

In 1809, instead of the Chancellorship of the Exchequer, he accepted the post of Secretary at War, as being 'more suited to a beginner'. Since this was in the middle of the Napoleonic Wars, this struck one of his biographers as richly comic (Guedalla 1926: 60). In fact it was not an unreasonable point of view. The Secretary at War was not the head of his department – that was the Secretary of State for War – and, at least in theory, had clearly defined duties looking after those aspects of the army for which Parliament was responsible, mainly financing it. In fact, because the whole system was in an awkward state of transition, Palmerston's sphere of responsibility was anything but clear and he spent many embattled years with rival vested interests. But he made little public mark and another biographer, Kenneth Bourne, seems entirely justified in saying that he emerges from these years as a 'bureaucrat' (Bourne 1982: 115). Amazingly, Palmerston remained in this hack position from 1809 until 1828. The Secretary at War did not usually rate a seat in the Cabinet (although Palmerston had been offered and declined one in 1809) but Canning brought him in to strengthen his rather weak Cabinet in 1827. For the first time Palmerston was able to see the whole range of papers relating to foreign affairs and his interest seems to have been caught.

He made one of his few important and effective speeches of this early period in June 1829 when he launched into a comprehensive attack on the policy of Wellington's government in Greece and Portugal. This may, or may not, have been, as Southgate believes, a deliberate bid for the Foreign Office (Southgate 1966: 7). But presumably it played its part in suggesting his name to Grey in 1830. In any case Grey, like Canning, meant to keep control of foreign affairs himself.

It might be more accurate to speak of British foreign policy between 1830 and 1834 as the policy of Grey rather than Palmerston. Contemporaries saw it in that light and looked to the confrontations between Grey and Wellington in the Lords, as the main debates on foreign policy in those years. Sir Charles Webster is a formidable authority with whom to disagree and he attributed more initiative to Palmerston but there is sufficient evidence, especially in the Broadlands papers, to suggest that Grey supervised Palmerston very carefully in the early years. He expressed himself with a tact which bordered on the deferential but the guidance was there and Palmerston heeded it.

Grey's policy was such as might have been expected from a Whig of his stamp. Men like Grey and Holland were basically pro-French. Here the situation was eased by the overthrow of the older Bourbon line, in the person of Charles X, and his replacement in July 1830 by Louis

Philippe, the son of Philippe Egalité, who had at the beginning supported the Revolution. The decision to recognise Louis Philippe had already been taken by Wellington's government (see below pp. 83–4). Louis Philippe, whose accession had only been grudgingly recognised by the three Eastern monarchies, felt sufficiently insecure in those early years to be glad to co-operate with Britain.

The first and most intractable problem was that of Belgium. Inspired by the revolution in Paris, the Belgians had risen to throw off Dutch rule. It was the first important territorial challenge to the Vienna Settlement. Here too Wellington's government had been prepared to come to terms with events. They had, however, hoped that the Belgians might be ready to accept some compromise, such as Home Rule, under a prince of the House of Orange. A barrier to France still seemed to them very important. Grey and Palmerston were more whole-hearted in their acceptance of Belgian independence. In fact they never seriously considered any alternative. But they played a clever and careful game to ensure that the French did not reap too much advantage from the situation.

The Belgians were prepared to accept a monarchical form of government which, as in the case of the former Spanish colonies, was more acceptable to Britain than a republic. The Belgians themselves wanted the duc de Nemours, a son of Louis Philippe, but the French king was prepared to veto his son's selection rather than offend Britain as well as the other powers. The crown went instead to Leopold of Saxe-Coburg. It is true that Leopold had English connections in that he had been married to the Prince Regent's only daughter, Charlotte, who had died in childbirth, but he was on the point of marrying Louis Philippe's daughter. He can therefore hardly be called simply an 'English' candidate and the British acceptance of Leopold was in itself an important compromise.

For a time it looked as if the Belgian crisis might well lead to a European war. At the outset both Russia and Prussia would have been prepared to use armed force to uphold the Vienna Settlement but they were distracted by a rising in Poland and discouraged by the opposition of both Britain and France to any armed intervention. The Belgians were hardly conciliatory and laid claim to Luxembourg which was a member of the German Confederation, as well as the property of the House of Orange.

An ambassadorial conference had met in London to consider the situation, originally under the chairmanship of the Duke of Wellington. It remained in being until 1839 and was the main forum in which the British government pursued its policy. It was hardly a revival of the conferences of the 1818–22 period since it was not attended by heads of government or even Foreign Secretaries – except for the British hosts – but it did continue to demonstrate that international crises were usually best met by round-table discussions.

As early as January 1831 the conference adopted a Protocol, accepting the independence of Belgium. William I of Holland was prepared to accept the January terms but, when they were modified in June by the Eighteen Articles, renegotiated by Leopold and giving further concessions to the Belgians, William determined to act. He invaded Belgium in August and won considerable success. The sympathy of British conservatives was on the side of William, whom they were beginning to see as the aggrieved party. Leopold appealed for French help and a French army entered Belgium. Conservative anger began to boil over at this setting aside of the Vienna safeguards. This was going too far even for Grey and Palmerston and France was effectively warned off. The method employed sheds a curious light on the tactics of the period. Palmerston wrote to Lord Granville, the British Ambassador in Paris, saying, 'One thing is certain – the French must go out of Belgium, or we have a general war, and war in a given number of days.' He then sent the letter by post, not by diplomatic messenger, in the (correct) belief that the French would open and read the letter (Bulwer 1871: vol. 2, 109; Ridley 1970: 130).

The Belgian question dragged on, although less in the centre of the stage, until 1839. The Belgians were then compelled to relinquish those parts of Luxembourg, which they had held since 1831, in return for more favourable financial terms. The special position of Belgium as an independent and neutral state was guaranteed by all the Great Powers. The precedent was the settlement of Switzerland in 1815 and the country against whom the guarantee was really provided in 1839 was, of course, France. It was an historic irony that the country against whom it actually became operative in 1914 was Germany.

Palmerston played a similar game of watchful co-operation with France in the Iberian Peninsula. Oddly parallel crises had developed in Spain and Portugal. In Portugal the conflict between the supporters of Miguel and of Maria dragged on. In Spain, on the death of Ferdinand VII the throne passed to his infant daughter, Isabella, with her mother, Christina, as Regent but Isabella's right to succeed was challenged by Ferdinand's younger brother, Carlos. Palmerston's priorities were the same as Canning's – to stop another power, more especially France, from taking advantage of the situation. Like Canning he acquired a reputation for supporting liberal and national causes, which grossly over-simplified the situation. The British press portrayed the parties of Maria and Isabella as the 'constitutional parties'. There were pleasant overtones of a fairy story – wicked uncle against innocent niece. Those with first-hand experience of Spain and Portugal saw the struggles much more as factional fighting and certainly Isabella and Maria proved themselves anything but constitutional rulers in the end. But Palmerston's support for the young queens was popular. In 1834 he secured a Quadruple Alliance between Britain, France and the governments representing Isabella and Maria. Palmerston was delighted – 'a capital hit and all my own doing', as he called it to his brother (Bulwer 1871: vol. 2, 186). But Palmerston's pleasure sprang from the fact that he had tied France's hands.

Portugal was easily settled. Miguel had never been a great fighter and he was finally expelled from the country in 1834. Carlos proved more difficult. Palmerston dissuaded Louis Philippe from sending an army. Instead an Anglo-French naval squadron appeared off the Spanish coast. Carlos actually surrendered to the British navy in 1834 and was brought to London. But, embarrassingly for Palmerston, he slipped away and rejoined his forces. The Carlists were not finally defeated until 1839.

The Near East proved even more difficult. At the time of the Russo-Turkish war of 1828–29, Palmerston had briefly believed that the sooner the Ottoman empire collapsed the better (Bourne 1982: 304). But by the time he came to the Foreign Office he was reverting to the then orthodox belief that the Ottoman empire must be bolstered up as long as possible. The greatest challenge to the Sultan now came from Mehemet Ali, the energetic pasha of Egypt, who was all the more the object of British suspicions because he was known to be a strong Francophile, who employed many French advisers. It is possible that Mehemet Ali had ambitions to become Sultan himself. Certainly he was angry that he had not received the rewards he had been promised for his intervention in the Greek war. In 1831 Ibrahim invaded and occupied Syria and Palestine and, by December 1832, he was in a position to advance on the Bosphorus and so on Constantinople itself.

In this extremity the Sultan appealed to Britain. Palmerston would have been prepared to respond but the European situation was dangerous because of the Belgian crisis and, at home, Britain was still in turmoil over the Great Reform Act. The Cabinet was not willing to authorise any intervention in the Near East. Instead the Turks turned to Russia – 'as a drowning man grasps a serpent' – and concluded the Treaty of Unkiar Skelessi of July 1833. Most of Britain's fears about secret clauses were unfounded but in return for a promise of Russian support against Mehemet Ali the Turks agreed to close the Dardanelles to foreign warships if the Russians requested it.

Grey finally retired from the premiership in the summer of 1834. His successor, Lord Melbourne, who returned to office again after the brief interlude of Peel's first government, never professed any particular interest in foreign affairs. Palmerston generally had a freer hand and by now his experience was beginning to outstrip that of his colleagues. Even so he could not always count on their unqualified support. The major crisis both within the British Cabinet and internationally came over the Eastern Question.

In 1839 the Sultan Mahmoud, realising that he did not have long to live, made a last effort to dislodge Ibrahim from Syria. He failed and when Mahmoud died in July 1839, to be succeeded by the youthful

Abdul Mejid, it looked as if the dissolution of the Ottoman empire might be at hand. Palmerston negotiated with both France and Russia but relations with France deteriorated sharply when Thiers became Prime Minister of France. Thiers was a man of a rather similar stamp to Palmerston himself and, moreover, he was looking for a foreign success to consolidate his position at home. The French still regarded themselves as the patrons of Mehemet Ali – a man Palmerston disliked and even regarded as a crook – and Palmerston suspected that the French were prolonging the negotiations to allow Mehemet Ali to present the world with a *fait accompli*. Palmerston therefore entered into a treaty, the Convention for the Pacification of the Levant, with Russia, Prussia and Austria, in July 1840, to which France was not a party. Mehemet Ali had twenty days to accept the terms offered. Egypt would become hereditary in his family (technically he was still a 'pasha' or governor, removable at the Sultan's will) and he would be allowed to keep Syria for his lifetime. If he did not accept the Great Powers would assist the Sultan against him. Mehemet Ali was obdurate and a British fleet bombarded Acre in November. Mehemet Ali accepted terms in December.

The French were furious. Thiers began to speak in war-like language and some military preparations were undertaken. In fact Louis Philippe dared not risk a war on such an issue and Thiers was replaced by the moderate and Anglophile, Guizot, who had been a well-liked ambassador in London. France joined with the other powers in the Straits Convention of July 1841 which forbade the passage of warships (with certain ceremonial exceptions) through the Bosphorus and Dardanelles, which in effect cancelled any special advantages which Russia had gained by the Treaty of Unkiar Skelessi.

Palmerston was very well satisfied with his Eastern policy. He had called Thiers's bluff and got the outcome he wanted. At home the Tories supported him. His troubles came with his own party. This making common cause with the despotic powers and humiliating France angered the Francophile Whigs. Some of the most senior among them, including Lansdowne and Holland, did not scruple to tell friends in the French government that they disapproved of Palmerston's policy. The British press, which also got its information from official leaks, via men like Charles Greville, the Clerk to the Privy Council, was generally critical. In the end Palmerston rather over-played his hand and lost the support of Peel and the conservatives by not responding to Guizot's more conciliatory overtures.

Palmerston's original reputation had been for diffidence. By 1841 it was quite the opposite. There were those who were beginning to regard him as a dangerous irresponsible. Charles Greville confided to his diary, 'There is a flippancy in his tone, an undoubted self-sufficiency, and a levity in discussing interests of such tremendous magnitude, which satisfies me that he is a very dangerous man to be entrusted with the uncontrolled management of our foreign affairs.' (Greville 1888: vol. 4, 308–9)

Britain was in fact dangerously over-extended in 1840–1. She was at war with Afghanistan from 1839 to 1842 and a British army was completely destroyed there in 1841. She was also at war with China from 1839 to 1842. It is known to history as the Opium War and opium smuggling was the trigger point but the issues were wider than that. Westerners were irritated by the Chinese refusal to open up what they regarded as normal diplomatic relations or to allow foreigners unrestricted access to their trade. Essentially it was a confrontation between two cultures and two ways of conducting affairs, with both sides convinced that theirs was the only proper way. The war began when the Chinese placed the British community at Canton, including the British consul, Charles Elliot, under a species of house arrest – the British saw it as a siege – because, according to the normal principles of their law, they held the entire community responsible for the misdemeanours of the smugglers. Palmerston admitted the right of the Chinese to take action against the smugglers but there is a hint of his later '*Civis Romanus sum*' position in his blanket defence of British citizens abroad.

A war with Afghanistan, a war with China and a possible war with France might seem to be enough but Britain was also on the verge of war with the United States. Here there was a whole series of quarrels but those relating to the suppression of the slave trade and to the Canadian boundary were the most serious.

Palmerston had a genuine hatred of the slave trade. Although it had been outlawed by the European powers at Vienna in 1815 and, separately, by the United States in 1807, its suppression in practice depended on the vigilance of the British West Africa squadron and British warships could only arrest slave ships belonging to other nations if they had specific treaty rights to do so. Britain had negotiated such treaty rights with many small nations and in 1838 Palmerston seemed on the verge of a great diplomatic triumph when all the Great Powers of Europe were about to agree to the Quintuple Treaty, which would have permitted a common 'right of search' over all slavers. In the end the French refused to ratify it because of the Eastern crisis. The Americans, apart from the vested interests of the southern slave-owning states, had always been very sensitive about maritime rights. Palmerston was particularly angered when slavers belonging to nations with whom Britain did have treaty rights, escaped by running up the American flag. He therefore argued for a 'right of visit', which would allow the British warship to verify the nationality of the suspected ship. Surely, he said, the Americans did not want slavers to escape simply by 'hoisting a piece of bunting'. The phrase caused anger in the United States where Palmerston was accused of calling the American flag 'a piece of bunting', and they remained adamant on the 'right of visit'.

The Canadian boundary disputes were even more explosive. In 1837 there had been two very small rebellions in Canada. They were local and easily suppressed but some Americans had never reconciled themselves to the presence of a British colony on North American soil. They ran guns to the rebels. Pursuing them a Canadian posse sank a steamer, the *Caroline*, on the Niagara river and killed an American, Amos Durfee. In November 1840 a Canadian, Alexander McLeod, was arrested in New York State and charged with Durfee's murder. It seems unlikely that McLeod had been present and, in any case, the British government had already told the Americans that the sinking of the *Caroline* was an official act for which individuals could not be held responsible. The American government replied that they could not intervene in the judicial processes of New York State. Palmerston gave the British Minister in Washington, Henry Fox, contingent instructions to leave.

In the midst of all this Melbourne's government resigned in September 1841. They had been brought down by domestic issues and Palmerston was furious. Whatever anyone else might think he was convinced that he had the situation under control and that his successor – Lord Aberdeen at the Foreign Office in a Peel government – would ruin everything.

Chapter 5

AN ALTERNATIVE TRADITION?

Palmerston's doubts as to whether Aberdeen would be either able or willing to continue his policy was partly personal – the two men had been rivals since their schooldays together at Harrow – but it was also the recognition of a different approach to foreign affairs. If Palmerston was the heir of the Canning tradition, which was increasingly becoming a chauvinistic and even a bombastic one, Wellington and Aberdeen were the obvious heirs of the Castlereagh tradition. It is now time to ask how much substance there was in this alternative tradition.

It may have owed something to personality but it owed nothing to social origins. Castlereagh, like Canning, came from an obscure Irish family. Wellington and Aberdeen, like Palmerston, were the sons of peers but their families had not previously been prominent in English politics. In each case chance played an important part in bringing them to the direction of British foreign policy.

Wellington, like Castlereagh, was born in Dublin in 1769, Arthur Wellesley, a younger son of the Earl of Mornington. He showed no particular talents as a boy and was destined for the army – a common fate of younger sons. At sixteen he was sent to the famous French cavalry school at Angers, where he acquired not only a fluent command of the French language but also an admiration of the culture of the *ancien régime* and a number of French friends. It may have been their death in the revolutionary turmoil of 1792 which inspired not only his hatred of revolutions but also his determination to pursue a military career seriously, although a purely personal concern – to win Kitty Pakenham as his bride in the face of her family's opposition – helped to turn him from a dilettante into an ambitious young man.

It was his successes as a soldier which brought Wellington the unique status that he was later accorded both in Britain and in Europe. The fact that his early service was spent in India also gave Wellington a particular perspective on Britain's world-wide interests and, more especially, coloured his attitude to the Eastern Question.

He arrived in India early in 1797, not long before his elder brother,

Marquess Wellesley, came out as Governor-General. Arthur's defeat of Tippoo Sultan of Mysore, a potential ally of the French, at Seringapatam in 1799 and of the Mahratta Confederation at Assaye in 1803 not only considerably increased the area of British control in India but also eliminated possible rivals. His early experiences in Europe were less happy. He had been a junior officer in the unsuccessful expedition to the Low Countries in 1794–95 and his reputation was nearly ruined by the Convention of Cintra in 1808 (see above, pp. 36, 61). But, from the time he was sent back to command the British forces in Portugal in 1809, his reputation began to grow until he was acknowledged as the greatest British commander since Marlborough.

He quickly made the transition to a formidable diplomat and statesman as well. In the spring of 1814 he became the British ambassador to the new royalist French government and, when Castlereagh had to leave Vienna, Wellington was regarded as his only possible replacement. He accompanied Castlereagh to Aix-la-Chapelle and was the obvious choice when Canning decided not to attend the Verona conference in person. It was Wellington whom Canning despatched to see the new tsar, Nicholas I, in 1826. After the death of the Duke of York in 1827, there seemed only one person to be the Commander-in-Chief of the British army, Wellington.

He was a less obvious choice as Prime Minister in the political crisis of January 1828. He was not a party man and his attitude was honestly enough summed up in his own comment, 'The King's government must be carried on.' A broad-based coalition seemed the best solution, although he made difficulties for himself by retaining the Canningites, and particularly the weak Lord Dudley at the Foreign Office. From the beginning he made it clear that he regarded Aberdeen, who took the mainly honorific post of Chancellor of the Duchy of Lancaster, as Dudley's 'coadjutor' and designated successor. Lord Ellenborough, who became Lord Privy Seal and later President of the Board of Control, was convinced that Wellington really wanted him at the Foreign Office but, for some unexplained reason, was stuck with Aberdeen (Ellenborough 1881: vol. 1, 146, 212, 213, 216). There is not the slightest evidence that this was so. Wellington thought Ellenborough a wild man, while he liked and trusted Aberdeen. Nevertheless, the publication of Ellenborough's diaries in 1881, dripping with venom as they were about his rival Aberdeen, did a good deal to damage the latter's reputation and also to give a distorted picture of the foreign policy of Wellington's administration. By 1881, twenty-five years after the Crimean War, Aberdeen was very vulnerable to the charge that he had been ineffectual from the beginning.

Aberdeen was born, like Palmerston, in 1784. His family, the Gordons of Haddo, had been staunch supporters of the Stuarts. Sir John Gordon was the first royalist executed in Scotland during the Civil War and his son, the First Earl of Aberdeen, was a non-juror, who refused to take the oaths of allegiance to William and Mary. The Second Earl died on his way to join the 'Forty-Five. But the Third Earl reconciled himself to the Whigs. The Fourth Earl always felt a sentimental regard for the Jacobite traditions of his family. Travelling on the continent during the brief peace of Amiens, he found the Stuart archives in Paris even more interesting than the Louvre and, in Rome, sought out the widow of the Young Pretender. He was always a royalist at heart, although by this time family loyalties had been sufficiently transferred to the House of Hanover for him, later in life, to become almost paternal in his feelings towards the young Queen Victoria.

But for a series of chance circumstances he too might well never have entered politics. The death of his father when he was only seven led eventually to his being brought up in England and becoming a ward of Henry Dundas and the Younger Pitt. Aberdeen always felt an unbounded admiration for Pitt. He joined with Castlereagh and others immediately after Pitt's death to form a party to continue Pitt's policies and, as Prime Minister himself in the 1850s, still proclaimed himself to be Pitt's disciple. It was Pitt's influence which persuaded him that public affairs was the only proper career. Pitt's premature death deprived him of his natural patron but he entered the House of Lords in 1806 as one of the sixteen Scottish representative peers (as a Scots peer he had no automatic right to sit there) after a hard-fought election, when he was the only candidate not on the 'government list' to be returned.

Unfortunately, this early promise was not maintained. He proved to be a very poor speaker in the House and it was partly this which suggested to his friends that he might make a better diplomat than politician. He had already established a reputation as an adventurous traveller and a remarkable classical scholar when, after accompanying William Drummond's embassy to Constantinople in 1804, he had embarked on a solo exploration of parts of the Ottoman empire. Perhaps he might have been a happier man if he had pursued his classical interests and his enthusiasms as a reforming Scottish landlord, where he transformed his neglected estate, and left politics to others. One of the problems in discussing the relative success of different approaches to foreign policy is that they cannot be entirely disentangled from personalities. Aberdeen's calm, judicial temperament and scholarly inclination to see all sides of a question were not ideally suited to the rough game of politics. A not unfriendly contemporary said of him that he made an excellent pilot in calm waters but in fairness it must be added that he also steered his country successfully through some very stormy seas until the final shipwreck of the Crimean War.

The Wellington administration of 1828–30 saw what was almost a rehearsal for the Crimean War in the Russo-Turkish War of 1828–29, which rose indirectly out of the Greek War of Independence. A general war was then avoided and in fact Aberdeen in 1853–4 constantly referred back to the precedents of 1828–29 to try to determine what should be done. The crisis also led to the first difficulties between Aberdeen and Stratford Canning, the ambassador at Constantinople, which were to have repercussions even at the time of the Crimean War.

Wellington's views were simple. Turkish power must be maintained to check the Russians and guarantee the 'balance' in the area. He was horrified by the battle of Navarino and insisted on describing it as an 'untoward' event in the King's Speech, despite the misgivings of Peel and others, and seized on a pretext to recall Codrington, the admiral responsible.

The situation deteriorated when, in April 1828, the Russians declared war on the Turks, nominally because of a dispute about shipping in the Bosphorus. Wellington, who had come to dislike the Treaty of London, took the view that the Russians, as belligerents, could no longer act as mediators between the Greeks and the Turks and the ambassadorial conferences, which were meeting in London to implement the treaty, were suspended. The Canningites took their stand on the Treaty of London and were indignant that, after they had resigned from the government in May, Wellington's line softened and the conferences were resumed. They under-estimated the influence of Aberdeen who was still, in his friend Earl Bathurst's words, 'a great Greek' (Chamberlain 1983: 207).

Although Aberdeen had not openly dissented from Wellington's views during the cabinets of the spring of 1828, he hoped to achieve as much as possible for the Greeks. It was this which led to the misunderstanding with Stratford Canning. Canning, together with the French and Russian ambassadors, had had to flee from Constantinople after the battle of Navarino, although there had been no formal break in diplomatic relations. The three ambassadors met on the island of Poros to attempt to work out a compromise peace between the Greeks and the Turks. Aberdeen encouraged Canning in private letters to try to get Athens included in the new Greek state, even though it was not at that point under Greek control. The ambassadors agreed on frontiers for Greece in the Protocol of Poros of December 1828, which would have drawn the boundary on a line from the Gulf of Arta to the Gulf of Volos and would have given the Greeks Crete, Samos and Euboea (Evvoia). The Duke was alarmed. He feared that an enlarged Greece might fall under Russian influence and that the Ionian Islands, then a British Protectorate and regarded as an important station in the eastern Mediterranean, would be threatened. He insisted that the Poros terms be rejected. Stratford Canning was furious. He felt, with reason, that he had done no more than he had been encouraged to do by the Foreign Secretary (Chamberlain 1983: 213–16). He is said to have danced with rage on the despatch repudiating his actions. He resigned and was replaced by Aberdeen's brother, Robert Gordon.

Wellington's attitude was in fact becoming unrealistic. The French had sent an army, with Wellington's reluctant consent, to save the

Greeks from Ibrahim's Egyptians. (Since the French were also Mehemet Ali's military advisers, French officers finished up fighting on both sides.) In the winter of 1828–9 the Russians, after some initial checks, began to advance rapidly against the Turks. Events in both Greece and the Near East generally were being decided by the Russians and the French, who had the military forces on the ground.

In August 1829 Robert Gordon suggested that a British fleet be sent up to Constantinople. Both Wellington and Aberdeen were opposed to the idea on the grounds that a Russian advance by land might catch the fleet in a 'rat trap'. What saved the situation in 1829 was that the Russians stopped short of Constantinople and made peace with the Turks. The astute new British ambassador in St Petersburg, William A'Court, Lord Heytesbury, had realised that Russian policy was now to keep the moribund Ottoman empire as intact as possible as a buffer state on their southern flank. Modern research has confirmed that interpretation but Wellington disbelieved it (Kerner 1937: 280–90; Chamberlain 1983: 210–11, 219).

In the Treaty of Adrianople of September 1829 the Russians were as good as their word in that they annexed no territory in Europe. But Wellington was temporarily in despair. He wrote to Aberdeen, 'It will be absurd to think of bolstering up the Turkish Power in Europe. It is gone in fact: and the Tranquillity of the World . . . along with it . . . All I wish is to get out of the Greek affair without loss of Honour; and without imminent Risk for the safety of the Ionian Islands.' (AP, BL, Add. MSS 43058: 4 October 1829.) What particularly aroused his suspicions were the autonomous status granted to the Danubian Principalities and the Russian acquisition of Anapa and Poti on the Asian shore of the Black Sea. Aberdeen's reaction was more moderate but he too thought that the dissolution of the Turkish empire might not be long delayed and his thoughts began to turn in the direction of an international agreement to prevent a *fait accompli* like the partition of Poland.

The Treaty of Adrianople was not concerned with Greece but it envisaged that Greece too would become autonomous within the Ottoman empire. Metternich, however, now preferred an independent Greece and his views were shared by Peel and Aberdeen. In February 1830 the powers agreed that Greece should be independent but with more restricted boundaries than had been envisaged at Poros. All were agreed that Greece must be a monarchy, and, after much diplomatic manoeuvring, the throne was offered to Leopold of Saxe-Coburg.

Wellington's government resigned in November 1830 before Greece was finally settled. Leopold withdrew his acceptance of the crown. The new wave of revolutions in Europe in 1830 made a settlement seem urgent. In February 1831 the three powers mainly concerned, Russia, France and Britain, accepted the Arta-Volos frontier, although Greece did not secure Crete, and guaranteed a large loan to the new Greek state. Unhappily they also invited the seventeen-year-old Prince Otto of

Bavaria to become king. Palmerston was enthusiastic, telling Grey, 'He is too young, but still he is of a good Race, popular in Greece, from a constitutional Country, and would bring some little pecuniary means with him.' (GP, Palmerston to Grey 30 June 1831.) Aberdeen, with his first-hand knowledge of the area, had realised that, although the Orthodox Greeks would reluctantly accept a Protestant ruler, they would loathe a Roman Catholic one. His religion apart, Otto had neither the experience nor the talent for the job and his appointment ensured that Greece would remain on the international agenda for many years to come.

The Eastern Question reached an acute stage at the time of Wellington's government. In western Europe the greatest problem was Portugal. Aberdeen had played an active rôle over Greece but over Portugal he was quite content to bow to the Duke's first-hand knowledge of the country. In fact both Wellington and Aberdeen were convinced that in Portugal they were not dealing with an ideological struggle at all but a simple contest for the succession between the two Braganza brothers, Pedro and Miguel.

In 1827 a compromise had been reached by which Miguel was to marry his niece, Maria – such marriages were regarded as acceptable in Portugal if accompanied by a papal dispensation – and in the meanwhile Miguel should act as Regent for his infant bride-to-be. Unfortunately when Miguel reached Portugal in the spring of 1828 he repudiated the new constitution and had himself proclaimed king in his own right.

The British minister in Lisbon, Frederick Lamb, the younger brother of Lord Melbourne, had committed himself heavily to the side of the 'Charter' and Maria. Wellington's views were very different. Miguel was in effective control of the whole country. (The civil war was not resumed until Pedro returned to Portugal in 1832, after being expelled from Brazil.) Miguel seemed to have the support of all the conservative forces, the Church, the army and the peasantry. Wellington suspected Miguel's opponents of being under French influence and disbelieved some of the atrocity stories which were being spread about Miguel. British merchants were assuring the government that they were receiving better treatment from Miguel than they ever had from his enemies. If Wellington's government had lasted a little longer, Miguel would have been recognised.

Suspicion of France was never far from Wellington's mind. He reacted sharply to the French invasion of Algeria in 1830. In the early nineteenth century Barbary pirates still preyed on European shipping in the Mediterranean. Britain herself had mounted a punitive expedition against Algiers in 1816 but the difficulty about punitive expeditions was that the pirates simply regrouped elsewhere. Although on the face of it Charles X's expedition against the Bey of Algiers in the spring of 1830 was just another reprisal for damage and insults to the French, from the beginning the British government suspected that more was afoot. The

An alternative tradition?

French now had an army in Greece. Mehemet Ali was their protégé. At one time the French even envisaged helping Mehemet Ali to take control of Algeria himself. The French expedition being assembled looked too big for a mere punitive raid. Old fears of the Mediterranean being turned into a French 'lake' revived. Wellington spelt out his views to Aberdeen very clearly. Europe had not united against Napoleon because 'of their fear of revolutionary principles ... They were apprehensive of his conquests, and they therefore leagued against him'. Aggressive action by the restored Bourbons would release Europe from any obligation to support them (AP, BL, Add. MSS 43058: 18 April 1830). The pragmatic nature of British policy could hardly have been more clearly stated.

The French expedition sailed on 25 May 1830. News of the fall of Algiers reached Paris on 9 July. This triumph encouraged Charles X to proceed with his *coup* against the newly elected French Chamber, whose composition was not to his liking. On 25 July Charles issued the Ordinance of St Cloud, dissolving the Chamber, changing the franchise and establishing a strict press censorship. Within days Charles had been overthrown and the Duke of Orleans elected king as Louis Philippe.

The crucial question for Europe was whether a new revolution in France and the overthrow of the older Bourbon line constituted the *casus belli*, which had been envisaged by the Quadruple Alliance in 1814, re-affirmed in 1815 and 1818. For several days it was difficult for the British government to get news out of Paris. The British ambassador, Lord Stuart de Rothesay, had not anticipated the rising and the revolutionaries deliberately obstructed the despatch of diplomatic messengers. Interestingly, the British government got its news from the Rothschilds, the bankers whose excellent network of couriers had also supplied them with important information during the Russo-Turkish war. The government would not have been adverse to the abdication of Charles X in favour of his infant grandson, the Duke of Bordeaux, but Wellington was angry when he discovered that Lord Stuart had been engaging in intrigues to support that to the point where he had almost compromised his diplomatic position. Aberdeen, his old Jacobite sentiments perhaps rising to the surface, seems to have had a sneaking sympathy for Stuart's activities (Chamberlain 1983: 238–40). But the official British position was one of strict neutrality and waiting on events.

According to Aberdeen's son and first biographer, it was his father who persuaded Wellington that they must accept the *fait accompli* of Louis Philippe's election (Gordon 1893: 100). In fact the two men seem to have reached the conclusion simultaneously, Aberdeen in London, Wellington at Walmer Castle, where he was staying in his capacity as Warden of the Cinque Ports. What mattered was peace and stability and a guarantee that France would not again become an aggressive nation. Both felt that Charles had put himself entirely in the wrong. A constitutional monarchy under Louis Philippe was certainly preferable to a republic which seemed the likely alternative. On this occasion the rest of Europe did wait for a signal from Britain. When the British government made clear that they would accept Louis Philippe's accession, their allies acquiesced, if not with enthusiasm, at least with relief.

During Peel's brief first administration of 1834–5, Wellington became Foreign Secretary – already one of the few offices a former Prime Minister could accept without loss of face – and Aberdeen went to the Colonial Office. Wellington eschewed new initiatives in foreign affairs. Despite his criticisms in the Lords of the Grey–Palmerston policy, he accepted it, including the 1834 Quadruple Alliance, as the working basis of his own policy.

When Peel returned to office in 1841 he would probably have again offered the Foreign Office to Wellington but Wellington had suffered a series of minor strokes in 1840 and, although much recovered, was still not well enough to take departmental office. Instead Peel turned to his own close friend, Aberdeen. To most people the accession of the calm, experienced Aberdeen came as a relief after what Professor Gash calls 'the last bellicose years of Palmerston's tenure of the Foreign Office' (Gash 1972: 287).

Britain was at war in China and Afghanistan. Relations with France were still bad as a result of the 1840 Eastern crisis. But the most immediate danger was war with the United States. From the British point of view the most dangerous foreign combination would be that of France and the United States. The Duke was not alone in talking of the coalition of 1778. Croker a little later wrote in panic, 'For God's sake, end it [the Oregon crisis]; for if anything were to happen to *Louis Philippe*, we shall have an American war immediately, and a French one just after, a rebellion in Ireland, real starvation in the manufacturing districts, and a twenty per-cent complication in the shape of Income Tax.' (AP, BL. Add. MSS 43239, 13 May 1846.)

Ironically, the conservatives had supported Palmerston over the substance of his Eastern policy in 1840. It was only when he seemed to go out of his way to continue to irritate the French that they parted company with him. It was actually Peel who, in a speech in the Commons on 10 August 1842 (3 *Hansard* lxv: 1280–2) held out the first olive branch to France, but both Peel and Wellington continued to be wary of France. Aberdeen judged the situation rather differently. He had distrusted the restored Bourbons and he was to distrust profoundly Louis Napoleon, but he believed the policy of Louis Philippe and of his minister, François Guizot, with whom he had formed a friendship when Guizot was ambassador in London, to be genuinely pacific. He calculated that it was worth some concessions to keep a peaceful ministry in office in France.

It was, however, relations with the United States which could not wait. On the McLeod case, Aberdeen took as firm a line as Palmerston.

He instructed the British envoy, Henry Fox, to leave Washington immediately if McLeod were executed. On 18 October 1841 a small group of senior ministers including Peel, Aberdeen and the Colonial Secretary, Lord Stanley, met to discuss the deployment of the British Fleet in the event of war. The American ambassador reported, 'There seems to be a general impression that war is inevitable.' (Chamberlain 1983: 312; cf. Bourne 1967: 93–6.) The crisis subsided when McLeod was acquitted.

The quarrel about the slave trade, already acute, was aggravated in the autumn of 1841 when an American ship, the *Creole*, sailing (legally) from Virginia to New Orleans with slaves on board, was forced into Nassau in the British Bahamas by a mutiny. The British authorities agreed to hold those accused of murdering members of the crew but freed the rest on the grounds that, since the abolition of slavery in the British empire in 1833, slavery was not a status recognised by British law.

Apart from the slave trade, the most serious quarrels centred on the boundaries between the United States and British North America. The frontier west of the Rocky Mountains, the so-called Oregon boundary, had never been defined, but the more acute problem related to the frontier between Maine and New Brunswick. No map had been appended to the Treaty of Versailles in 1783 and the wording was capable of different interpretations. As the area was opened up, belligerent lumberjacks from both sides confronted one another. Various unsuccessful attempts had been made to resolve the question, including an arbitration by the Dutch king in 1831. Aberdeen concluded that nothing further was to be gained by searching the records and proposed a compromise line.

The McLeod case had alarmed both governments and made them conscious that, unless there was a comprehensive settlement of disputes, they might well stumble into war. Daniel Webster, the new Secretary of State, was well disposed and sent the conciliatory Edward Everett to London to replace the bellicose Stevenson. Aberdeen was happy to respond. There were some practical advantages in the negotiations taking place in Washington near the scene of the disputes and, since Fox was on nearly as bad terms with the Americans as Stevenson had been with the British, it was agreed that a special envoy should go out. The choice of Lord Ashburton, a friend of Daniel Webster, was a clear signal that the British wanted a settlement. Ashburton was married to an American and was a member of the great banking firm of Baring Brothers, which had extensive American interests.

In the event the negotiations were dominated by the Maine boundary. Wellington took strong exception to Aberdeen's proposed line on the grounds that it would cut the road from Halifax to Quebec and bring the Americans on to the hills 'overlooking Quebec'. In the end the British saved the areas insisted on by the Duke by concessions elsewhere. The

British probably got a very good bargain in the Webster–Ashburton treaty of 1842 since later research has tended to support the American, rather than the British, case.

The North-East boundary negotiations occupied so much time that other matters were overshadowed. The *Creole* case led eventually to the conclusion of an extradition treaty between Britain and the United States. The right of search and the right of visit controversy was apparently settled by an exchange of explanatory notes. Ashburton would have liked a more radical solution, which would have involved Britain renouncing the right of impressment and accepting that five years' residence made a British subject an American citizen. Aberdeen, usually a flexible negotiator, refused. He had a case for declining to make such a fundamental change in British law as an incidental result of other negotiations but he was probably unduly nervous, after his experiences in 1814, of touching any aspect of maritime rights. Despite the exchange of notes, the problem continued to give trouble. The settlement of the Oregon boundary was postponed.

The Ashburton treaty was generally well-received at home. Most of the issues did not rouse strong feelings in Britain. As Charles Greville put it, 'there was a universal desire to settle our various differences with America upon such terms as would conduce to the restoration of good humour and good will.' (Greville 1888: vol. 2, 109.) Palmerston's attempt to whip up feeling against the 'Ashburton capitulation' fell flat. The Whig leaders all came out against him and his attempt to censure the government's conduct when parliament met in the spring of 1843 came to an ignominious end when the House was 'counted out' for lack of a quorum.

In fact relations with America did not run entirely smoothly, especially when the comparatively conciliatory administration of President Tyler, with Webster as his Secretary of State, was replaced by the belligerent and inexperienced President Polk. Texas was one problem. Texas had broken away from Mexico in 1836 and formed an independent republic. Whether the Texans would join the American Union hung in the balance for a decade. The British hoped they would not. For one thing, they would have liked to see Texas becoming a major cotton-producing area, outside the United States' tariff system. For another, British abolitionists hoped that Texas would end slavery, where it had never been important, in return for commercial and other concessions. The Americans resented what they saw as British meddling in Texan affairs. For Britain, arrangements with Texas were never as important as maintaining good relations with the United States and they acquiesced, although reluctantly, when the United States annexed Texas in 1845. Meanwhile America and Mexico were drifting towards war and the Mexicans made a desperate play for British support in 1845 by offering to cede California to Britain. Lord Ellenborough, just returned from being Governor-General of India and now installed as First Lord of the Admiralty, was keen to accept. Even Aberdeen was tempted by the magnitude of the offer. But caution prevailed.

Texas and the West Coast had become intermeshed in American domestic politics and, by 1845, Oregon was a key issue. Until the United States gained San Francisco in her war with Mexico in 1848, she had no satisfactory harbour on the West Coast. In the early 1840s it was believed, erroneously, that the Columbia River might provide a major outlet to the Pacific and the Columbia was central to the North-West boundary dispute between Britain and the United States. Technically, the ownership of all the land north of California and south of 54° 40', the boundary of Russian America, was unsettled. In practice, the dispute was confined to the triangle of land north of the Columbia and south of the 49th parallel. Here Britain had better claims than she had to the disputed land in the north east. In so far as the area had been opened up, it had been mainly by the Hudson's Bay Company. But, when Polk was elected in 1845 on the belligerent slogan of '54° 40' or fight', the British again chose compromise, settling the boundary on the 49th parallel, with a diversion to leave the whole of Vancouver Island to Britain. The motives were much the same as in 1842. The details of the settlement mattered much more to the Americans than to the British. American settlers were beginning to pour west. British North America was not yet ready for any significant westward expansion. For Britain what counted was once again 'the restoration of good humour and good will'.

Aberdeen extended much the same policy to Europe, to problems like Greece and Spain. With a few exceptions, good relations mattered, details did not. This was the issue on which Palmerston attacked him so fiercely and where the differences in their policies become more evident. Palmerston shared Ellenborough's suspicions that Aberdeen would let the country down 'not by any flagrant error, but by being always under the mark' (Ellenborough 1881: vol. 2, 87). In fact Aberdeen was not a weak man nor, despite the deep impression made on him by his experiences of 1813–14, a pacifist. He was the only nineteenth-century British Prime Minister, apart from Wellington himself, who had ever seen a battlefield and he had no doubt that war could only be justified when every resource of diplomacy had been exhausted. But he did not question that every country had vital interests which must in the last resort be defended and he was prepared to face up to the likelihood of war, as with the United States in 1841.

What he was not good at was bluff. Some of the continental diplomats had noticed that in 1813–14. Palmerston was appalled by his weakness in this direction. For Palmerston it was a vital tactic. He once told Bulwer that every country would give up three questions out of four rather than go to war but one must never let one's opponent guess which. Palmerston sometimes over-played his hand, particularly towards the end of his life, but he could not understand the attitude of a statesman who discarded this weapon. Aberdeen's approach was quite different. He believed that most international problems could be settled by rational discussion. For this purpose he continued to cultivate cordial relations with foreign statesmen and diplomats, Daniel Webster and Edward Everett, Metternich, or François Guizot. It should also perhaps be remembered that the 1840s were a period of particular tension at home, with the Chartist troubles rising to their height, and that, as Professor Gash points out, one of Aberdeen's most important functions was to keep foreign affairs tranquil while Peel undertook important reforms at home.

France was the key to the problem. Peel made the first overture in August 1842 but the idea of a close relationship between Britain and France – not normally a Tory policy – became associated with Aberdeen and Guizot. Some practical but important matters – an extradition treaty, a fisheries agreement, a postal convention – were settled without too much difficulty. But Britain was unable to secure French ratification of the Quintuple Treaty on the right of search and a commercial treaty also proved unattainable. Britain was forced, for practical purposes, to accept the French position in Algeria but a French attempt to bring Belgium into a customs union with her – a subtle thwarting of the Vienna Settlement – was brought to nothing.

The revolution in Greece in 1843 was more testing. Aberdeen's first reaction was one of qualified approval. The blame, he felt, attached to Otto and he wrote to his brother Robert, now British ambassador in Vienna, 'I am no lover of Revolutions ... but in truth, it is only the fulfilment of promises made by the three Powers, and by the King, many years ago.' (Chamberlain 1983: 358.) It soon became apparent that the revolution had brought the pro-French party into the ascendancy. Guizot showed Aberdeen copies of the despatches from Paris to Athens to demonstrate that the movement had been spontaneous and not the result of a French intrigue. Aberdeen believed him and took the view, as in Portugal in 1829, that it was a matter for the Greeks.

The year 1843 was generally a good one for Anglo-French relations. In the summer Queen Victoria paid an informal visit to the French royal family at the Château d'Eu in Normandy. The visit was repeated in 1845, and, in 1844, Louis Philippe visited Windsor. From this sprang the idea of the *entente cordiale*. The phrase itself became invested with meaning by accident. In the autumn of 1843 the comte de Jarnac, the French chargé d'affaires (himself an Anglophile with estates in Ireland, and well known in British society), was staying at Aberdeen's country home, Haddo House in Aberdeenshire. Aberdeen showed him a letter he had just written to his brother, Robert, in which he spoke of 'a cordial, good understanding' with France. Jarnac and Guizot translated the phrase as *entente cordiale* and Louis Philippe used it to the French Chamber in December. Strangely, when Victoria used the phrase 'good understanding' in her Speech from the Throne a few weeks later, it disappointed the French who called it '*courte et froide*'.

In fact the *entente* remained an aspiration rather than a reality. In the summer of 1844 Anglo-French relations deteriorated almost to the point of war. There were two flash-points. In 1840 Britain annexed New Zealand. The French were beginning to take an interest in the Pacific again after a generation of indifference. The development of steam navigation led them to search for new stations, since steam ships required more elaborate facilities than sailing vessels and, although Britain already had missionary and trading interests in New Zealand, it was one of the places the French had considered. In 1842 a French naval officer, Captain (later Admiral Dupetit-Thouars), was sent out to annex the Marquesa Islands. He decided that the Marquesas were inadequate and proclaimed a protectorate over Tahiti. Dupetit-Thouars, who had exceeded his instructions, saw it as 'tit-for-tat' for the British annexation of New Zealand. This kind of independent action by a French officer foreshadowed many clashes between Britain and France during the period of the 'new imperialism' at the end of the century.

Tahiti was, as Aberdeen said, 'almost an English island' but Britain had refused Tahitian requests to be taken under British protection in 1822 and 1826. It was therefore difficult, despite strong protests from British missionary interests, to do other than accept a *fait accompli*. But, in 1844, Dupetit-Thouars converted the protectorate into outright annexation and imprisoned the British consul, a missionary called George Pritchard, whom he accused of stirring up rebellion. Popular anger boiled over. The story had everything to rouse the British public: a Protestant missionary persecuted by a Catholic power, a British diplomat insulted by the French, an Englishman torn from his family and imprisoned in a dirty blockhouse by dubious authority.

Peel and Aberdeen were angry too but, from the government's point of view, French actions in Tahiti were less important than a simultaneous crisis in Morocco. The British government had made it clear that, although they could do little about the French occupation of Algeria, they would not tolerate the extension of French influence to Morocco, with its strategically important position at the western end of the Mediterranean. But in August 1844, the French, after accusing the Moroccans of aiding the Algerian rebel leader, Abd-el-Kader, bombarded Tangiers. It was all the more unacceptable because the British Consul, Drummond Hay, was trying to mediate at the time.

However great his indignation – and he was indignant – Aberdeen was clear that the quarrels were not worth the horrors of war, if an honourable settlement could be arrived at. He negotiated patiently and the French agreed to withdraw the annexation of Tahiti and compensate Pritchard. More importantly, they agreed that they would not annex a yard of Moroccan territory. The whole episode helped to confirm Aberdeen's conviction that diplomatic solutions were usually possible and that excited public opinion was a very bad guide in foreign affairs.

Wellington, however, was becoming increasingly suspicious of

French intentions and deeply alarmed at the state of British unpreparedness. Here again steam navigation was the problem. If the British fleet
could be decoyed away, even for a matter of hours, it was argued, a
'steam bridge' could be thrown across the Channel and a French army
landed. Britain's arsenals and dockyards were almost completely
undefended. At first Peel had tended to side with Aberdeen against
Wellington but, after the crises of 1844, he too became impressed by the
argument *Si vis pacem, para bellum*, if you wish for peace, prepare for
war. The chasm grew so wide that Aberdeen tendered his resignation but
Peel pronounced his loss 'irreparable' and persuaded him to stay on.
The question was never resolved and Aberdeen and Wellington's
policies were pursued in tandem, as it were, until the Corn Law crisis
drove all other matters off the agenda (Chamberlain 1983: 371–4).

The Anglo-French crisis of 1844 had one rather unexpected spin-off.
The Tsar Nicholas I visited London at the height of the quarrel. He saw
it as an excellent opportunity to reach an understanding with Britain
about the Eastern Question, to bolster those agreements he already had
with Austria and Prussia. He still felt that the Ottoman empire was the
best possible buffer state in such a sensitive area but he feared that it
might collapse of its own weakness and the European powers should
therefore have contingency plans. On his return to Russia he instructed
his Chancellor, Nesselrode, to put the understanding he believed he had
reached with Peel and Aberdeen in writing. This document, the
Nesselrode Memorandum, was never the basis of a formal agreement
between the two countries but simply a record of informal conversations.
At the time Peel and Aberdeen were satisfied by it – the Tsar had
acknowledged the desirability of keeping the Turkish empire intact and
it committed them to nothing but discussions if a crisis arose – but they
do not seem to have attached great importance to it. It only assumed a
crucial significance when it was made public, unexpectedly and
misleadingly, on the eve of the Crimean War.

The dangers of private and informal 'understandings' between
governments, although they were common enough in eighteenth- and
early nineteenth-century diplomacy, became very evident over the
Spanish marriage question. Spanish politics were still turbulent but
Aberdeen took the view, as he had done over Greece, that the Spaniards
should be left to settle matters for themselves and that it should not
become the scene of a contest between British and French influence. The
immediate problem centred on finding a husband for the young Queen
Isabella and her still younger sister, the Infanta. The latter was
important because Isabella's health was such that it seemed doubtful
whether she would bear an heir. The British wished to exclude a
marriage between Isabella and a French prince. The French wished to
exclude a Coburg marriage. Aberdeen was therefore prepared –
although still protesting that it was really a matter for the Spaniards and
no one else – to come to an informal arrangement with Guizot that

Isabella's choice should be restricted to descendants of the House of Bourbon (excluding Louis Philippe's sons) and that the Infanta should only be free to marry a French prince when Isabella had issue – whether one or more children was meant was left ambiguous and subsequently became a matter of fierce controversy.

Unfortunately Henry Bulwer, the British ambassador in Madrid, allowed himself to be drawn into an intrigue to re-instate Leopold of Saxe-Coburg in the list. When Palmerston succeeded Aberdeen at the Foreign Office in the summer of 1846, one of his first acts was to write a despatch in which he named Leopold as a possible candidate. Although Aberdeen had explained his informal understanding with Guizot on the subject, Palmerston does not seem to have regarded his despatch as a breach of this and actually showed it to de Jarnac. However it gave Guizot the opportunity he had been looking for, for some time, to break the agreement. The notorious double wedding was arranged at which Isabella married her cousin, the Duke of Cadiz – who, contrary to some later reports, had at one time been regarded as a perfectly acceptable candidate by the British – and the Infanta married the Duke of Montpensier, a younger son of Louis Philippe.

The whole controversy was an anachronism in the 1840s – although some indignant critics in Britain wished to appeal to the Treaty of Utrecht of 1713 to declare the Infanta's marriage invalid – and became of no practical importance when Isabella had children. But it played an important rôle in finally ending the first *entente cordiale* between Britain and France.

Historians have tended to accept Palmerston's judgement of Aberdeen and accuse him of failing to stand up for national interests, allowing his dislike of war to be too well known, and relying too much on personal contact. But it is as well to remember that this was not the judgement of contemporaries. In 1846 Aberdeen was regarded as a sound statesman, who had extricated Britain from potentially dangerous quarrels with France and the United States, kept the Eastern Question quiet, safeguarded Britain's trading interests from China to South America and, except over the particular question of re-armament against France, retained the support of Wellington and Peel, neither usually judged to be weak men. It was Palmerston who failed to inspire confidence.

Chapter 6

THE YEARS OF REVOLUTION

Palmerston still roused fears in his own party. When Peel first tendered his resignation in December 1845, Russell's failure to form a government was partly due to Earl Grey's refusal to join a Cabinet in which Palmerston returned to the Foreign Office. Palmerston did some rapid fence-mending when he visited Paris and made his peace with leading French politicians, including Guizot, in the spring of 1846. The Court too was beginning to have misgivings and, in December 1845, Palmerston wrote a long letter addressed to Lord Melbourne but intended for the Queen's eyes, in which he deplored 'the notion that I am more indifferent than I ought to be as to the risk of war' (LQV 1908: vol. 2, 68).

Between 1846 and 1851 Palmerston often lived dangerously both in his relations with foreign powers and with his colleagues but, until his quarrel with Russell in 1851, his luck held. Arguably the fiasco of the Spanish marriages resulted from Palmerston's own clumsiness in giving Guizot an excuse to seize on the revival of the Coburg candidature but public anger in Britain, from the Court down, was directed at the French and some of it spilled over onto Peel's government for being taken in by the French. The deterioration in relations between Britain and France compelled Guizot to align his policy more closely with that of the Eastern Powers. When both Guizot and Louis Philippe fell in 1848, Palmerston gleefully made the connection between this unpopular conservatism and the downfall of 'the Plotters of the Spanish Marriages' (Guedalla 1926: 283). The reality was a good deal more complicated than that but Palmerston's reaction was symptomatic of his belief that luck was with him.

He escaped unscathed from two potentially very embarrassing developments. In 1846 Austria annexed the tiny republic of Cracow, the last remnant of an independent Poland. This was both a breach of the Treaty of Vienna and an affront to western liberal opinion but Palmerston was well aware that there was nothing Britain could do about it, since both Russia and Prussia had accepted it. But he satisfied

British opinion by a stern denunciation of Austria's action in his speech at the Lord Mayor's banquet.

Portugal, that supposed showpiece of British liberalism in action, was even more embarrassing. The radical party, the Septembrists, had won the general election in 1845. Queen Maria, now married to a cousin of Prince Albert, dissolved the Portuguese parliament, the Cortes, annulled the constitution, and conferred dictatorial powers on Marshal Saldanha. In October 1846 the Septembrists seized control of Oporto. Maria promptly appealed to France and Britain under the terms of the Quadruple Treaty of 1834. Palmerston stalled as long as he could but, in May 1847, he allowed the British navy to assist Maria's forces to blockade Oporto. In return Maria agreed to restore the constitution but this was an empty promise since Saldanha remained in control. Palmerston, however, retained his reputation as the friend of constitutions.

He also escaped from a potentially disastrous involvement in Swiss affairs with an enhanced reputation. In the autumn of 1847 he sent his close friend, Lord Minto, on a special mission to the Pope. The main purpose of the mission was to ask the new, and unexpectedly liberal, Pope Pius IX for his assistance in calming the situation in Ireland, which was still in the throes of the potato famine. But Minto was also to suggest that the Pope should use his influence to further the cause of reform in Italy and ease the crisis in Switzerland by voluntarily withdrawing the Jesuits. On his way to Rome Minto visited the Swiss capital, Berne.

The Swiss Confederation had been guaranteed by the Treaty of Vienna but, by the 1840s, serious conflict had arisen between the Federal government in Berne, where the twelve Protestant cantons had a majority, and which wanted liberal reforms, and the seven more conservative Catholic cantons, the Sonderbund. The quarrel had come to centre on the rôle and status of the Jesuits. When in Berne, Minto urged caution on the government but, almost immediately afterwards, they launched a successful attack on the Catholic stronghold of Fribourg. The Catholic powers of Europe would probably have come to the Sonderbund's assistance the following spring but for the fact that they had by then been overtaken by revolution themselves.

Palmerston got the blame, or credit, for instigating the attack on Fribourg. He was soon to be credited with triggering the Italian risings, which heralded the great revolutionary year of 1848, through his emissary, Minto. In fact Minto had only advised various Italian rulers that the fear of Austrian disapproval should not deter them from necessary reforms, on the good Whig principle that reform staves off revolution. Minto did once cry 'Long live Italian independence' from a balcony in Genoa but this must be understood in its context. In the summer of 1847 the Austrians, angered by Pius IX's early reforms, had sent troops to Ferrara, just beyond the border of Venetia. Britain and France sent fleets to Naples and Charles Albert declared he would fight the Austrians if necessary. In Palmerston's eyes, it was Austria who was exceeding her rights. He was not advocating an Italian revolution; still less, a unified Italy.

The revolution began with a rising in Sicily in January 1848. The same month saw the so-called Tobacco riots in Milan. These, a protest against tobacco taxes, were a minor affair and easily suppressed. But, in February, the rulers of both Tuscany and Naples were compelled to grant their peoples liberal constitutions. On 14 March the Pope too granted a constitution.

By then what was happening in Italy was eclipsed by events in Paris, where the government of Louis Philippe was overthrown on 22 February, and in Vienna, where the rising on 13 March compelled Metternich to make his ignominious escape in a laundry basket. The Italians seized control of Venetia and most of Lombardy from the Austrians. On 18 March the revolution reached Berlin and the king, Frederick William IV, not only promised a liberal constitution but agreed to place himself at the head of a German national movement and promised that Prussia would 'merge' herself in Germany.

In retrospect it seemed that only Britain and Russia had escaped the general overthrow of the old order. At the time it was by no means clear that the revolution would not spread to Britain. Ireland was a powder keg that might ignite at any time. As in 1792 there were outbreaks in Scotland, notably in Glasgow. But the greatest danger was apprehended from the huge Chartist demonstration in London, planned for 10 April, which some believed was meant to be an insurrection to establish a provisional government on French lines. The government had reason to suspect that there were links between Irish and French revolutionaries. When the Chartist demonstration collapsed without serious result, the government breathed more easily but nervousness remained for months.

In domestic affairs, Palmerston reacted like any other Englishman of property – with complete hostility to any potential rebels. He took command of the force of special constables assigned to defend the Foreign Office and rejoiced at the collapse of the movement. He was notably unforgiving towards the Irish Chartists and, for many years, unsympathetic to any suggestion that those who had been transported should be pardoned. It is therefore surprising that, in the eyes of European conservatives, he was coming to be regarded as the devil incarnate, who was responsible for stirring up most of the trouble on the continent, and all the more so that this interpretation was accepted by many British radicals.

Palmerston seems to have made his great breakthrough in the management of British public opinion in 1847, the year before the revolutions. From 1835 until his death, Palmerston was the MP for the Devon constituency of Tiverton. The Chartists had considered Palmerston a villain since the Eastern crisis of 1840. (The strong line he took on the suppression of the Newport rising in 1839 may also have influenced them.) In the 1847 general election the leading Chartist spokesman on foreign affairs, Julian Harney, decided to challenge Palmerston in his own constituency. The two met in a great set-piece debate on 31 July. Harney accused Palmerston of being a dyed-in-the wool reactionary, who had defended the unspeakable Sultan against the reforming Mehemet Ali; of weakly allowing independent Cracow to be extinguished; of supporting Maria of Portugal against the constitutionalists; and of an utterly immoral war against China in defence of the opium smugglers. Palmerston replied in a witty, well-informed (although not entirely truthful) speech, which lasted three hours (Ridley 1970: 323–7). There is no question about the importance Palmerston attached to this speech. He had invited a large audience of journalists and supplied them with copies. He also published it as a pamphlet. He set out to refute Harney's charges one by one. It was not really open to him to argue that inaction, or even the support of the conservative side, might sometimes actually be in Britain's best interests because that side of the argument had already been pre-empted by Aberdeen. Instead he tried to cut the ground from under the feet of his radical critics by proclaiming that he had been the consistent champion of liberal causes. He found that the British public loved it, although it confirmed all the awakening suspicions of European conservatives.

Both sides interpreted Palmerston's actions throughout the crises of 1848 in the light of his own publicly stated position, even though his actual policy was cautious, often neutral and frequently ineffective. It was in Italy that Palmerston became most involved. Like many upper-class Englishmen he had visited Italy; he could read and speak the language, and may even have been taught it by an Italian nationalist (Bourne 1982: 6). But he never forgot that the reason for the Austrian presence in Italy – even if they had abused it – was to keep the French out and that consideration still had priority. The divisions between the Italians and the vacillations of their only plausible leaders, the Pope and Charles Albert of Piedmont, meant that they had little chance of success, once the Austrians had rallied their forces.

In the spring of 1848 the Italian national movement had looked unstoppable. The Austrian commander, Marshal Radetzky, had retreated to his final defence line, the fortresses of the Quadrilateral. Tuscany, Parma and Modena declared war on Austria. Ferdinand II of Naples and his former Sicilian subjects – although the latter refused to re-unite with Naples – also declared their support for Charles Albert. In April Palmerston suggested that Austria should cede Lombardy to Piedmont and grant Venetia Home Rule. The Austrians sent an envoy, Baron Hummelauer, to London to discuss the possibility of British mediation but negotiations were overtaken by events. The octogenarian Radetzky defeated Charles Albert at Custozza on 25 July 1848. Palmerston now proposed a joint Anglo-French mediation with the intention of preventing any unilateral French intervention.

The Pope, who had refused to join in the war against Austria in April 1848, was forced to leave Rome in November and in February 1849 a republic was proclaimed there, under the leadership of Mazzini and Garibaldi. The Pope fled to Neapolitan territory and asked the Catholic powers to come to his aid. Radetzky began to march towards Rome. Charles Albert, against Palmerston's advice, re-entered the war but was again defeated by Radetsky at Novara in March 1849. He was compelled to abdicate in favour of his son, Victor Emmanuel.

By the summer of 1849 the status quo had been restored virtually throughout Italy. If Palmerston had really been the advocate of a united Italy under a liberal form of government, he would have suffered a great defeat. In fact, he was not. He wanted to maintain a balance here, with some amelioration of political conditions in some states. Even so he had given two serious hostages to fortune. The first was Rome. Instead of the Austrians, the French had occupied it. The new president of France, Louis Napoleon Bonaparte, the nephew of the great Napoleon, had decided to make a play for clerical support by restoring the Pope. What sort of policy was this, asked English conservatives, which left France in control of central Italy?

The other hostage was Sicily. The British had felt an interest in Sicily since the time of the Napoleonic Wars, not unlike their interest in Portugal, because Sicily too had been a British base. They had even tried their hands at constitution-making there. In 1848 Palmerston came very near to giving *de facto* recognition to the Sicilian rebels. In the winter of 1848–49 the British and French fleets for a short time enforced an armistice in the Straits of Messina and prevented the Neapolitan army from crossing. Palmerston, whether deliberately or inadvertently is not clear, allowed a large quantity of British arms to be shipped out to the Sicilians. Nevertheless, they were eventually defeated and exposed to the full force of Ferdinand's revenge. Once again, British conservatives had an opening to charge Palmerston with having achieved the opposite of what presumably he wanted – first encouraging, then abandoning, the Sicilians.

Palmerston did not attempt to play any significant rôle in Germany in 1848–9, when the Frankfort Parliament met and tried to bring about a united and liberal Germany, only to shipwreck on its divided objectives and lack of material power. He watched the restoration of the status quo in the Austrian empire with equanimity. A strong Austria was essential to the balance of power in Europe. His objections to Austrian proceedings in Italy – apart from a genuine belief that Austria was bolstering up bad governments there – derived from his conviction that Italy had over-extended Austrian resources and that she should concentrate on her rôle in Germany and on the Danube, in particular, to provide a counter-weight to Russia. It was therefore highly regrettable that the Austrians had had to seek Russian help to put down the

Hungarian rebels in 1849. (The conservatives complained that, if Palmerston had not been playing with fire and encouraging rebellion in Italy, the Austrians would not have needed Russian help in Hungary.) Palmerston himself suggested that the Austrians should have offered the Hungarians something like the Dual Monarchy, which was in fact created in 1867, recognising the autonomy of the ancient kingdom of Hungary.

Although they were almost universally defeated, the 1848 revolutions left a legacy of excitement and tension in Europe and, although this is less often appreciated, in Britain too, which influenced both attitudes and events over the next few years. In the autumn of 1849 a number of leading Polish and Hungarian rebels fled to Turkey. The Russian and Austrian ambassadors demanded their return. The British ambassador, Stratford Canning, backed by Palmerston, persuaded the Turks to refuse. The Turks were, however, nervous and the British fleet under Sir William Parker (the same man who had commanded it in the Straits of Messina) entered the Dardanelles, in breach of the Convention of 1841, under a very transparent pretext of stress of weather.

British public opinion was particularly indignant about Austrian repression in northern Italy and when one of the men responsible for it, General Haynau, visited London in 1850, the draymen at Barclay's Brewery caused a famous scandal by throwing him into a horse trough. Palmerston was only with difficulty persuaded to send a formal apology to the Austrians. The offence was compounded the following year when Louis Kossuth, the Hungarian nationalist leader, visited Britain and was given a hero's reception and Palmerston was only just dissuaded from receiving him. It is, however, worth noting that this contrasted very sharply with Palmerston's treatment of Kossuth in 1853 when he suspected him of organising terrorist activities from Britain (Ridley 1970: 411–12).

But in 1848–9 many conservatives in Britain were becoming extremely uneasy at what they saw as Palmerston's irresponsible policy and increasing tendency to play to the gallery of public opinion. His best-known quarrel was with the Court which deplored what they mistakenly regarded as his 'anti-Austrian' attitude. Up to this time Palmerston's personal relations with Aberdeen had been friendly enough, despite the rather intemperate attacks he had made on Aberdeen's policy in the early 1840s. But, by 1849, Aberdeen saw Palmerston as a dangerous man.

British politics were themselves in a very fluid state after the split in the Conservative party, following the repeal of the Corn Laws in 1846. The Protectionists commanded the largest number of seats in the Commons but lacked leaders, since the well-known and experienced Conservatives had almost all followed Sir Robert Peel out of the party. The protectionist leader, Lord Stanley, made several determined attempts to persuade Aberdeen to rejoin the Conservative party and become his Foreign Secretary, if they could form a government.

Aberdeen was undoubtedly tempted by the offer and Stanley and Aberdeen co-operated in staging the assault on Palmerston in the summer of 1850.

The occasion was the rather ridiculous Don Pacifico affair but it was rightly recognised as the great debate about Palmerstonian policy. The affair itself can be quickly described. Don Pacifico, a Portuguese Jew with a technical claim to British citizenship (he had been born in Gibraltar) and a well-established reputation as a confidence trickster, undoubtedly lost some property in anti-Semitic riots in Athens in 1847. He eventually appealed to Palmerston for help. Palmerston was not sorry for an excuse for a show-down with the Greeks. They had defaulted on the 1831 loan and they had treated several British citizens badly. They were also under suspicion of stirring up trouble in the British Protectorate of the Ionian Islands, which they claimed as Greek territory. Against this the fact that even Palmerston soon became convinced that Pacifico's claims were exaggerated did not weigh heavily. Palmerston ordered Parker's fleet to proceed from the Dardanelles and, if necessary, blockade Athens. Palmerston does seem to have been completely carried away. He wrote to Thomas Wyse, the British envoy in Greece, ' ... at one Time it was thought that a landing of Marines & sailors at some town might enable us to seize & carry off public treasure of sufficient amount. Of course Pacifico's claim must be fully satisfied.' (Chamberlain 1987: 72–3.) Russia and France, Britain's fellow guarantors of an independent Greece, reacted sharply. At one point the French recalled their ambassador from London.

Informed opinion in London felt that this time Palmerston had carried intervention and gun-boat diplomacy entirely too far. The condemnation of Palmerston's policy in the Lords in the debate led by Stanley and Aberdeen, was a fair reflection of this. It ranged over the whole of Palmerston's policy, not just Don Pacifico, and Palmerston was censured by 169 votes to 132.

The Prime Minister, Lord John Russell, although he too had many misgivings about Palmerston's policy, could not allow this condemnation of his Foreign Secretary to go unchallenged. The radical, John Arthur Roebuck, moved a motion in the commons, praising Palmerston. The ensuing debate lasted four days. Gladstone spoke against Palmerston. Peel, who had hitherto refrained from attacking Palmerston because he feared bringing down the Russell government and bringing in the Protectionists, now defended Aberdeen's careful policies against Palmerston's wildness. Palmerston was fighting for his political life and he had at long last mastered all the techniques of public speaking. His speech, one of the greatest of his life, lasted nearly four hours. He turned the weakest part of his defence – the Don Pacifico case – to his advantage. British subjects abroad must always feel secure of British support, just as a Roman citizen could claim protection, as St Paul had done, by simply declaring 'Civis Romanus sum' – 'I am a Roman citizen'.

He won his vote of confidence in the Commons but his real victory was in the country. Palmerston was now the personification of Victorian 'John Bullish' policy.

Foreign statesmen criticised Palmerston for hypocrisy as well as bullying. These charges of double standards went back at least to 1848. When Palmerston rebuked the new Austrian Chancellor, Schwarzenberg, in November 1848 for Austrian actions in Milan, Schwarzenberg gave as good as he got. He was not, he said, telling the British what to do in Ireland and 'we are tired of his [Palmerston's] eternal insinuations, of his tone now protective and pedantic, now insulting . . .' (Ridley 1970: 350).

Schwarzenberg kept up this line of attack on British 'hypocrisy'. When Gladstone wintered in Naples in 1850–1 his sympathies were aroused by the treatment of the Neapolitan liberals, particularly a lawyer named Poerio, who had been imprisoned. He asked Aberdeen to use his personal influence with the Austrians to intercede for them. Schwarzenberg in fact undertook to use his influence with the Neapolitans so long as the matter was kept absolutely confidential. Unfortunately his reply was delayed – ironically because Schwarzenberg wanted to send it by special messenger to avoid any possibility of 'interception' and publicity. Gladstone grew impatient and made the matter public himself. As a result the conditions of the Neapolitan liberals actually worsened. Even in his friendly reply to Aberdeen, Schwarzenberg had pointed out that Poerio's position was not very different from that of Ernest Jones, a Chartist lawyer, whose health had broken down in prison. (Jones happened to be well known on the continent because his father had been an equerry to the King of Hanover.) He also again commented on the British treatment of Irish and Ionian rebels. If the Austrians had flogged Italians, the British had flogged Ionians. Aberdeen had also made that point in the Don Pacifico debate. It was generally believed that Admiral Parker's fleet had called into the Ionian Islands only to deliver the naval cat-o'-nine-tails.

Despite his co-operation with Stanley in the Pacifico debate, Aberdeen did not rejoin the Conservatives. There were two reasons for this. Immediately after the debate in the Commons Peel met with a fatal accident. Aberdeen became the accepted leader of the Peelites. As an individual he might have broken away but, as the leader, he felt compelled to negotiate for the whole group. Secondly, Stanley, while pressing Aberdeen to join him, let slip that otherwise he would turn to Palmerston. For Aberdeen this made nonsense of the whole negotiation which, so far as he was concerned, was based on the proposition that Palmerston was a dangerous man who must be removed from the Foreign Office.

In fact, Palmerston was to be removed from the Foreign Office by Russell and it was France which was to prove his undoing. When Louis Philippe was overthrown in February 1848, the British government's first instinct, as in 1830, was to remain neutral and see what happened.

But 1848 was not 1830. That had been a mere dynastic change, but 1848 began to look like 1792 with a possible transfer of power from one class to another and all the consequences that that implied for the propertied classes throughout Europe. Socialist ideas had gained a modest following among intellectuals and the small urban proletariat which was emerging in France. The Constituent Assembly, which met early in May 1848, was predominantly moderate Republican in sympathy, but the National Workshops, established in Paris soon after the revolution to provide work for the Paris unemployed, had had the unintended result of drawing thousands of men to Paris. The Socialists staged an abortive *coup* on 15 May. On 22 June the Provisional Government decided to close down the Workshops. For four days – the notorious 'June Days' – the unemployed workmen and a mixed force of National Guards and regular soldiers, under the command of General Cavaignac, fought on the streets of Paris. Cavaignac won to the undisguised relief of conservative Europe.

But, almost immediately, a new danger appeared. The Constituent Assembly drew up a constitution which provided for the election of a President for a four-year term on the American model. Louis Bonaparte, Napoleon's nephew, who had previously been regarded as a figure of fun for his two unsuccessful attempts at *coups* at Strasbourg in 1836 and at Boulogne in 1840, decided to stand. He won a huge majority against Cavaignac and the Socialist, Ledru-Rollin. It was clear that it was the Bonaparte name which had won for him. Therein lay the danger. Could Louis Bonaparte retain power without giving the French the military victories they associated with his uncle? Many people feared not. Aberdeen wrote to Princess Lieven in December 1851, after Bonaparte's first *coup* to extend his Presidency.

> The President has made his Uncle the model of his imitation ... the President must find employment for his army, or he must disband it ... Perhaps Brussels and Chambery may satisfy him; but he does not forget that his Uncle has been at Vienna, Berlin, and Moscow. Possibly he may take a fancy to revisit London in a new character; and Waterloo is still unavenged. (Jones Parry 1936: vol. 2, 607.)

Aberdeen believed, as did many people, that the majority of the French, outside Paris and a few large towns, were still royalist at heart. The problem was that there were now two claimants for the throne, Charles X's grandson, the Duke of Bordeaux, and Louis Philippe's grandson, the Count of Paris. Aberdeen co-operated with Guizot and Louis Philippe, both in exile in Britain, to try to persuade the French royalists to unite behind the Duke of Bordeaux, known to his supporters as Henri VI. Louis Bonaparte, however, struck first and arrested the man who was intended to play the part of General Monk, General Changarnier (Chamberlain 1983: 396–8).

Aberdeen was out of office but Palmerston in office acted with the caution which usually characterised his deeds, although not his words. He had accepted both the proclamation of the Second Republic and Bonaparte's election as *faits accomplis* and properly only a matter for the French. Arguably the agreement at the end of the Napoleonic wars should have automatically triggered a European coalition against the return of the Bonaparte dynasty but the extraordinary circumstances of 1848 precluded any thought of that. Palmerston did his best to keep in step with the French, particularly over Italy, just as he had done over the Iberian Peninsula in the 1830s. The French occupation of Rome in 1849 showed the fragility of that policy.

Ironically, it was Bonaparte's *coup* in December 1851 which brought down Palmerston. The British cabinet decided to maintain a neutral attitude but Palmerston, still bent on working with Bonaparte, told the French ambassador in London that he approved of his action. Lord Normanby, the British ambassador in Paris, complained that he had been put in an impossible situation.

Russell decided that the time had come to act. For several years both Russell and Victoria had hoped that Palmerston could be persuaded to accept the Lord Lieutenancy of Ireland with a peerage, which would gracefully remove him from both the Foreign Office and the Commons. Palmerston refused the compromise and Russell asked for his resignation. Palmerston was furious and kept a mass of press cuttings and letters, which showed that there was genuine widespread indignation at his dismissal (BP. GMC/47–106). The *Morning Advertiser*, the paper beloved of publicans, spoke for many in deploring the 'sacrifice' of 'the most *English* minister' to appease 'the despotic Courts of the Continent'.

When Parliament re-assembled in February 1852 Russell hoped to discredit Palmerston with the public and his radical admirers by revealing that in fact Palmerston's resignation had been precipitated by his recognition of Bonaparte's despotic *coup*. At the time Palmerston was disconcerted and did not reply effectively. A shrewd observer, Benjamin Disraeli, thought he was finally finished. But, a month later, Palmerston joined with the Tory opposition to bring down Russell's government on the Militia Bill.

Stanley, now Lord Derby, formed an administration with Disraeli at the Exchequer and Lord Malmesbury, the grandson of Palmerston's first mentor, at the Foreign Office. Malmesbury was an old friend of Louis Bonaparte and he was also willing to accept advice from Palmerston. Significantly, Palmerston told him to keep on good terms with France and to remember 'what a power of prestige England possesses abroad' and that it was his 'first duty to see that it does not wane' (Malmesbury 1885: 238). Malmesbury had less than a year to profit by the advice. British politics were still unstable. No party could command a secure majority. In December 1852 Aberdeen formed his coalition government of Whigs and Peelites, in which Palmerston, to many people's astonishment, went to the Home Office.

Chapter 7

THE CRIMEAN WAR: THE TRIUMPH OF LORD PALMERSTON?

The Aberdeen Coalition is best remembered, often only remembered, for the Crimean War. It can be regarded as the point where there was a disastrous clash between the two traditions, now represented by Aberdeen and Palmerston, and there is substance in that interpretation. If either Aberdeen's or Palmerston's policy had been consistently followed, it is possible that war could have been avoided.

Ironically, there was little difference on foreign policy between the two men when the coalition was formed. Both thought that the danger came from France and that Britain should prepare for war. Aberdeen no longer rejected the maxim *Si vis pacem, para bellum.* The France of Napoleon III was very different from that of Louis Philippe. The Commons were quite unusually willing to vote for increased Service Estimates, which should have been, but was not, seen as a danger sign. Aberdeen and Palmerston agreed the money should be spent on the defence of dockyards and arsenals to guard against a French invasion. The possibility of a war with Russia did not initially occur to either of them. The Tsar was intensely unpopular with liberals in the West because of his actions in Poland and Hungary. Both Palmerston and Aberdeen disliked those actions but saw nothing they could do about it.

It was in fact Napoleon III who set the house of cards in the Near East toppling. Still anxious to win favour with the French Catholics, he backed the claims of the Roman monks, against those of the Greek Orthodox monks, to have certain rights over the Holy Sepulchre and other 'Holy Places' in Palestine. In the course of putting pressure on the Sultan he sent the French ambassador to Constantinople on an impressive French warship, the *Charlemagne*, which was a breach of the spirit, although not the letter of the Straits Convention of 1841. Austria also successfully put pressure on the Sultan in a dispute over Bosnia. It is not altogether surprising that the Tsar felt that, if Russia's influence was not to fall away, he too must make his voice heard. The result was the Menshikov mission.

The Tsar was not seeking a war. Nor is there any evidence that he had any immediate designs on Constantinople. Neither Aberdeen nor Palmerston supposed he was or had, but any crisis in the Near East could escalate quickly. Palmerston believed that the Tsar must be warned very clearly, by fleet movements, of the limits of what Britain would tolerate. Aberdeen believed that the matter must be settled by quiet diplomacy. Russia was not Greece or Naples. The Tsar was unlikely to compromise or retreat if he had been publicly challenged in a way which would make him lose face.

Even before the Aberdeen Coalition came into office, the Tsar alerted by Napoleon III's actions, tried to open discussions with the British ambassador, Sir Hamilton Seymour, on contingency plans for the dissolution of the Ottoman empire, basing himself on the understanding he supposed he had reached with the British government in 1844. Seymour was suspicious at the time although the Tsar, who had always taken the 1844 conversations more seriously than the British, may have thought Seymour had invited him to discuss the matter.

Rather better-founded suspicions surrounded the Menshikov mission. Was Menshikov simply asking for a re-affirmation of Russia's undoubted treaty rights from Kuchuk Kainardji onwards or was he asking the Sultan to acknowledge that the Tsar had a vast and undefined right to 'protect' the millions of Orthodox Christians within the Ottoman empire? Either way, Menshikov had a bullying manner which the Turks resented and he left empty-handed. The French sent a fleet to the Eastern Mediterranean but the British Cabinet decided against similar action.

The differences within the Cabinet were beginning to reveal themselves as early as the spring of 1853. The Aberdeen Coalition worked together remarkably harmoniously on domestic questions but the fissures appeared on foreign policy. The fact that Britain gave fatally contradictory signals during the run-up to the Crimean War owed much to British domestic politics. The Protectionists, led by Derby in the Lords and Disraeli in the Commons, were still the largest party, but without an overall majority. The Whigs, led by Lord John Russell, could command a majority if they had the support of either the Irish members or the Peelites but Russell had recently quarrelled with both the Irish and some of his own supporters on domestic issues. It was this which led to the Coalition being formed under a Peelite, Aberdeen. As a result of the 1852 election the Peelites had been reduced to a very small band but they still included some of the most talented men in politics. Despite the disparity of their numbers in the Commons, the Whigs and the Peelites were roughly equal in number in the Cabinet. Generally, although not in every case, the Whigs were the 'hawks', the Peelites the 'doves' in the Eastern crisis. Because of the parliamentary arithmetic, Aberdeen was effectively deprived of a Prime Minister's ultimate weapon, the threat to dissolve the government. On the contrary, Russell was increasingly impatient to claim back the premiership, which he felt was rightfully his.

It was Russell, rather than Palmerston, who began to play with fire and exploit differences about foreign policy to further his own ambitions. Palmerston's temporary resignation from the government in December 1853 was, as he said, because he could not stomach his colleagues' proposals for parliamentary reform, on which he now held near-fanatical views. It was not about foreign policy, although that was how it was interpreted in the country.

Part of Aberdeen's reluctance to give place to Russell arose from his desire to settle the Eastern Question first. He felt that he had the best chance of arriving at a negotiated settlement and his track record in diplomacy over the previous quarter of a century made this a perfectly reasonable proposition. There was no question that the situation was becoming dangerous.

Late in May 1853 the Tsar threatened to occupy the Danubian Principalities and, in July, he carried out his threat. Contrary to what is sometimes stated, the Tsar had no treaty rights to do this and the British Cabinet agreed that the Sultan would have been within his rights in declaring war but they counselled prudence. In June both the British and French fleets moved to Besika Bay just outside the Dardanelles. In July the ambassadors of the Great Powers, meeting in the Austrian capital, prepared a compromise solution, the Vienna Note. The Russians accepted it but the Turks rejected it. The Turks no doubt knew that the very experienced British ambassador in Constantinople, Stratford Canning (now Lord Stratford de Redcliffe) was doubtful about the note but he behaved with scrupulous correctness in urging the Turks to accept it. In September a diplomatic leak revealed that the Russian Chancellor, Nesselrode, was interpreting the Vienna Note to mean the acceptance of the whole Russian claim to exercise a protectorate over all the Orthodox subjects of the Sultan.

This revelation had a critical effect in the British Cabinet. Hitherto Aberdeen had urged restraint. He now agreed to the despatch of a British fleet to Constantinople, ostensibly to protect westerners in the city, and made no real attempt to urge serious discussions of the Olmütz proposals by which the Tsar, in effect, repudiated Nesselrode's interpretation of the Vienna Note. Late in October the Turks declared war on the Russians, although negotiations continued between the European Great Powers.

On 30 November a Russian squadron sank a Turkish fleet at Sinope. The encounter was accidental. The Russian squadron was looking for ships running guns to rebels in the Caucasus. It is sometimes said that, since Russia and Turkey were at war, the Russians had every right to attack a Turkish force but this was not quite how the matter appeared to British diplomats and ministers at the time. The Tsar had assured the other powers that, despite the Turkish declaration of war, he would do nothing to escalate the conflict before the continuing diplomatic negotiations had had a chance to succeed. At first sight, Sinope looked not only like a breach of this, but like a deliberate Russian attack on the Turkish Black Sea coast of a kind which even the more pacific members of the British government had always believed would have to be resisted.

The French were urging action. While Palmerston was absent because of the quarrel about parliamentary reform, the Cabinet agreed to send the British fleet into the Black Sea. Ironically, if Palmerston had been present he might have urged caution, since his actions were always more cautious than his words. But fears of attacks from Palmerston outside the Cabinet probably stiffened its resolve to act. To prevent any further descent on the Turkish coast, they demanded that the Russian fleet return to its base at Sebastopol. Russell saw no reason why they should not engage the Russian fleet without a declaration of war. Aberdeen, with his long experience of diplomacy, was horrified at this proposed breach of international law. In fact, a number of members of the Cabinet, notably Gladstone, became anxious about the legal basis of their presence in the Black Sea and preferred to switch the grounds for the quarrel back to the Tsar's original illegal act, the occupation of the Principalities. It was the Tsar's rejection of the Anglo-French ultimatum that he should evacuate the Principalities which led to the Anglo-French declaration of war on 27/28 March 1854.

The first British army detachments sailed for the Near East late in February. The intention had been to assist the Turks to regain the Danubian Principalities and, incidentally, block the most obvious line of advance to Constantinople. But this strategy was thwarted by an Austro-Russian agreement in June 1854 by which the Austrians withdrew and left the Principalities in the temporary guardianship of Austria. Strictly speaking, all the original objectives of the war had been accomplished by September 1854. The Russians had evacuated the Principalities and Constantinople was for all practical purposes safe. Only Aberdeen and those like Richard Cobden, who had opposed the war from the beginning, thought that the sensible thing would have been to make peace. Public excitement was much too great.

Aberdeen should, of course, have resigned when he found that he could not prevent the outbreak of the war and, still more, when he found himself conducting a war which he could not whole-heartedly support. In retrospect he was bitterly aware of that himself. His motives for not resigning were entirely honourable. The Queen, to whom he felt an almost paternal protectiveness, begged him, literally with tears, not to leave her to the war party. He had every reason to distrust the wilder ideas which were now being put forward and still believed that he had the best chance of bringing the war to a negotiated conclusion before too much damage was done.

In March 1854 Palmerston wrote to Lord Clarendon, the Foreign Secretary, greatly widening the objectives of the war from the defence of Constantinople or even the preservation of the Ottoman empire. Poland could be re-established in its ancient limits as an independent state;

Finland restored to Sweden; the mouth of the Danube, either restored to Turkey or given to Austria; the Crimea returned to Turkey; Circassia made independent and Georgia given either to Circassia or Turkey. Aberdeen thought this was fantasy. Such terms, he pointed out, could only be dictated at the gates of Moscow. He did not bother to add that he, unlike Palmerston, had seen Napoleon's army after the retreat from Moscow. Palmerston, however, believed that most of the Cabinet agreed with him on Poland and affected horror that Aberdeen did not.

Palmerston's ideas for widening the conflict (and Aberdeen's rejection of them) reveal much about the Crimean War. In part it was, as late nineteenth-century British historians tended to assume, about the defence of India; not so much the defence of the Mediterranean route – the Suez Canal was not yet built – but about the British fear of an increase of Russian influence round the Black Sea and into Asia Minor which, combined with Russian pressure on Persia, might one day bring Russia into a commanding position on the ancient invasion route of India from the north west. But India was very rarely mentioned either in the letters of cabinet ministers or in the public debate. At the time the conflict was felt to be mainly about the balance of power in Europe.

Public opinion in Britain was in a quite extraordinarily febrile state. There had been a very small precursor of this in 1844 at the time of the Tahiti crisis but it is difficult to avoid the conclusion that public excitement had mounted in Britain in 1848–49, as it had on the continent, but because there had been no blood-letting as there had been on the continent, it was still dangerously pent up in Britain. Because of his rôle in 1848–49 the Tsar, Nicholas I, was the bogy-man of the whole European left, about whom they would believe anything. Aberdeen in no way shared that belief. So far as he was concerned, Russia was still an essential component in the European balance with whom Britain had no necessary quarrel. Palmerston's views had become much more complicated. In part he still wanted to preserve the Vienna Settlement. Indeed he was still defending it just before his death in 1865. In part, as his letter of March 1854 shows, he had become a revisionist. Prince Albert suspected him of also being ready to use the Crimean War to force the Austrians out of Italy, although here the Prince's suspicions were probably exaggerated. But Palmerston had become imbued with public distrust of Russia to the point where he was prepared to hail Turkey, whose corruption he had so castigated in the 1840s, as a reformed state, more 'western' than Russia. He was even prepared to throw in his lot with Napoleon III of France, whom Aberdeen continued to distrust. Throughout the tortuous events of 1853–54, it was Aberdeen who was consistent in his attitudes, Palmerston who performed a somersault. But it was Palmerston who was in tune with the public.

The hysteria about Russia was incarnated in that extraordinary figure, David Urquhart, who even persuaded himself that Palmerston was a Russian secret agent. More seriously, a press campaign against the coalition had been launched even before the Eastern crisis became acute, by Disraeli in his new journal, *The Press*. Disraeli's motives lay in domestic politics but he chose to portray Aberdeen as belonging to the 'Kremlin School', the friend of foreign statesmen and so by definition unpatriotic, and Palmerston as the 'English minister'.

The press moved into the centre of the stage at the time of the Crimean War. (For a general discussion of the rôle of the press see Koss 1981; for the Crimean War period, Martin 1963.) But, as Cobden saw, the new militaristic tone of the press reflected rather than led public opinion. 'To change the press,' he wrote 'we must change public opinion.' (Koss 1981: 101) Palmerston had long appreciated the importance of maintaining good relations with the press. In the 1830s he principally used the *Globe*. As Professor Webster remarked, 'Few journals have had the Secretary of State for Foreign Affairs as a regular contributor.' (Webster 1951: vol. 1, 50) The *Courier* and the *Morning Chronicle* also supported him. Palmerston, like all British Foreign Secretaries, was aware that it was easier to get news into the papers than to persuade editors to leave embarrassing items out. Very occasionally secret service funds were used to influence the press but the usual coinage was 'exclusive' information.

Aberdeen did not share Palmerston's skill at press management. In the 1840s he had a great windfall in public relations when *The Times*, then easily the most influential newspaper, under its powerful editor, John Thaddeus Delane, consistently supported his foreign policy despite often being critical of Peel's domestic policies. At the beginning of the Eastern crisis in 1853 Delane still supported Aberdeen but eventually *The Times* too surrendered to the pressure of public hostility to Russia. By the 1850s Palmerston had close personal links with the *Morning Post* through the Borthwicks. Other Whig and radical papers like the *Morning Advertiser* and the *Daily News* supported him. As the crisis developed even Tory papers, such as the *Morning Herald*, swung to Palmerston's side because of what they regarded as Aberdeen's appeasement.

Into this excited atmosphere dropped the revelations about the Seymour conversations and the Nesselrode Memorandum. It was at first supposed that the leak had come from the British Foreign Office but *The Times* in fact picked up the story from the *St Petersburg Gazette*. The government's decision to publish the Nesselrode Memorandum was taken to prevent any further leaks but it gave the document a significance it had never previously possessed and created the impression that the Tsar had long been plotting the dissolution of the Turkish empire with the connivance of Aberdeen. Derby made it the centre-piece of his attack on the government in April 1854, insisting (which may or may not have been true) that the Conservative government had not even known of the existence of the Memorandum when they were in office.

Militarism and xenophobia seemed triumphant in the winter of 1853–54. Pamphlets and broadsheets flooded onto the streets. The hysteria culminated in the rumours that Prince Albert had been committed to the Tower as an enemy agent. Public opinion howled for a military triumph. Even after the Russian withdrawal from the Principalities a negotiated settlement was out of the question. Instead the government decided on the destruction of the Russian Black Sea naval base of Sebastopol. This had been considered as a possibility as early as February 1854 but the decision was not taken until June. All members of the Cabinet were asked for their opinion in writing. These crucial memoranda are now among Palmerston's papers and it may be significant that he contrived to retain control of them, rather than leaving them, as would have been more natural, with the papers of the Prime Minister, Aberdeen, or the Secretary of State for War, the Duke of Newcastle. They make it clear that the man who was pressing most strongly for the Sebastopol attack was Palmerston himself. They would, he said, 'lose caste in the world' if, having entered the war, they concluded it with 'small result'. It was getting late in the season to risk a land attack but the alternative, destruction by naval bombardment, was held to be impractical by Admiral Dundas commanding the British fleet. The Cabinet decided, on the face of it sensibly, that the decision whether to go ahead that year must be left to the men on the spot, Dundas and Lord Raglan. (BP CAB/65–79; for detailed analysis of these crucial memoranda see Chamberlain 1987: 94–6.)

Raglan did go ahead with disastrous results. In some ways he was unlucky. The destruction of the British supply fleet by a gale in November 1854 was unexpected. The Crimean winter of 1853–54 was worse than intelligence reports had led them to anticipate. But the basic problem was the unpreparedness of the British army. Disease claimed more lives than fighting. In fact, the Crimean War was not any worse in its horrors, or probably in its incompetence, than the Napoleonic Wars. The difference was that it was fought in a glare of publicity. William Howard Russell of *The Times* for the first time brought home to the British public what war really meant. Wars were now covered by journalists, and even photographers. There was, for practical purposes, no censorship. (No country made that mistake in any future war.) The impact on the British public was similar to the impact of the television coverage of the Vietnam War on America.

The public naturally turned on the government. Aberdeen was the worst possible man to handle the situation. He had tried from the beginning to give parliament a rational explanation of how the war had come about, not concealing the fact that there had been mistakes on all sides, and had not disguised the fact that his first objective was to restore peace. No Prime Minister of a country at war could hope to get away with such a thing. Queen Victoria had a better political instinct. She told him, ' ... the public, particularly under strong excitement of patriotic feeling, is impatient and annoyed to hear at this moment the first Minister of the Crown enter into an *impartial* examination of the Emperor of Russia's character and conduct.' (LQV 1908: vol. 3, 34–5.) But it was divisions within the cabinet itself which eventually brought Aberdeen down. In January 1855 the radical, John Arthur Roebuck, brought forward a motion in the Commons for a parliamentary enquiry into the conduct of the war. Most members of the Cabinet wished to resist it. It was Lord John Russell, the Leader of the House, still angry that Aberdeen had not yielded the Prime Minister's chair to him, who said he could not meet it. Instead he resigned. His colleagues' anger at what some did not hesitate to call his treachery in fact cost Russell the succession to the premiership.

Palmerston on the contrary led the government's defence in the Commons. In spite of that, Roebuck's motion was carried by 305 votes to 148, a larger majority than had been expected. Paradoxically, the House was voting for Palmerston. He had become, in his own phrase, 'l'inévitable' (Ashley 1876: vol. 2, 77). Even so, his assumption of the premiership was not easy. The Queen still so distrusted him that she tried to find almost any other leader – Derby, Russell or even the very aged Lord Lansdowne. Palmerston would probably have been unable to form a government if Aberdeen had not persuaded his fellow Peelites, Gladstone, Sir James Graham, the Duke of Argyll and Sidney Herbert, to stay on, at least during the early critical days.

In fact, the change of government made much less difference to the conduct of the war than the public supposed. Most of the reforms at the War Office had already been put in train under Newcastle. Sebastopol did not fall until September 1855 and that owed more to the French army, and perhaps to Russia's declining commitment to the war after the death of Nicholas I the previous March, than to any new-found efficiency in the British army.

The Crimean War was brought to an end, as Aberdeen had always supposed it would be, more by international diplomacy than by military success. The terms finally agreed were not very unlike those already under discussion before the fall of the Coalition government. The fact that the Peace Conference at the end of the war was held in Paris, to the great gratification of Napoleon III, was a public recognition of the fact that in the eyes of most of Europe, it had been a contest between France and Russia more than between Britain and Russia.

Negotiations had gone on throughout the war, mainly in Vienna. The British and French had tried very hard to bring Austria in on their side and the Tsar's conduct had been influenced by his desire to continue to appear moderate and reasonable in Austrian eyes. In November 1854, negotiations had begun on the basis of the Four Points, by which Russia would renounce her claim to special rights in the Principalities and Serbia, the navigation of the Danube would be free, the Straits Convention would be revised and Russia would renounce her claim to a blanket protectorate of the Orthodox Christians within the Ottoman empire. A year later, the allies were asking for rather more, the neutralisation of the Black Sea and the Russian cession of Bessarabia. The revised Four Points were the basis of the Treaty of Paris of 1856. The most important part, from the British point of view, was the neutralisation of the Black Sea. No arsenals or naval dockyards were to exist on its shores. Sebastopol was not to be rebuilt as a naval base and the Russian Black Sea fleet was to cease to exist. It was a remarkable restraint upon the freedom of action of a Great Power (and provided a precedent for demanding the permanent disarmament of Germany in 1919). For a time it probably did inhibit Russia's influence in the area but it was a comparatively short-lived provision. Russia was able to take advantage of the Franco-Prussian war in 1870–71 to secure its abrogation (see below p. 130). In the meantime, it had the disadvantage of making Russia a 'revisionist' power which, like France, wanted to alter rather than uphold the European treaty system. The wider 'aims' of the Crimean War, to restore the Crimea to Turkey, or even to re-instate the independent kingdom of Poland, were quietly forgotten. Palmerston even surrendered Britain's interpretation of 'maritime rights', mainly the right to intercept neutral vessels, which had occasioned so much trouble in the past (Semmel 1986: 53–9). He was no doubt right in thinking that they could never again be enforced. Aberdeen, when he heard the details of the treaty, remarked philosophically that the country would accept terms from Palmerston for which they would have 'cut my head off'. In fact it was not a popular peace. When the heralds proclaimed it in the City of London, it was hissed.

Aberdeen never returned to office but the popular picture of him sinking to his grave under a burden of guilt is exaggerated. He did blame himself because he felt that war had been resorted to before diplomacy had been exhausted but the well-known story, related by his son, of his refusal to build a church because he felt that, like King David, he had become a 'man of blood' comes from his last sad months when public and private sorrows overwhelmed him. Between 1855 and 1860 he continued to play an active rôle behind the scenes, advising Clarendon at the Foreign Office, at Clarendon's request, and working to ensure that Gladstone would become leader of the Liberal party, which was emerging from the fusion of the Whigs and Peelites.

Palmerston's fate was very different. At the age of seventy he had become Prime Minister and he retained that office for ten years, with one short break. Those years were almost a blank in English domestic reform. Palmerston not only opposed parliamentary reform. Once he became Prime Minister, he showed none of the zeal for practical measures, such as prison reform or smoke abatement Acts, which he had manifested as Home Secretary.

But Palmerston remained popular with the public. Perhaps it was partly sheer longevity. He was an institution. People could not imagine

British politics without him. But his real hold on the public imagination was that of an incarnation of John Bull. He would keep Britain in her rightful place as the leading world power. It was, of course, a benevolent power which would uphold 'free' governments and check tyrannies. The picture was an amalgam of Palmerston's supposed attitude in 1848–49, Don Pacifico and 'victory' in the Crimean War, despite disappointment at the actual peace terms. In fact there were not many triumphs in the years 1855–65 and Britain often stood on the side lines while great events were decided in Europe or North America.

The Crimean War had scarcely ended when Britain found herself at war with Persia. A Persian force had occupied the strategic centre of Herat, long in dispute between Persia and Afghanistan. The Russians had been cultivating good relations with Persia during the Crimean War and Palmerston agreed with Ellenborough that Russia was the 'prompter and secret backer'. A British naval force was sent to Bushire to compel the Persians to renounce any claim to Herat. 'We are,' Palmerston told Clarendon, 'beginning to repel the first opening of trenches against India by Russia.' (Ashley 1876: vol. 2, 128.)

The war against Persia was easily won and may have consoled some who were disappointed by the modest outcome of the Crimean War but it may also have lighted a dangerous fuse in India itself. Disaffected Indians had noted the mediocre performance of the British army in the Crimea. Troops were removed from India for both the Crimean and Persian campaigns. In May 1857 the Indian 'Mutiny' broke out. In part it was an army mutiny, centring on the army of Bengal. It certainly stopped far short of a national war of independence. Two of the three Presidencies (Provinces) of British India, Bombay and Madras, were scarcely involved and even in Bengal most of the population stood aloof or even sided with the British. By 1858 Britain had regained control of the situation.

The British authorities dealt with the mutineers or those suspected, sometimes wrongly, of aiding them, with a severity which far exceeded that of the Austrians in Italy. Villages were burnt; men executed without trial; strange punishments, such as blowing men from guns, were devised. It would be untrue to say that this attracted no protest in Britain. William Howard Russell of *The Times* exposed the excessive 'severities', as he had exposed the incompetence of the Crimean War. But, for most people, they were over-shadowed by the well-publicised crimes of the mutineers, especially the massacre of the women and children at Cawnpore.

Thirty thousand troops were despatched from Britain to deal with the crisis in India but Palmerston turned down all offers of help from the continent, even Napoleon III's suggestion that the troops should travel across France and embark at Marseilles to cut the journey time. Some critics felt that he was taking the crisis remarkably lightly. In fact Palmerston was probably very conscious of the immense threat to

Britain's position in the world. The loss of India in 1857 would have been a greater blow than the loss of the American colonies in 1783. As it was, he wrote to Clarendon in November 1857 that throughout Europe for the last six months, Britain had been 'talked of, and written of, and printed of as a second-rate power' (Ashley 1876: vol. 2, 140). It was not unreasonable to suppose that Russia wanted revenge for the Crimean War and, by an unfortunate coincidence, Britain had become involved in a serious quarrel with the United States about British claims to the Mosquito Coast on the borders of Honduras and Nicaragua.

As if Britain was not already over-extended enough she was also involved in a war with China, and many British critics were very doubtful about the moral justification for the war. In October 1856 a Chinese official had arrested the crew of a small sailing ship, the *Arrow*, on suspicion of piracy. They claimed immunity from his jurisdiction on the grounds that the ship was registered in Hong Kong and flying the British flag. Sir John Bowring, the Governor of Hong Kong, ordered the navy to bombard Canton. The Chinese retaliated by putting a price on the head of any Englishman found in Canton. News of these events did not reach London for some months. When it did the Law Officers were unanimous in their opinion that Bowring had acted illegally. But the double standard of judging Europeans and non-Europeans, which had been apparent during the discussion of the Indian Mutiny, became even more evident. Palmerston held, and most of the Cabinet agreed with him, that whoever had been in the right, the Chinese must be taught a lesson.

A number of other countries were glad to join Britain in putting pressure on the Chinese, who were still unwilling to open their country up freely to Europeans. In 1857 a joint Anglo-French force occupied Canton. The following year, joined by the Americans and the Russians, they took Tientsin, on the way to Peking. The Chinese agreed to the opening up of more treaty ports, the establishing of western-style diplomatic relations, and free access and protection for missionaries and other travellers. But hostilities were renewed in 1859. The Chinese held a number of British and French hostages within the Emperor's summer palace in Peking. When the allied forces got there, Lord Elgin committed one of the most notable acts of vandalism of the nineteenth century by ordering the burning of the palace in retaliation. The Chinese agreed to the confirmation and extension of the Tientsin terms, in the Convention of Peking. In the short run the allies got what they wanted but at the cost of destabilising the Chinese empire, where the Manchu dynasty was already beginning to lose control, and so creating another 'dying empire', similar to that of the Ottomans, over which the Great Powers could haggle and perhaps fight.

Palmerston had to face his critics in England. In February 1857 Richard Cobden proposed a motion of censure. Cobden spoke with his usual measured seriousness and condemned not only the violence and immorality of the British action, and the foolishness of supposing that the Chinese, the oldest civilisation in the world, were 'barbarians' who understood only force, but also the practical stupidity of imagining that, in the long run, British commerce could be furthered by this kind of force (3 *Hansard* cxliv 1391–1421, 26 February 1857). Cobden was supported not only by Gladstone, who shared his moral views, but also by men like Russell and Disraeli, whose motives were more nakedly political. Palmerston concentrated his fire on Cobden. He accused him, as he had accused other opponents, of lack of patriotism, and he tried to repeat his Don Pacifico triumph by ignoring other aspects of the question and re-affirming that the British government's first duty was to protect British citizens. He failed in the Commons and lost the vote, although fairly narrowly, by 247 votes to 263.

In the course of the debate Disraeli had challenged him to go to the country. Palmerston did just that. If Parliament was beginning to have qualms about Palmerston's style, the electorate had none. It was a single issue campaign. Palmerston fought on the question of China but really it was about Palmerston himself. His victory was overwhelming. His supporters won a clear majority of 85 seats in the Commons – the first absolute majority since Peel's in 1841 – but, more importantly, his leading critics, Cobden and Bright, lost their seats. Russell and J. A. Roebuck (not this time on Palmerston's side) only just retained theirs. The country was almost delirious in its support for Palmerston and that support ran across all classes and geographical divisions. On this the City of London and the industrial north felt much the same.

It would have seemed incredible at the time that a year later Palmerston would be ignominiously thrown out of office. There was poetic justice in the fact that it was because he could not control the wild fever of patriotism and contempt for other nations which he himself had done so much to foster. In January 1858 an Italian nationalist, Felice Orsini, threw a bomb at Napoleon III, which killed a number of bystanders, although Napoleon himself escaped. The explosives had come from London. Since 1848 London had been suspected of being the terrorist capital of the world and continental conservatives had begged successive British governments to check their activities. Englishmen tended to reply that they were proud to offer asylum to political refugees and, in 1853, even the conservative Aberdeen had tartly told the Austrians (after an attempt on the Austrian emperor's life) that English law was quite adequate to deal with criminal conspiracies and needed no amendment. But in 1858 Palmerston yielded to French pressure and brought in the Conspiracy to Murder Bill. He was suddenly confronted in the Commons by a totally unexpected coalition of conservatives and radicals and defeated by nineteen votes.

Palmerston was now seventy-three and it seemed unlikely that he would ever return to office. Essentially he owed his return to the continuing instability of British politics. The 1859 election left Derby, who had succeeded Palmerston as Prime Minister in 1858, without a clear majority. Palmerston and Russell achieved their famous reconciliation at Willis's Rooms in June 1859 and, before the month was out, Palmerston was once again in Downing Street, heading a mixed Cabinet of Whigs and Peelites. Russell went to the Foreign Office. One question which had been important in reconciling Palmerston and Russell, and decisive in bringing Gladstone in, was Italy. All three men were now well disposed to the cause of Italian independence, although that was still not quite synonymous with Italian unification.

Palmerston's sympathy for Italy at the time of the Crimean War had alarmed the Prince Consort but there were very obvious difficulties in opening the Italian question when Britain and France wanted Austrian support against Russia. Piedmont–Sardinia had contributed a small (but welcome) force to the allied armies and gained a seat at the Paris Peace Conference but with no substantial result. Two years later, however, the Piedmontese Prime Minister, Cavour, secured Napoleon's consent to the Pact of Plombières, by which France would help to expel the Austrians from northern Italy; Lombardy, Venetia, Parma and Piacenza and the Romagna would join Piedmont; and France would be compensated by the cession of Savoy and Nice. The Austrians were manoeuvred into war in April 1859 and quickly defeated in two particularly bloody battles, Magenta and Solferino, but Napoleon made peace with the Austrians by the Armistice of Villafranca in July. He did not have his uncle's stomach for war and had been sickened by the slaughter, but he also feared that Piedmontese success was outrunning anything he had envisaged. By the Villafranca terms Austria was to keep Venetia, and the Pope the Romagna.

During the 1859 election campaign Palmerston had appeared to come out quite strongly for the Italians, although he had been careful to hedge his bets. No one, he said, could properly set out to deprive Austria of Lombardy and Venetia but she should stop interfering in other parts of Italy and, if she were defeated after an unprovoked attack on Piedmont (the Franco-Italian cover story), it would be reasonable to demand that she retreat north of the Alps. This left most of his options open.

The real test for British policy came in May 1860 when following a rising in Palermo, Garibaldi sailed from Genoa to Sicily with his thousand Redshirts. Palmerston at once suspected another secret agreement between France and Piedmont, with possibly extensive 'compensation' for France involved. His first instinct was to support the King of Naples (the relatively inoffensive Francis II) against the invaders. On 17 May he suggested to Russell that a British fleet should be sent to the Straits of Messina with a watching brief. He was surprised when the French ambassador suggested that the British and French fleets should co-operate to prevent Garibaldi crossing to the mainland. Napoleon had been moved to intervene by fears of the reaction of the clerical party if the Papal States were invaded but his overture relieved

Palmerston of the fear of a secret French deal with Piedmont. Russell persuaded him that, if the Neapolitans supported Garibaldi, such an intervention would destroy British influence in southern Italy. In the event neither Britain nor France intervened. Garibaldi crossed to Naples and Cavour sent an army into the Papal States to forestall him. Plebiscites were held throughout much of Italy in the autumn of 1860 and generally produced overwhelming majorities in favour of uniting with Piedmont. The first Italian parliament, representing the whole country except Venetia (which was still Austrian) and Rome itself (still under the direct rule of the Pope), met in Turin in February 1861.

Palmerston had played no more active rôle in creating Italy in 1860 than Aberdeen had done in creating Greece in 1828–30 – indeed arguably less – but the impression left in Britain was very different. A British fleet had been on the scene but the public probably had a very hazy idea of what it had done, and they felt no disinclination to disbelieve Palmerston's carefully cultivated impression that he had always been not only the friend of Italian independence from foreign interference, which was true, but also an important friend and architect of the new Italian national state, which was extremely dubious.

Palmerston's Italian policy had always been tempered by suspicion of France. Despite the co-operation of the two powers in the Crimean War, British distrust of France had intensified by 1858. The French had been building their navy up since the war and the danger of a 'steam bridge' across the Channel which would convey a large French army to Britain's still ill-defended shore, was becoming ever more apparent. By 1859 excitement had reached a pitch which could properly be called a war scare. Palmerston persuaded his reluctant Chancellor of the Exchequer, Gladstone, to spend £9 million on coastal defences in Britain and Ireland.

Once again it seemed possible that a crisis in relations with France might coincide with a crisis in relations with the United States. In 1861 the United States split apart in the Civil War. At the time the issues appeared more confused than they were to do with hindsight. Not until 1863 did the struggle clearly become one for or against slavery. The original break had come over the question of Federal against State rights. Palmerston, like most Englishmen by this time, hoped to see slavery abolished but he had much more mixed feelings about the right of the Southern States to secede from the Union, if they wished. It was the wisdom of the day that large-scale secessions always succeeded, as the American colonies had broken from Britain or Texas from Mexico. From the British point of view, there was a good deal to be said in favour of the break-up of the United States, which would establish a balance of power on the American continent and, more particularly, help to prevent the erection of a tariff barrier round the continent. Britain was already acutely aware of her dependence on American cotton. One-fifth of the whole British labour force was employed directly or indirectly in the cotton industry.

This in itself did much to determine British policy. An accommodation with the South was more urgent than one with the North. In May 1861 Britain risked offending the North by proclaiming her neutrality – which, in itself, tacitly recognised the South as belligerents, not rebels. In the autumn of 1861 the South sent two of their leading politicians, James M. Mason and John Slidell, to Europe to secure formal recognition. It was the North's seizure of Mason and Slidell from the British mail steamer, *Trent*, which brought Britain and the United States close to war.

Over the *Trent* case, Palmerston does seem to have shown the reckless belligerence which his critics complained was characteristic of his later years. Russell wrote an aggressive demand for satisfaction to Washington, even though the Law Officers' initial opinion was that, since Britain had recognised the legality of the North's blockade, it was debatable whether the seizure was improper. The Prince Consort, in one of his last acts before his premature death, persuaded the government to tone down the despatch. But troop re-inforcements were sent to Canada and pressure was kept up through the British press. Palmerston was believed to have written one particularly strong article in the *Morning Post* himself (Ridley 1970: 55). But, Mason and Slidell were released and Palmerston could plausibly argue that his bluff, if it was a bluff, had worked.

The North believed that Britain had breached her neutrality by allowing the South to buy armaments. The main controversy centred on the ship, later known as the *Alabama*, ordered by Southern agents in Liverpool in 1861. The North complained, basing their objections partly on the British Foreign Enlistment Act of 1819. The British Law Officers eventually upheld the American complaint but, in the meanwhile, the *Alabama* had slipped away from Liverpool. When the Southerners attempted to buy more ships, particularly the 'Laird rams', that is ships with 'rams' designed to pierce the wooden hulls of the guardships blockading the Southern ports, the British government intervened to buy the ships themselves to avoid any legal debate. The more accommodating attitude of the British government was clearly linked to the realities of the war. By the winter of 1864–65, it looked as if the North would win.

Palmerston had gained a certain propaganda victory with the British public by his firm stand on the *Trent* affair but Britain had not exerted any decisive influence on the outcome of the war itself. The government had trimmed to events. The Lancashire cotton operatives who had consistently supported the North and the anti-slavery cause, despite the hardships they had to endure as the raw cotton supplies dried up, had shown more resolution and certainly more altruism.

The bluster which had worked over Mason and Slidell was to betray Palmerston in the next international crisis. This time he was up against a man who was perfectly willing to call his bluff, the new Prime Minister of

Prussia, Otto von Bismarck. Palmerston, like most Englishmen of his class, had cherished some sympathy for the Italians but he knew and cared little about the cause of German nationalism. Despite the suspicions of the Court, he was content to see Austria play a leading rôle in Germany.

By 1863 Palmerston was in fact prepared to commit himself very strongly to continuing to uphold the Vienna balance. In 1863 the Poles were once again in the throes of a rebellion against the Russians. Napoleon III tried to persuade Palmerston to join him in a protest and, in November, put forward what Palmerston regarded as a very dangerous suggestion for a new Congress of the powers to revise what he called the 'decayed' treaties of 1815. The British government returned a very sharp answer. Palmerston's attitude in 1863 is not consistent with his suggestion in March 1854 that the Crimean war might be used to re-open a whole range of questions, including Poland. But in 1863 fear of France once again predominated and Palmerston feared that the whole treaty structure of Europe might be brought into question. He told Leopold of the Belgians that Russia would want to revise the Treaty of Paris; Italy ask for Venetia and Rome; France demand the Rhine frontier; Austria seek Bosnia and the Danubian Principalities; Greece want Thessaly and Epirus; Spain demand Gibraltar; Denmark expect Schleswig and Holstein; and Sweden claim Finland (Ashley 1876: vol. 2, 241). The snub over Poland annoyed Napoleon and made him unwilling to support Britain over the next crisis, Schleswig-Holstein.

The ramifications of the Schleswig-Holstein dispute were such that few people any longer claimed to understand it. The two Duchies were joined to the Crown of Denmark by a personal union, although both had large German populations and Holstein was actually a member of the German Confederation. Complications were bound to ensue when the childless King Frederick VII died since different heirs would inherit, because the Salic Law, barring inheritance through the female line, applied in the Duchies but not in Denmark. The same thing had happened when Victoria inherited the British throne and her uncle, Cumberland, the Electorate of Hanover. But the Danish royal family was not prepared to relinquish the Duchies. When the crisis became acute in the 1840s, Palmerston played a major role in securing the settlement of 1852, by which Christian of Augustenberg was persuaded to renounce his claim to the Duchies to Christian of Glücksberg, the heir presumptive to the Danish throne. In March 1863 the Danish king, Frederick VII, had the unlucky inspiration of making assurance doubly sure by incorporating Schleswig into Denmark. The German Confederation took strong exception and threatened military intervention. It was an unfortunate coincidence that the Prince of Wales had just married Alexandra, the daughter of Christian of Glücksberg. It was therefore difficult for the British government to shrug the matter off entirely. Palmerston advised Frederick to withdraw the new constitution incorporating Schleswig but he also made his famous speech in the Commons, warning that if anyone interfered with Danish independence, 'it would not be Denmark alone with which they would have to contend' (3 *Hansard* clxxii 1252, 23 July 1863).

The speech was taken more seriously in Denmark than in Britain. In November the Danish Parliament ratified the incorporation of Schleswig. Two days later Frederick died. Christian of Augustenberg's son, Frederick, immediately revived his claim. The following month Saxon and Hanoverian troops, acting on behalf of the German Confederation, entered the Duchies to demand the abrogation of the new constitution and the enforcement of the Treaty of London of 1852.

The Danes looked to Britain for assistance. By this time Russell was much more bellicose than Palmerston. He suggested joint intervention with France. Britain should send a fleet to Copenhagen. Palmerston had no intention of agreeing. He deeply distrusted Napoleon's ambitions on the Rhine but, in any case, Napoleon preferred a deal with Berlin. An armistice was agreed in May but the Danes, still apparently expecting British support, refused to make concessions. On 25 June the British cabinet was equally divided on the proposal to send a fleet to Copenhagen. Palmerston gave his casting vote in favour but then conceded that it was impossible to act on such a narrow majority. The war continued and by the Treaty of Vienna of October 1864 the Danes surrendered the Duchies into the keeping of Prussia and Austria. In 1871 they were incorporated into a united Germany.

Palmerston faced the recriminations in the Commons. Disraeli introduced a motion of censure which had already been carried in the Lords, roundly indicting every aspect of Palmerston's policy. The debate lasted, like the Don Pacifico debate, for four days. Once again Palmerston denounced his opponents as unpatriotic but he won the day this time, not by his oratory, but by clever parliamentary tactics. He accepted an amendment to Disraeli's motion, in favour of non-intervention between Germany and Denmark. It divided his opponents. The Cobdenites could not fail to vote for it and Palmerston won by 18 votes.

It was almost his last triumph. He won the general election in the summer of 1865 but died in the October, just short of his eighty-first birthday and still Prime Minister.

Russell succeeded him as Prime Minister and Clarendon went back to the Foreign Office. By far the most important development in Europe between the death of Palmerston and the fall of the Russell administration the following June was the deterioration of relations between the two Germanic powers, which was to culminate in the Austro-Prussian war. Warned by their ill success in the Danish crisis, the British remained on the side-lines. Clarendon told the Queen on 31 March 1866, 'The country would not tolerate any direct interference in a quarrel with which we had no concern' and the Cabinet had been unanimous against it (LQV 2nd Ser, 1926: vol. 1, 315). The incoming conservative administration endorsed that. Lord Stanley told the Commons, 'Ours will be a pacific policy, a policy of observation rather than action. I think there never was a great European war in which the direct national interests of England were less concerned.' (Kennedy 1982 12–18 for full discussion.) Bismarck did not even regard it as necessary to buy British diplomatic support, as he secured that of France and Italy.

III. A NEW AND MORE DANGEROUS WORLD

III. A NEW AND MORE DANGEROUS WORLD

Chapter 8

THE TURNING POINT

From the Treaty of Vienna in 1815 to the death of Palmerston in 1865, Britain could reasonably be described as a 'satiated' power in Europe and, for the most part overseas, with no particular ambitions to pursue. The industrial revolution had given her a long lead over her potential rivals and the British wanted peace and stability in the world and the general triumph of free trade ideals. Free trade had come to assume the status almost of a gospel in Britain, where it was believed that it would ensure not only universal prosperity but also universal peace. Its virtues were argued most persuasively by the leaders of the Manchester School, Richard Cobden with his almost unanswerable logic, and John Bright, who added the emotional salt of his Quaker beliefs. Ironically, it was in the 1860s, when free trade ideals seemed to have at last triumphed in Europe, when even France was dismantling her protectionist system and had signed a free trade treaty with Britain, negotiated by Cobden himself, that the first cracks began to appear.

So far as Europe was concerned Britain had been content to uphold the Vienna balance; despite their differences on tactics, which could be considerable, that had been the basic aim of Canning and Palmerston as well as of Castlereagh and Aberdeen. The ideal rôle of the Foreign Secretary was, as Lord Salisbury later described it, 'floating lazily down stream, occasionally putting out a diplomatic boathook to avoid collisions' (Cecil 1921: vol. 2, 130). The country to be watched, and if necessary checked, was France, although various methods could be employed, friendship, precautionary alliances or frank armaments. Russia was intensely unpopular with the public, especially the radical public, but governments were generally less alarmed. In that sense the Crimean War was a messy accident which could have been avoided by diplomacy, as Aberdeen always believed that it should have been. (For an interesting new argument on this see N. Rich (1985).) Britain's mild preference for constitutional states – a preference which could be overridden when other strategic factors came into play, as they did in Italy in 1848–49 – was not unconnected with the belief that a powerful middle class, usual in a constitutional state, made for good trading relations.

This equilibrium, which suited Britain very well, was about to be overturned. The British were so oblivious to what was happening that they do not seem to have had any very clear view of the matter, never mind any ambition to intervene to influence events. The unification of virtually the whole of Italy in 1861, although unexpected by the British government, was rightly felt to be no particular political or economic threat in the foreseeable future. (It was only in the 1980s that the Italian standard of living passed the British.) The Italians lacked the coal and iron resources requisite for the first industrial revolution and had difficulty in making good their claim to be regarded as a fully fledged Great Power. They were well disposed towards Britain and might be a useful, if subordinate, force in the balance of power. In the meantime Britain, well taught by Palmerston, could rejoice in the triumph of nationalism and liberalism.

The victory of the North in the American Civil War was seen as rather more of a mixed blessing. The high tariffs put on during the war were never really relaxed and it required no exceptional powers of prophecy to see that the United States, now secure from the Atlantic to the Pacific and from the Caribbean to the Canadian border, had the resources to become a formidable industrial rival. Nor was it by any means certain that the United States could be regarded as a friendly power. The Americans still resented the presence of British colonies in the western hemisphere, as had been quite recently demonstrated over the Mosquito Coast and their now considerable Irish population had particular reasons to be anti-British. The 1860s were to see the Fenian raids across the border into Canada. But the British had been neither able nor anxious to play any decisive rôle in the war. The public could, however, once again console themselves with the thought that the righteous side, in this case the anti-slavery side, had won.

The rise of a united Germany was to be the decisive factor in overturning the world balance of power which had been on the whole very favourable to British interests, yet here again the British public and government watched with a mild interest, which gave no hint of any appreciation of the significance of what was happening. There was not the same reservoir of sympathy among the upper classes for German nationalism as there was for Italian nationalism. As far as they could see the Germans were not being oppressed by foreigners, as arguably the Italians were by the Austrians. The German Confederation seemed to give the Germans as much opportunity for collective action as it was assumed most of them, reasonably content with their own states, were likely to want. Those Britons who cared about the matter at all probably regretted the failure of liberalism, rather than nationalism, in 1848–9. At the same time the British were generally well disposed towards the Germans. The Germans had frequently been their allies against the

French, most recently in the Napoleonic Wars. The British had a feeling of cousinship for the Germans, fostered by recent scholarship, which often emphasised Britain's Anglo-Saxon past. The British stood aloof from both the Austro-Prussian War and the Franco-Prussian War which together created the new German Reich and made Prussia, not Austria, the dominant German power. (For discussion of the British attitude to the Franco-Prussian War see below pp. 129–30.) In the eighteenth century Britain had been drawn into continental wars of far less moment.

In the 1860s Britain seemed equally passive in her attitude to the world outside Europe. The eighteenth century had seen strenuous contests for empire between the European maritime powers. At the end of the Napoleonic Wars Britain had been prepared to use most of her colonial gains – except those on the route to India – as mere bargaining counters. With the triumph of free trade it became the received political wisdom to say that colonies were expensive burdens of no benefit to the mother country which should be disposed of as soon as possible. It has, of course, been pointed out that no European country acted on this axiom. Britain did not merely not get rid of her colonies in the first half of the nineteenth century; she acquired more, especially in the 1840s (Robinson and Gallagher 1953).

It is, however, true that Britain declined to acquire a number of territories which were offered to her and Robinson and Gallagher are convincing in their argument that Britain preferred 'informal suasion' to actual political control so long as informal influence was adequate to protect her trading interests (Robinson and Gallagher 1953, 1981). The Niger delta provides a perfect example of this. Britain had important trading interests there, the export of textiles and metal goods in exchange for vegetable oils. Until the 1880s no other European power had any significant presence there. From 1849 the British consul, a remarkable man named John Beecroft, won for himself an extraordinary position as an arbitrator in the region (Dike 1956: 93–6). But not until the Berlin West Africa Conference internationalised the question in 1884–5 did Britain make any attempt to claim formal authority. Equally, there is no reason to question the sincerity of the 1865 Parliamentary Select Committee which recommended that Britain should on no account acquire any more West African territory and that it would be sensible to dispose of her existing stations there, with the possible exception of Freetown in Sierra Leone, with its excellent naval harbour. Within ten years of that report British policy was to begin to change dramatically.

Britain could no longer be regarded as a 'satiated' power in the imperial field. In the last quarter of the nineteenth century she acquired over 4 million square miles of territory and the total population of the empire grew by perhaps 90 million subjects. Population statistics for the remoter areas were vague. But there was no question that by 1914, with a total population in the region of 400 million (of whom only one-tenth lived in the British Isles), it was the largest empire in both geographical area and population that the world had ever known. On the face of it British policy in the last quarter or so of the nineteenth century was dynamic, not simply reactive as it had been during the previous three-quarters of a century.

The irony is that, far from being an overflowing of pride and national spirit – as it was often represented at the time by supporters and critics alike – it was essentially defensive, an expression of weakness, not of strength. Britain was now being challenged by powers which were potentially much stronger that she was, the United States and Germany. It became apparent to the British that they could only remain a Great Power, if they too were the centre of a great empire. For obvious geographical reasons in their case, this must be a maritime, not a land-based empire. They seemed to have at least a sporting chance of remaining among the greatest powers. They already had a navy, which still commanded the seas, and a world-wide empire. They governed the sub-continent of India – their greatest prize from the eighteenth-century contests for empire. They still had a stake in the American hemisphere in Canada and the West Indies; control of Australasia; and the strategic base of the Cape of Good Hope which had grown into another major colony of settlement. Britain was to acquire the largest single share of the African continent. She was well placed to take part in the Scramble for China, which seemed likely to succeed the Scramble for Africa. It was the scramble for the other 'dying empire', the Ottoman, which was to put Britain together with the European powers on the course for disaster.

The conservative government of Derby and Disraeli came into office in the middle of the Austro-Prussian war. They were no more inclined than Russell's government to intervene but Disraeli explained their abstention in rather different terms. He told the electors,

> The abstention of England from any unnecessary interference in the affairs of Europe is the consequence, not of her decline of power, but of her increased strength. England is no longer a mere European Power; she is the metropolis of a great maritime empire, extending to the boundaries of the farthest ocean. It is not that England has taken refuge in a state of apathy ... She interferes in Asia, because she is really more an Asiatic power than a European. She interferes in Australia, in Africa, and New Zealand, where she carries on war often on a great scale.

But he added, 'We are interested in the peace and prosperity of Europe, and I do not say that there may not be occasions in which it may be the duty of England to interfere in European wars.' (Monypenny and Buckle 1916: vol. 4, 467.)

Disraeli was making a virtue of necessity and doing it with a skill which showed him to be a worthy successor of Canning and Palmerston but there was also truth in what he said. Britain would concentrate on her overseas interests but she could not allow the situation in Europe to become too unfavourable to her. This same point is emphasised by a modern historian, Professor Martel in his study of Rosebery, when he says, 'Rosebery was convinced that Britain's position as an imperial power could be maintained only through the balance of power in Europe.' (Martel 1986: 223.) This made a nonsense of the proposition that Britain would prefer 'splendid isolation' but it meant that the balancing act she had to perform eventually between the Dual Alliance and the Triple Alliance was a very complicated one. Gladstone's attempt to ensure that it would never become necessary, by maintaining the old 'open' concert system, failed.

This diplomacy was too complicated to present to an uninformed public. Where a Castlereagh or an Aberdeen might have taken refuge in a lofty professionalism, both Gladstone and Disraeli, faced with a greatly extended electorate, had to find new ways of presenting their policies to the public. For Gladstone this meant the Midlothian campaign; for Disraeli, a new emphasis on Britain as an imperial power.

Only in the very recent past, in books such as M. Swartz's *The Politics of British Foreign Policy in the Era of Disraeli and Gladstone* (1985), has the relationship of domestic and foreign policy in Britain in this period begun to be examined as the relationship in Germany has been examined by writers such as H.-U. Wehler (1969, 1985). The crudest and most obvious way in which foreign policy can be exploited to influence domestic politics is that which was known to Victorian England as Bonapartism, a deliberate pursuit of a 'glorious' foreign policy to unite the nation and to distract attention from domestic grievances. This element was not entirely absent from late Victorian foreign policy. But the new enthusiasm for imperialism had altogether deeper roots. From 1873 onwards it was increasingly obvious that there was something seriously wrong with the British economy and that this might have grave social consequences. Not everyone came to believe that the empire, and the empire alone, could solve Britain's domestic ills but by the late 1890s this was the orthodoxy of the great majority.

Chapter 9

'IMPERIUM ET SANITAS' VERSUS MIDLOTHIAN

The great protagonists at the beginning of this new period were William Gladstone and Benjamin Disraeli. A dramatist could not have chosen two more contrasting characters. Gladstone seemed to be the epitome of high-minded Victorian earnestness, a religious man who brought all political issues to the bar of moral judgement and made no concessions to his audience. He expressed his views in long, rolling and, to modern taste, cumbersome sentences but, by all contemporary accounts, his speeches were effective. Queen Victoria might complain that he addressed her like a public meeting, but the electorate was captured by his ability to speak to them, not as 'a miner or a boiler-maker brooding over the hardships of his life but [as] a classless man whose mind is playing freely, able to give a disinterested study to a great issue' (Hammond 1938: 706). Disraeli projected, indeed cultivated, quite the opposite image, brilliant, witty, possibly meretricious, apparently at any rate frivolous in his approach to life. In foreign affairs, he proclaimed himself the disciple of Canning (Blake 1966: 571, 615).

Of the two, Gladstone had by far the more orthodox background. Like Peel he came from a middle-class family, which had become sufficiently wealthy to give its sons an upper-class education. Despite being sent to Eton and Oxford, Gladstone never quite lost the attitudes of his Scottish family, who had become successful Liverpool merchants. His friend, Lord Acton, could still discern the 'stumps' of his Calvinist ancestry, despite Gladstone's own conversion to the High Church movement. Gladstone may have exaggerated the extent to which he was turned away from a career in the Church by his family (Shannon 1982: 28–9) but his religious cast of mind was such that he always had to view his political campaigns as 'missions'. Unlike most men, he became steadily less conservative as he got older. In the 1830s he was, in Macaulay's famous phrase, 'the rising hope of the stern, unbending Tories'. He finally left office in 1895 as a Liberal Prime Minister, whose back benchers included David Lloyd George.

Gladstone was a man of strong intellect, who thought out his principles for himself. The basis of his liberalism differed from that of most of his contemporaries. He found his prophets, not in John Locke, Adam Smith, Jeremy Bentham or J. S. Mill, but in Aristotle, St Augustine, Dante and Bishop Butler. His belief in the universal dignity of man sprang from his classical studies as well as from his Christian beliefs and there was a European dimension to his thought which made him able to see the Irish question in a way most of his contemporaries could not, from a European standpoint (Morley 1903: vol. 1, 207; Hammond 1938: 533–7, 53–65). Within British politics the strongest influences on the development of his views were, in domestic affairs, Peel and, in foreign affairs, Aberdeen. Peel was Gladstone's first important political patron and, as Morley said, they 'were in the strict line of political succession' (Morley 1903: vol. 1, 269) but it was Aberdeen, of whom Gladstone said to the Duchess of Sutherland in 1855 'I love [him] like a father, while I reverence him almost like a being from another world.' (Magnus 1963: 120.)

Disraeli was a very rare phenomenon in British politics, the complete outsider who rose to the top. Jewish by birth, but for his father's quarrel with the local synagogue, he would never have been baptised into the Anglican Church and become eligible to enter the House of Commons. A failed lawyer, a failed stock exchange speculator and, apparently, a failed novelist, he went on a tour of the Near East in 1830, which included visits to Turkey and Egypt. His imagination was captured. One difference which is often overlooked between the 'imperialist' generation and their predecessors is that the younger men had often travelled outside Europe. Their predecessors very rarely had. This was to be even more true of Charles Dilke and Lord Rosebery than of Disraeli.

On his return Disraeli stood for Parliament as a radical. His switch to the Conservatives in 1835 was not quite so cynical as it appears at first sight. Leaving aside the fact that the Tories were slightly less oligarchical than the Whigs – and therefore easier for an outsider to penetrate – the influential reformers within the Whig party, the Benthamites, were a type of radical particularly obnoxious to Disraeli. He felt much more affinity for the popular radicals, like William Cobbett or Orator Hunt who, in their different ways, hated the results of the industrial revolution. His first attempt at party building was the Young England party of rather sentimental young aristocrats, looking back to a largely imaginary past. Disraeli himself could probably never have expected much more than a Taper or Tadpole 'man of business' rôle but for the split in the party on the repeal of the Corn Laws, which left him almost the only man of real political talent among the Protectionists. Even so, it was not until ill-health compelled Derby's resignation in February 1868 that Disraeli was finally recognised as the leader of the party.

When Russell's government was forced to resign in June 1866, after failing to carry a parliamentary reform measure, it was the Derby–Disraeli ministry which brought off a famous *coup* by passing the

Second Reform Act which, together with a separate measure for Scotland in 1868, approximately doubled the electorate to (excluding Ireland) rather over 2 million voters, or approximately 36 per cent of the adult male population (Evans 1983: 379). It was still a very narrow franchise by modern standards but the more astute politicians had already begun to see that they would have to widen their appeal. It has been suggested (Harcourt 1980) that the Derby–Disraeli ministry embarked on one foreign adventure, the Abyssinian campaign, which was a direct appeal to popular sentiment, as well as a public affirmation that Britain was not negligible as a military power, despite her passivity in the recent European crises, including the Austro-Prussian War. The case for intervention was a strong one, to the Victorian mind an overwhelming one. The Abyssinian emperor, Theodore, had imprisoned and ill-treated the British consul, Captain C. D. Cameron, and a number of other Europeans. A rescue expedition was mounted from India, under the command of Sir Robert (later Lord) Napier. It was a classic hostage situation and the main British fear was that the expedition might fail or the captives be killed (DP. B/XVIII/H). In fact a serious miscalculation by Theodore delivered his army into Napier's hands, his capital Magdala was captured, and Theodore committed suicide. The expedition attracted a number of young men following the new profession of war correspondent, among them the Welsh-American, Henry Morton Stanley, better known for his own explorations, and there was extensive press coverage.

To what extent the Abyssinian campaign was a deliberate attempt to provide the British public with a 'national' cause, which would appeal to the extended electorate and distract public attention from the dangerous economic and social problems which were emerging, is not an easy question to resolve. It is true that the so-called 'Battle of Hyde Park' in 1866, concerned with the struggle for the extension of the franchise, was the first serious political challenge to public order in London since the Chartists. It is also true that the middle classes were becoming increasingly aware of the potentially dangerous forces penned up in the slums. Dr Harcourt dates the beginning of the general sense of crisis to the great banking crash of Overend and Gurney in 1866 (Harcourt 1980: 89) but this seems early. Although the mid-Victorian period of prosperity was certainly not the seamless web it was at one time supposed to be (Church 1975) the 1860s do seem on balance a fairly optimistic decade and it was not until after the European financial crisis of 1873 that serious doubts set in. Certainly those giving evidence to the extremely detailed Royal Commission enquiry into the state of depression in trade and industry in the 1880s (PP. 1886, xxx, 1, 231; xxii, 1; xxiii, 1), almost unanimously dated the beginning of the crisis to the mid-seventies.

Nevertheless, something was stirring in the late sixties and this was reflected in the reviving British interest in the empire. This was not at first directed to any ambitions for a great expansion of empire, such as happened twenty years later, but to a sober interest in the British colonies of settlement. One symptom was the founding of the Colonial Society, later the Royal Colonial Institute, an expert body with a prestigious membership from both Britain and the colonies. Like a number of other quasi-scientific organisations, it easily passed into being a pressure group (Reese 1968). Another symptom, to which Bodelsen long ago drew attention (1924, 1960) was the sudden increase of articles on colonial matters appearing in the press and periodicals.

It was this new interest, rather than any change of government policy, which led to the charges that Gladstone's first government of 1868–74 was actively trying to break up the empire and put into practice those doctrines of separation, which had long been fashionable but never acted upon. The government was reluctant to send troop re-inforcements to aid the New Zealand colonists in their quarrel with the Maoris, not least because the Colonial Office, drawing some of its information from missionary sources, suspected that the colonists were the aggressors. Casual speeches by officials in Canada and South Africa, expressing sentiments which would have been regarded as unexceptionable for the previous forty years, were seized upon as evidence of 'separatist' designs. It is true that the governments of the time, Conservative as well as Liberal, were anxious to give the larger colonies more responsibility for their own affairs, which it was hoped would mean that they would take more responsibility for their own defence and remove some of the burden from British shoulders. The British North America Act of 1867 which brought the Confederation of Canada into being, proposed by the Canadians for a mixture of political and economic reasons, was attractive to the British partly because they thought it would make the Canadians more able to resist the Americans. Similarly, the internal self-government, which was virtually thrust upon Cape Province in 1872, was a deliberate attempt to make the South Africans stand upon their own feet.

As emigration to the colonies of settlement increased with the economic depression at home (and by about 1900 British emigrants were beginning to turn more to the colonies and less to the United States), the working classes felt more involvement with those countries, in which a close relative might well be living. This helps to explain why the new interest in empire was by no means confined to the upper classes or to those with generally right-wing views.

Disraeli began to associate the Conservative party with the empire in 1872, in a speech in Manchester and in the better-known one at the Crystal Palace. The imperial theme did not predominate in either and only in retrospect did they come to seem important. Both may have been what modern political slang would call a 'kite-flying' exercise but they fitted in with Disraeli's general policy of associating the working classes with the Crown and representing the Conservative party as the party of national interest, in contrast to the Liberal representation of sectional, mainly middle-class, interests. It has been suggested that there was blatant electioneering in this; that Disraeli tried to rouse the voters against Gladstone on the old cry of 'The Church in danger', following Gladstone's disestablishment of the Irish Church in 1869 and, only when this failed, did he try the new cry of 'The Empire in danger'. This is possible, although not entirely proven, but even if true, it shows that such a seasoned campaigner as Disraeli saw that there was now electoral advantage to gain by playing the empire card.

It has also been argued that there was no 'conversion', cynical or otherwise on Disraeli's part but that he had always valued the empire and that the two pieces of evidence usually quoted to the contrary (his letter to Malmesbury in 1852, when he referred to the colonies as 'millstones', and his letter to Derby in 1866, when he suggested financial retrenchment at the expense of the empire) have been taken out of context (Stembridge 1965). His 1866 speech (quoted above p. 123) is certainly striking evidence for this and, even in the 1850s, he made fairly frequent references to the empire. Koebner and Schmidt (1964: 46) conclude, 'Among the rising politicians of the day Benjamin Disraeli stood out as manifesting a personal allegiance to the name of the empire.' But he evoked little public response in the earlier period, his ideas are rather ambiguous and it probably remains true that only in the 1870s did he devote much real thought to imperial questions.

It was Gladstone, not Disraeli, who wrote in 1878, 'The sentiment of empire may be called innate in every Briton. If there are exceptions, they are like those of men born blind or lame among us. It is part of our patrimony: born with our birth, dying only with our death; incorporating itself in the first elements of our knowledge, and interwoven with all our habits of mental action upon public affairs.' (*Nineteenth Century*, 1878: vol. 4, 569.) But he went on to deplore 'excess' in the imperial spirit, which could easily lead to disaster, as he believed it had done in the American War of Independence. Basically, Gladstone's view of empire was the Peelite one, that it was a duty and a responsibility that could not be shrugged off, but that there was likely to be little advantage in extending it. Britain's strength lay at home in her own people, not in 'territorial aggrandisement'.

Foreign adventures lead to militarism and war, and war was not only horrible in itself but it ate up the resources of a nation, which were needed for the betterment of its people. One of the charges sometimes brought against Gladstone was that he regretted the Crimean War mainly because it destroyed the financial strategy of his 1853 budget. That had been one of his objections and a perfectly reasonable one. The 1853 budget had been intended to inaugurate a new and more rational deal in the national economy. In the same 1878 article Gladstone pointed the finger at France, which had suffered for its militarism. 'The dominant passion of France', he wrote 'was military glory. Twice, in this century, it has towered beyond what is allowed to man; and twice has paid the tremendous forfeit of opening to the foe the proudest capital in the world.' (*ibid.* p. 570.) The second forfeit was, of course, the Franco-Prussian war.

At the time of the war, Gladstone's first government had been in office. Lord Clarendon had died and had been succeeded at the Foreign Office by Lord Granville only a fortnight before the war broke out. The British were taken by surprise and found it easy to believe Bismarck's allegations that Napoleon III was the aggressor. Indeed the initial debate hinged on whether a firmer British warning to France could have averted the war (Mosse 1958: 382–8). Bismarck could produce convincing evidence of Napoleon's manoeuvres to gain control of Luxembourg and even Belgium, which fitted in with the suspicions Britain had had of him since his 'revisionist' proposals of 1863. In these circumstances it seemed logical to make respect for Belgian neutrality the test of the intentions of the two powers. Once both had said that they would observe it, Britain declared her neutrality. In fact Britain did not have the military force available to intervene in any effective way in a short continental war such as the Franco-Prussian, like the Austro-Prussian war, proved to be.

Russia took advantage of the war to denounce the clauses of the Treaty of Paris of 1856, neutralising the Black Sea. Once again there was nothing that Britain could do to prevent this, particularly as Russia had obtained Bismarck's agreement. All Gladstone could do was to insist that the clause be formally abrogated by an international conference sitting in London, rather than by Russia's unilateral declaration. This face-saving manoeuvre did not much impress the British public, who were beginning to contrast the apparent passivity of Gladstone and his new Foreign Secretary with the vigour they had grown accustomed to from Palmerston. Palmerston would probably have acted much as Gladstone did in this particular dilemma but he would have carried it off with a flourish. It may well have been this, rather than any feeling that Gladstone was unsound on the empire, which opened the way for Disraeli's attacks (Ensor 1936: 5).

From Gladstone's point of view, the reference to an international conference was much more than a manoeuvre in public relations. Just as he had wanted to inaugurate a new era in fiscal policy in 1853, so he now wanted to inaugurate a new era in international affairs. His views were not fully worked out, or at least not expounded to the public, until the Midlothian campaigns of 1878 and 1879 but they underlay his policy from the beginning and they were not a matter of pious rhetoric but were intended as a perfectly practical framework for the conduct of international affairs. They depended upon the general acceptance of a code of international law, which would provide a means for the peaceful settlement of disputes and which implied both great respect for the sanctity of treaties and a willingness to return to conference diplomacy.

From this standpoint it was very important that the Treaty of Paris should be formally revised and not merely disregarded by one of its signatories.

Another aspect of Gladstone's concern for a new deal in international relations, and one for which he was prepared to defy public opinion, was the question of arbitration. Referring disputes to various kinds of arbitration was already a well-established procedure but Great Powers had often refused to accept the results, if the judgment went against them. Gladstone was convinced that arbitration provided an important alternative to conflict. The *Alabama** case, based on the damage the ship had inflicted on northern commerce after her escape from Liverpool in 1862, had been sent to arbitration in 1871. When the judgment was delivered the following year, many people felt that the damages awarded were excessive even if it was conceded that the British government was liable – in itself a disputed point. Gladstone, however, determined to accept it in order to uphold the principle of arbitration, in the spirit in which one would accept a dubious court decision rather than challenge the authority of the courts. The *Alabama* decision did in fact inaugurate an era in which practically all disputes between Britain and the United States were settled by arbitration (Bemis 1955: 405–31).

It is ironic that, as Professor McIntyre made clear in his *The Imperial Frontier in the Tropics* (1967), it was Gladstone's not Disraeli's, government, which laid the groundwork for a forward movement in both West Africa and parts of the Pacific, notably Fiji and Malaysia, although in each case they were responding to unexpected challenges.

Since the seventeenth century Britain had had a base at Cape Coast Castle on the Gold Coast. Her trading partners were the Fante people, who were at odds with their inland neighbours, the Ashanti Confederation. The British had already fought several wars with the Ashanti. In 1872 the Dutch, who had maintained much better relations with the Ashanti, relinquished their stations on the Gold Coast to Britain. Early in 1873 an Ashanti army advanced and defeated the Fante. The 'Cardwell policy' of strictly limited commitments in West Africa, or even withdrawal, which had found expression in the 1865 Select Committee report, was in disarray. Late in 1873 a British expedition was sent out, which attracted very extensive press coverage. Its commander, Sir Garnet Wolseley, was one of the best generals of the late Victorian period and the campaign was a text book success. Most of the credit redounded to Disraeli's ministry, which came to power in February 1874.

Events in Malaysia and Fiji were less spectacular but even more far-reaching. Both countries had suffered civil turmoil, as the result of disputed successions. In 1873 Gladstone's Colonial Secretary, Lord

---

*Strictly speaking the case involved other ships as well, notably the *Florida* and the *Shenandoah*; the last had been repaired in Australia in 1864.

Kimberley, appointed Sir Andrew Clarke as Governor of Singapore. Clarke was an active and ambitious man and by the summer of 1873 Kimberley had become convinced that something must be done about Malaya. Clarke took his instructions to the limit and, by the Pangkor Engagement of January 1874 recognised one of the contenders, the Raja Muda Abdullah, as Sultan of Perak and inaugurated the policy of appointing British 'Residents', or advisers, to the Malay States. Kimberley also sent Commodore Goodenough to Fiji and, although Kimberley's successor, Lord Carnarvon, urged caution on him, Goodenough had arranged the British annexation of Fiji by October 1874. Fiji was to cause further international complications. Attempts had been made by British, American and German entrepreneurs to develop Fiji as an alternative source of cotton during the American Civil War. After the British annexation, bitter complaints were received from both America and Germany that their investors were being discriminated against. Indeed Fiji may have played an important rôle in convincing Bismarck that Britain would be the enemy of German colonisation plans.

Many key decisions had been taken before Disraeli returned to office in February 1874 but whereas Gladstone was always faintly embarrassed by 'forward' actions, Disraeli knew how to milk them for publicity even when, as happened in the late 1870s, they went wrong. The two overseas adventures with which Disraeli's administration was to be indelibly associated were in Afghanistan and South Africa.

Since her defeat in the Crimean War, Russia had been expanding into Central Asia, subduing the Uzbek Khanates of Kokand, Bukhara and Khiva. In 1865 they captured Tashkent and began to organise their province of Turkestan. By 1868 they had conquered Samarkand. They were now on the frontiers of Afghanistan. A threat to Britain's Indian empire, which had at one time seemed remote and theoretical, began to look increasingly real; and even imminent. Gladstone's government tried to negotiate and, for a time in 1873, it looked as if they had secured Russian assent to a 'hands off' policy in Afghanistan (Thornton 1953).

British military experts were sharply divided in their views on how best to defend India. They resolved themselves into what were nicknamed, by friends or enemies, the 'masterly inactivity' and 'mischievous activity' schools. The former believed that the British in India should sit tight behind easily defensible frontiers, to which supplies could now be delivered by the new strategic railways, and should avoid over-extending either their frontiers or their communications. Let the Russians wrestle with the problems of controlling and defending the difficult terrain of Central Asia and its proudly independent people. The latter believed that to allow the Russians to approach the existing frontiers of India would, in the long run, be disastrous. The British must go out to meet them, particularly in Afghanistan.

The new conservative Viceroy, Lord Lytton, who took up his appointment in 1876, very emphatically belonged to the 'mischievous activity' school, but his appointment cannot necessarily be taken as proof that the government had made up its mind to endorse that policy. The resignation of the previous Viceroy, Lord Northbrook, had been unexpected and Lytton was not the government's first choice to replace him. They would have preferred Carnarvon or Dufferin, both men of very different views. On his way out Lytton bombarded the government with inordinately long letters, explaining what he thought should be done. The Secretary of State for India, Lord Salisbury, was not altogether impressed. He told Disraeli that he was 'telegraphing hastily back to prevent the immediate annexation of Central Asia' (DP. B/XX/Ce, 31 October 1876) but he did agree that Afghanistan could not be 'neutral territory'; it must pass to either Britain or Russia (NP. MSS Eur G 144, 30 April 1875).

The crisis came in 1878 when the Amir of Afghanistan received a Russian, but refused a British, mission. In November a British force invaded Afghanistan. The campaign was very successful and made the reputation of General, later Field Marshal, Roberts. The Amir fled and his son concluded a treaty, which allowed the British to control his foreign policy and to appoint a Resident in his Capital, Cabul. Everything seemed to have been satisfactorily concluded from the British point of view. But in September 1879 the British Resident, Sir Louis Cavagnari, and his whole staff were murdered. Roberts was once again despatched to retrieve the situation but hostilities were still going on when Disraeli's government was defeated in the 1880 election.

Whatever may have been the Conservative government's intentions in Central Asia, they were not looking for a forward policy in South Africa. Britain had retained the Cape in 1815 as a staging post to India. There had been some half-hearted attempts to encourage British emigration to establish an English population and Britain had moved swiftly in the 1840s to annex the east coast, Natal, to stop the disaffected Boers from establishing an independent settlement there, which might have opened relations with a rival European power such as France. When the Boers moved inland to what became the Orange Free State and the Transvaal, the British were quite content to conclude arrangements, the Sand River Convention (1852) and the Bloemfontein Convention (1854), which gave them internal autonomy, although Britain never considered surrendering control of their external relations.

European settlement in southern Africa had a disruptive effect on the politics and society of the Africans, who were already engaged in titanic struggles among themselves for the control of the region (cf. Morris 1966). The outlines of those struggles are only now becoming apparent to historians. Even at the time, Europeans could not ignore the Zulus, the most formidable and highly organised of these African nations. British governments, Conservative or Liberal, were anxious to avoid being drawn into the morass and wished that the colonists would stand on their own feet. Gladstone had tried to make Cape Province assume the onus with his grant of responsible government in 1872. Carnarvon had a different solution to propose. He had been immensely impressed by the success of Canadian Confederation and was convinced that a federation would be equally successful in South Africa.

In the spring of 1877 the Boers of the Transvaal found themselves in a desperate condition. They were almost bankrupt and on the verge of war with their Zulu neighbours. Carnarvon sent Sir Theophilus Shepstone to Pretoria to negotiate with them. Carnarvon was clear both that such a war would probably engulf the whole of southern Africa and that the Transvaal would be better off within a federation. In April 1877 Shepstone annexed the Transvaal. Almost at the same moment Sir Bartle Frere began negotiating with the Zulus and arranged most of the outstanding disputes but he then demanded that the Zulus should stand down their army. Demobilisation would have been a reasonable request in a European context but it made little sense for a military monarchy like Ceshwayo's Zulus. In fact, Frere had almost certainly decided that there would be no permanent peace until the Zulus were suppressed one way or another.

Disraeli's cabinet were reluctant to back him. They were already at war in Afghanistan and Europe had barely emerged from the Eastern crisis (see below pp. 136–8). But they seem to have been equally afraid of a charge of leaving Frere in the lurch. The reinforcements he had asked for were sent, although with a strict injunction that they were to be used for defensive purposes. In January 1879 Lord Chelmsford marched into Zululand. His army had a rash contempt for the enemy and the result was the disaster of Isandhlwana in which a British camp was surprised, with the loss of about 1,500 men. When the news reached England, the fact that Frere had exceeded his instructions became unimportant beside the need to 'avenge' Isandhlwana. Large additional reinforcements were sent and, within a few months, the Zulu army was defeated and Zululand itself broken up into eight different units. A 'forward' policy in South Africa, as in Afghanistan, seemed costly in both lives and money. The Liberals, led by Gladstone, were prepared to argue that it was also morally indefensible.

Historically, Britain had been interested in South Africa because of the need to protect the Cape route to India and, even late in the nineteenth century, many were still prepared to argue that it would be the most reliable route in time of war. But the argument was profoundly affected in 1869 by the opening of the Suez Canal. The British had always opposed its building for the good reason that, while the Royal Navy could command the high seas, it could not control a 'ditch' through someone else's territory. But British opposition carried on to the end meant that the Canal was built by French capital and French technology. The French had been better established in Egypt than the

British since the time of Mehemet Ali, who had relied on them heavily for advice and support but the opening of the Suez Canal enormously increased the strategic importance of Egypt. Soon most of the trade to or from Europe with India and the East in general passed through Suez and over three-quarters of that trade was British.

In the 1870s Egypt, still part of the Ottoman empire, began to go bankrupt. The problem originated with the Khedive Ismail's attempts to modernise and develop his country too fast, not with mere extravagance as Victorian historians were prone to assert. In fact, in Egypt as in Fiji, the acute phase of the problem began with the attempt to develop an alternative supply of raw cotton during the American Civil War, which came to an abrupt end in 1865, although it was compounded by Ismail's attempts to consolidate Egypt's control over the Sudan, first established by Mehemet Ali.

Throughout the 1870s it was France which took the lead in the attempt to solve, or at least manage, Egypt's financial problems. Salisbury, first as Secretary of State for India and subsequently as Disraeli's Foreign Secretary, was very cautious in his approach to Egypt. He summed it up later in a famous letter to Sir Stafford Northcote,

> When you have got a neighbour and faithful ally who is bent on meddling in a country in which you are deeply interested – you have three courses open to you. You may renounce – or monopolise – or share. Renouncing would have been to place the French across our road to India.
> Monopolising would have been very near the risk of war. So we resolved to share. (Cecil 1921: vol. 2, 331–2.)

There was only one grand gesture – when Disraeli bought the Khedive's shares in the Suez Canal in 1875. There was speculation at the time that this was intended as a preliminary to a British annexation of Egypt. If Disraeli had any such thought in his mind, he covered his traces well, but it was rather strange that when, the following year, the Khedive asked for the loan of two British Treasury officials to advise him on his finances, Disraeli sent instead a Cabinet minister, Stephen Cave. Cave produced a judicious report in which he said that the Egyptian economy was fundamentally sound; the crisis was a financial one, brought about by the very high rates of interest the Khedive was having to pay to European speculators; and advised the bringing in of more European officials who 'would be checks upon the adventurers who have preyed upon Egypt' (PP 1876: lxxxiii, 100). The late 1870s saw the establishment of what came to be called the Anglo-French Dual Control of the Egyptian finances, by which they supervised both the collection and expenditure of the revenue. Evelyn Baring, later Lord Cromer, became the British Commissioner, although the British government, unlike the French, declined to make the appointment official, maintaining that it was the Khedive's arrangement.

Whatever the temptations to 'meddle' in Egypt, they were held in check by the fear of destabilising the whole Ottoman empire and when that crashed down, it seemed very likely that there would be a European war. A very dangerous situation was already developing in the Balkans. A rising took place in Herzegovina in the summer of 1875. The powers of the *Dreikaiserbund*, Germany, Austria and Russia, urged reforms on the Sultan, in a document known as the Andrassy Note, to avert further rebellion. Britain, although resenting the fact that she had not been consulted, agreed to support the Andrassy Note but when the Eastern powers put further pressure on the Sultan in the Berlin Memorandum of May 1876, Disraeli dissociated himself from the action. He even ordered the British fleet to take up its station in Besika Bay outside the Dardanelles. In fact, the British government was deeply divided as to how best to handle the situation but, because of its deep distrust of Russian, and to a lesser extent German, intentions, it was drifting in to an uncritically pro-Turkish position. Some of the preliminaries of the Crimean War seemed about to be re-enacted by a government headed by one of the severest critics of that war.

British fears of a partition about which they would not be consulted were not unfounded. After Serbia declared war on Turkey in July 1876, the Tsar Alexander II and the Austrian Emperor, Franz Josef, met at Reichstadt to discuss just such a partition. In fact the plan was premature. The Turks defeated the Serbs.

It was against this background that the news of the risings in Bulgaria and their savage repression by the Turks reached London. Apart from the fact that he may have been misled by the pro-Turkish ambassador in Constantinople, Sir Henry Elliott, Disraeli could not afford to come out against the Turks. When the full story of the 'Bulgarian horrors' became known, it provoked one of the most extraordinary campaigns ever seen in England (Shannon 1975), inaugurated by Gladstone's *The Bulgarian Horrors and the Question of the East*. It touched deep nerves in the Victorian psyche. It not only brought Gladstone back into the forefront of politics (he had resigned the leadership of the Liberal Party in 1875), it forged an entirely new relationship between him and the public.

Although Gladstone's famous advice to the Turks to get out 'bag and baggage' related only to Bulgaria, not to the Ottoman lands in general, it signalled the end of liberal support for the belief that the stability of the Near East could best be guaranteed by maintaining the Ottoman empire. For Disraeli, actually in office, the dilemma was acute. The British public would not back the 'unspeakable Turk'. In the winter of 1876–7 Lord Salisbury attended the Constantinople Conference on behalf of Britain. The conference once again tried to press reforms upon the Turks but they, apparently persuading themselves in the face of Salisbury's clear warnings that Britain would not leave Turkey to her fate, evaded the issue.

In April 1877 Russia declared war on Turkey. Britain proclaimed her neutrality but on conditions. Russia must recognise the inviolability of Constantinople and the maintenance of free navigation through the Dardanelles. She must also exclude Egypt and the Suez Canal from the sphere of military operations. There were now two focal points of British policy in the Near East, Cairo and Constantinople and Cairo was soon to assume the greater importance. The British Cabinet was deeply divided in its response to the crisis. In November 1877 Disraeli complained to the Queen that there were seven different parties in a Cabinet of twelve (Monypenny and Buckle 1920: vol. 6, 194). The Queen, like the British public in general, began to veer towards support for Turkey, once the war had begun. Two members of the Cabinet, Carnarvon and Derby, found the possibility of defending Turkey intolerable. Both resigned in the spring of 1878: Derby had previously been communicating the Cabinet discussions to Shuvalov, the Russian ambassador, with the deliberate intention of thwarting the war party. Blake sees it as 'the last occasion in the age of nationalism when two grandees, each equally contemptuous of the Chauvinism in their respective countries, could co-operate so closely in trying to preserve peace' (Blake 1966: 623).

Salisbury succeeded Derby at the Foreign Office and peace between England and Russia was preserved although the treaty which Russia concluded with Turkey at the end of the war, the Treaty of San Stefano of March 1878, created the 'Big Bulgaria', which it was assumed would be under Russian control, was entirely unacceptable to Britain. Fortunately for the British government, it was unpopular with other countries too and enjoyed only divided support in Russia itself.

Russia was prepared to come to the conference table and, in June 1878, the Congress of Berlin met. It was the most important international conference since Vienna in 1815 and both Disraeli and Salisbury attended in person. Its venue recognised that Berlin was now the diplomatic capital of Europe. But in fact most of the critical decisions had been agreed in advance of the conference, some of the most important between Salisbury and Shuvalov in London. These preliminary negotiations had the full backing of Bismarck, who had no wish to have to make a public choice between his two allies, Russia and Austria.

Disraeli had felt a particular interest in the Near East since his travels in 1830. For him the British empire meant above all India and the route to India. Berlin provided him with his greatest personal triumph in foreign affairs. He was fêted there and persuaded to address the conference in English as the 'greatest English orator' of his generation. (No one told him that it was because his French was so bad, his colleagues feared it would be incomprehensible.) He probably did not break a deadlock by ordering a special train to take him back to England (Blake 1966: 648) but, in spirit, the story was true. The Russians did give way in the face of British intransigence, supported by Bismarck.

Bismarck, who had previously met Disraeli in the 1850s, undoubtedly respected him and understood him in a way in which he never understood Gladstone.

On the face of it the outcome of the Congress of Berlin was satisfactory to Britain and Disraeli was justified in his famous boast to the cheering crowds in Downing Street that he had brought back 'Peace with Honour'. The Big Bulgaria was broken up, part going back to Turkey. Even the independent Bulgaria which emerged did not prove to be as subservient to Russia as had been expected. Austria gained a protectorate over Bosnia-Herzegovina. Russia retained some territory at the expense of Roumania.

In the Balkans the Berlin settlement stored up more trouble for the future than was apparent at the time. It may also have lit the slow-burning fuse which was to lead to the Scramble for Africa. Britain was still uneasy about the safety of the Suez Canal and her existing Mediterranean base, Malta, was too far west to be of much immediate help in a crisis. By one of the secret preliminary agreements to Berlin, the Sultan 'leased' the island of Cyprus to Britain in return for a guarantee of Turkey's Asian (as distinct from European) lands and the promise of military 'consuls' or advisers. In order to win French support for this, Britain agreed to withdraw her objections to the extension of French influence from Algeria to Tunis.

Gladstone's retort to Disraeli's apparent triumph at Berlin was the Midlothian campaigns of 1879 and 1880. These campaigns developed naturally from the Bulgarian agitation. As Shannon puts it, 'the sense of a deep and urgent moral responsibility enunciated, fostered, symbolised dramatically by Gladstone in the Midlothian campaigns, was a direct legacy of the great movement of 1876.' (Shannon 1975: 273, but for a caution on over-simplifying the connection see 266–7.) Gladstone deliberately chose to contest the marginal Midlothian seat against Lord Dalkeith, the son of Scotland's premier peer, the Duke of Buccleuch, even though he had a safe seat guaranteed in Leeds, in order to have a platform which would attract national attention.

His carefully planned speeches in Scotland in November and December 1879 were not entirely devoted to foreign affairs but it was the sections, which had been designated in Gladstone's rough notes, 'Indictment agt. the Govt. a. abroad – everywhere!' (Swartz 1985: 114), which lived in public memory. Some of his attacks went back to the Eastern crisis, the British government's failure to join the other powers in compelling Turkey to reform and the cynical deal about Cyprus but much of his fire was concentrated on Afghanistan and South Africa. 'Remember', he told the people of Edinburgh 'that the sanctity of life in the hill villages of Afghanistan . . . is as inviolable in the eye of Almighty God as can be your own.' In Glasgow he condemned the 'baseless quarrel' picked with the Amir of Afghanistan or the 10,000 Zulus slain 'for no offence than their attempt to defend against our artillery with their naked bodies their hearths and homes' (Morley 1903: vol. 2, 592, 595; for full text see Foot (ed.) 1971).

Gladstone did not confine himself to an attack upon conservative policy. He also enunciated what he regarded as the fundamental principles which should guide British foreign policy. Peace, of course, was basic but it should be peace based on justice, which respected the rights of smaller nations and acknowledged the rule of law in international affairs. His attitude to the empire was still Peelite. While condemning the jingoism of the Disraeli government he aligned himself with the 'love of freedom' of Canning, Palmerston and Russell. At the same time he denounced unnecessary interventions and 'entangling engagements' but he re-affirmed his deep commitment to the principle of the Concert of Europe.

The Liberals won a clear majority in the 1880 general election although it is very doubtful whether foreign affairs played such an important rôle in the outcome as some contemporaries assumed (Swartz 1985: 120–2). The Queen was horrified. She told Sir Henry Ponsonby, 'She will sooner *abdicate* than send for or have anything to do with that *half-mad fire-brand* who would soon ruin everything, and be a *Dictator*.' (Magnus 1963: 270.) Some of her objections were to Gladstone's domestic politics but the most startling political innovation to those accustomed to the political conventions of the first half of the century, was this 'stumping' the country and this clear appeal to a mass public, many of whom still did not have the vote. Gladstone's Scottish tour had attracted audiences of thousands – it was estimated that 20,000 working men and women heard him in the Waverley Market in Edinburgh on 29 November. That was the real change in politics.

However reluctantly, Victoria had to accept Gladstone as her new Prime Minister. Gladstone's principles were now to be put to the practical test. Were the ideals proclaimed in Midlothian merely pious rhetoric or did they provide a real basis for the conduct of foreign policy? Britain faced a Europe increasingly dominated by Bismarck's Germany. Despite the Berlin Congress, the reverberations of the Eastern crisis had not quite died away. Professor Medlicott argued a powerful case (Medlicott 1969) that Bismarck and Gladstone fought a crucial battle to determine the direction of European diplomacy, which Bismarck won, with ultimately disastrous consequences for the whole continent.

Gladstone's return to office was greeted with almost as much dismay at Berlin as at Windsor. Both Britain and Germany had angled for each other's friendship during the last years of the conservative administration although neither was willing to pay too high a price and the overtures had come to very little in practice (Kennedy 1982: 34–7, 157–9). Bismarck profoundly distrusted Gladstone. This owed something to his belief that the importation of Gladstonian liberal ideas into Germany, supposedly favoured by the heir apparent, the Crown Prince

Frederick, would wreck his own carefully constructed conservative Germany. It owed something to a personality clash. Neither man ever understood the other, although each came to appreciate that the other seemed to be playing to a totally different set of rules. But it arose essentially from the incompatibility of their European objectives. Gladstone, who in Bismarck's opinion was becoming dangerously 'Slavophil', was determined that Greece and Montenegro should receive all that they had been promised under the Treaty of Berlin; in the case of Greece, a large part of Thessaly. To ensure this he was prepared to see an allied naval demonstration in the Adriatic in the autumn of 1880 and even an expedition to Smyrna. On the face of it the policy was almost Palmerstonian and Greece in fact gained Thessaly. But the thinking behind it was very different. This was enforcement of a treaty by the Concert of Europe, that body intended to 'neutralize and fetter and bind up the selfish aims of each' (Foot (ed.) 1971: 115). Bismarck sneered and promised to 'pray' for the Smyrna expedition. He was intent not on turning the Concert of Europe into the standing machinery for the resolution of all European questions but in creating, first, the Austro-German alliance and, second, the *Dreikaiserbund*, of Germany, Austria and Russia, which he believed would best ensure Germany's security. Bismarck's system of tight alliances triumphed and, so long as Bismarck himself directed it, maintained the peace of Europe, even if in reality he had 'made a deadlock and called it peace', but his successors were less skilful men (Medlicott 1969: 1–4, 17–24, 30–4, 305–6, 315–321, 336–7).

Gladstone, when in opposition, had relentlessly condemned the Conservatives' policy in both Afghanistan and South Africa. Once in office, it was not easy to extricate himself. Apart from the ambivalence of public feeling, not even all Gladstone's own Cabinet was in any hurry to withdraw. By October 1879 Roberts had once again occupied Cabul but even Disraeli's government was shrinking from the idea of trying to control the whole of Afghanistan and considering a deal by which Persia would supervise Herat and the north of the country. While the Liberals hesitated as to how best to resolve the situation, a British force was overwhelmed at Maiwand, and the British garrison at Candahar besieged and only relieved by a spectacular march by Roberts from Cabul. In the end the Liberals secured an unexpectedly satisfactory settlement, retaining control of the Khyber Pass and some other strategic points but recognising the independence of the new Amir, Abdur Rahman. This in itself was a gamble since Abdur Rahman's previous connections had been Russian, rather than British, but the new Amir proved to want only genuine independence. The Russians, whose forward move in 1878 had been connected with the crisis in the Near East, were content to let Afghanistan revert to being a buffer state.

Gladstone had no such luck in South Africa. The Transvaalers, relieved of the Zulu threat, wanted to resume their independence and protested, not entirely accurately, that they had never consented to annexation in 1877. They expected immediate independence from Gladstone but Bartle Frere was not at once recalled and the Liberal government still entertained some hope that federation might solve all South Africa's problems. In February 1881 the Transvaalers resorted to arms. Sir George Colley, the Governor of Natal, and a small British force were defeated at Majuba Hill and Colley himself killed. 'Revenge Majuba' became the angry cry of a large part of the British press. Gladstone was now confronted by a dilemma. Should he avenge Majuba or 'make peace, conceding to force what he had refused to reason, and leaving the Boers arrogant as well as injured?' (Ensor 1936: 69.) He chose to ignore Majuba and conclude the Convention of Pretoria, which restored internal autonomy to the Boers, while leaving Britain in control of their foreign policy. Generations of historians were left to argue how far the 'arrogance' thus engendered in the Boers led to the second Boer War of 1889–1902 (Ensor 1936: 69; Pakenham 1979: 18–19, 70).

In opposition the Liberals had also condemned the Cyprus Convention. Gladstone changed the military consuls to ordinary consuls but he did not cancel the lease of Cyprus. In 1881 the French finally moved into Tunis, alarmed by Italian interests in the country. The French invasion of Tunis had a further destabilising effect in Egypt. In 1879 the Khedive Ismail had been deposed by the Sultan in favour of his son Tewfik, a well-meaning but weak man. Nominally the British occupied Egypt in 1882 to protect Tewfik from his mutinous army. In retrospect the best-informed Englishmen, including Lord Cromer, did not doubt that what they had really confronted in Egypt was a genuine nationalist movement, angered by the impoverishment of the country by foreign intervention. It had in fact been anti-Ottoman before it was anti-European and even looked to the west for sympathy. Gladstone never recognised it for what it was, a parallel to the nationalist movements in the Balkans. This was partly hidden from the Liberals by the fact that it was spear-headed by the army. Joseph Chamberlain who, contrary to popular belief, was deeply divided in his mind about the intervention, could only square his conscience by supposing that there were two rebellious movements, the army which must be suppressed and a constitutional one which must be fostered (Chamberlain 1976: 240–3). The campaign, commanded by Garnet Wolseley, was once again a text-book one and, after the battle of Tel-el-Kebir, Britain was in control of the whole of Egypt.

The British had intended to withdraw immediately, as the French had done after a similar intervention in Syria in 1860. Instead they were trapped in Egypt until the middle of the next century. They had created a power vacuum and dared not withdraw, first, in the face of the Islamic *jihad* being proclaimed from the Sudan, and, second, from the fear that another Great Power might take their place. Until the very last minute it had been intended that it should be a joint Anglo-French intervention but the French had drawn back, fearful that it was a Bismarckian manoeuvre to weaken them on the Rhine. At first the French attitude had been almost apologetic but when the British abolished the Dual Control and proceeded to administer Egypt themselves, although without regularising their position in international law by assuming a protectorate, a breach was created between Britain and France which was not healed until 1904.

Coming only three years after Midlothian, a staunch critic of the occupation, Frederic Harrison, was perhaps justified in saying that he seemed to hear 'a hollow and ghostlike laugh of derision ... as from a certain quiet vault at Hughenden', where Disraeli had been buried the previous year (Chamberlain 1981: 23). In fact Gladstone had tried to 'internationalise' Egypt through a conference in Constantinople but the Sultan, angry with France over Tunis and Britain over Cyprus, had been obstructive and the other powers had declined to allow Britain to act as the 'mandatory' of Europe – with Italy if France would not move.

In Egypt matters went from bad to worse. A further dogged attempt to internationalise the control of the Egyptian finances in 1885 meant that all the major European powers had a hand on the purse-strings while Britain continued to try to adminster the country. It was, as a later British Foreign Secretary, Sir Edward Grey, put it, 'a noose' round Britain's neck which any other country could tighten at will. The declaration that the Suez Canal was an international waterway, through which the ships of all nations could sail in war as in peace, finally agreed to in 1888 survived until the Arab-Israeli conflicts after the Second World War. But Gladstone's hope that Egypt might become an 'Eastern Belgium' proved unattainable. Its strategic importance was too great in the new global strategy which was developing.

The British occupation of Egypt attracted remarkably little criticism at home at the time. Only later were the arguments marshalled that it had been an intervention, not even to protect the Suez Canal, but to protect the British bondholders, who had been battening on Egypt. The very fact that Gladstone was Prime Minister silenced many of the groups who would have denounced such an action by Disraeli.

Public condemnation of the Liberal government's policy came over something very different, the death of General Gordon at Khartoum. Gordon, already a popular hero, had been sent to extricate the remaining Egyptian garrisons in the Sudan. Once there, he pursued his own policy. Whether he could, or should, have left Khartoum earlier and whether the government could, or should, have mounted an effective relief expedition sooner, was bitterly debated in the press. Gladstone's government barely survived the ensuing outcry.

Did the British occupation of Egypt trigger the Scramble for Africa? Not in the simple way first posited by Robinson and Gallagher in 1961. The French government did not deliberately take their revenge for Egypt by starting a scramble for West Africa (Stengers 1962; Newbury 1962). Crucial French decisions to endorse a forward policy were taken before the summer of 1882. Bismarck, probably persuaded by a mixture of domestic and diplomatic considerations, decided to enter the colonial field in 1884. The maverick activities of Leopold of the Belgians in the Congo also set a long chain of events in motion.

Africa assumed the centre of the stage with extraordinary suddenness. Salisbury complained that, when he left the Foreign Office in 1880, no one gave a thought to Africa, when he returned in 1885, no one talked of anything else. The partition of practically the whole continent was carried out between the European powers, Britain, France, Germany, Portugal, Spain, Italy and Belgium, between 1884 and 1891. The Scramble proper began with the Berlin West Africa Conference of 1884–5. In the spring of 1884 Britain and Portugal had concluded a treaty to regulate the navigation of the Congo and to recognise Portugal's historic rights in the region. In the past Britain had refused to recognise them (largely because of Portugal's bad record on the slave trade) but the desire to stop any French advance now took priority. This bilateral agreement about one of Africa's main waterways was unacceptable to other European powers and Bismarck was glad to have the opportunity of putting pressure on Britain whom he suspected, on the whole wrongly, of trying to thwart German colonial ambition.

The British went to Berlin not unwillingly. Gladstone still hankered after international agreements on the great rivers of Africa, similar to that established over the great rivers of Europe at Vienna in 1815. The Berlin Conference can be regarded as primarily a manoeuvre in European politics (Crowe 1942) but it also had dramatic consequences for Africa. Informal 'influence' virtually ceased. Powers now felt compelled to state formally their territorial claims and to provide some 'effective occupation' to justify them.

Almost immediately after the Conference, Britain staked a formal claim to the Niger delta and to the territories which became Kenya and Uganda. Since the Treasury wished to pay as little as possible for these new possessions, the old device of the Chartered Company, which many thought had become extinct with the East India Company in 1858, was revived. The North Borneo Company (1881) was joined by the three African companies, Royal Niger, Imperial British East Africa and British South Africa; the last opened up the Rhodesias.

In the midst of this, in June 1885, Gladstone's government fell on a domestic issue. Salisbury formed a minority government which lasted until February 1886. The Liberals won an apparently decisive majority in the 1886 general election but Ireland soon split the party and Gladstone's third administration only lasted until August, when Salisbury returned to power with a conservative administration which remained in office until 1892.

In this context, it is significant that there was no important change in British policy in Africa during the switches between Liberal and Conservative governments in 1885–86. Many critical decisions were outstanding when the Liberals left office in June 1885, among them the grant of the Royal Niger Company's Charter. Negotiations on this and other matters carried on as if there had been no change of government. For two parties which now professed totally different approaches to the management of foreign policy, this was remarkable, and must imply that deeper forces were impelling the country into the new competition for empire.

Chapter 10

THE GREAT GAME

When Salisbury came into office in June 1885 he surveyed what he regarded as the wreckage of British foreign policy and commented on his immediate predecessors, 'They have at least achieved their long desired "Concert of Europe". They have succeeded in uniting the continent of Europe – against England.' (Cecil 1931: vol. 3, 136.)

Salisbury's return to office marked the return to a more traditional approach to foreign policy. Gladstone had tried to apply the standards of morality, which would be normal in private life, to international affairs. Christian values, he would have argued, should reign supreme in both. Salisbury, although in his private life as devout as Gladstone – and within the same narrow English High Church tradition, which was as hostile to Roman Catholicism as to 'Protestantism' – viewed the matter differently. Nations stood to one another as men had done, according to Thomas Hobbes, in the 'State of Nature', that is to say, in a state of anarchy with no commonly accepted authority. Self-preservation was the first duty. Salisbury believed in *realpolitik*, as thoroughly as the eighteenth century or his contemporary, Bismarck, did, even if it meant aggression against a neighbour. 'It is puerile', he wrote in the *Quarterly Review* in 1881, defending British action in Afghanistan and Ireland 'to apply to the dealings of a nation with its neighbour's territory the morality which would be applicable to two individuals possessing adjoining property, and protected from mutual wrong by a law superior to both.' (Smith 1972: 53–4.)

Salisbury was arguably the most aristocratic incumbent of the Foreign Office in the nineteenth century. He was the direct descendant of Elizabeth I's great minister, Lord Burghley and his son, the First Earl of Salisbury, but the Cecil family had produced no notable figure since. Lady Gwendoline Cecil tartly remarked in her perceptive and revealing life of her father, 'the general mediocrity of intelligence which the family displayed was only varied by instances of quite exceptional stupidity' and suggested that both vigour and intelligence came back into the family through the female line. Whatever else he was, Salisbury was never mediocre. On the contrary, he was a man of exceptional intelligence, whose caustic and often destructive wit combined uncomfortably with (as a young man) poor health and an inability to form easy relationships. It was a much tried Disraeli who once described him as 'a great master of gibes, and flouts, and jeers'. (For a stimulating analysis of Salisbury's personality see Smith 1972: 9–20.)

The future third Marquess was a younger son who only succeeded to the title because of the deaths of his two elder brothers. Himself a frail, premature infant, he lost his mother as a child. He was, apparently, bullied unmercifully at school to the point where his father removed him from Eton. He was happier at Oxford but went down with an 'honorary Fourth Class' degree after two years, again for reasons of health. In 1851–53, he was despatched on a world cruise to South Africa, Australia and New Zealand but he seems to have been bored a good deal of the time and certainly did not undergo a conversion to the imperial cause as Rosebery did in Australia thirty years later.

When he returned home he was found a parliamentary seat in the family borough of Stamford, which he occupied until he went to the Lords in 1868. As a young man he supplemented his income by journalism and wrote regularly for the conservative *Quarterly Review*. He was, as Smith says 'writing for a partisan review, to stimulate and encourage a largely converted audience' and he defended his own invective on the grounds that, writing for money as he was compelled to do, he must command his audience's attention (Smith 1972: 6, 9). The articles were clever, often cynical, often pessimistic. He did not share the popular belief in human progress. He did to some extent share Marx's belief in class warfare. On this he knew where he stood – to defend the propertied, educated, cultured minority against the poor and the ignorant masses. Democracy was the enemy. But, after the 1867 Reform Act, which he deplored, democracy was advancing. It must be managed, rather than blindly resisted. As Prime Minister, he contrived, as the ageing Palmerston had done, to do remarkably little in the domestic field. He too found his métier in foreign affairs.

In the *Quarterly Review* in 1862 Salisbury wrote a stout defence of Castlereagh, praising him for his achievements in holding the Coalition together and contributing to a peace which prevented war for so long. He vigorously condemned an interventionist policy. 'All the failures that have taken place [since Vienna]', he wrote 'have arisen from one cause: the practice of foreign intervention in domestic quarrels.' Like Castlereagh, he believed that diplomacy was a confidential and even secret profession and that the diplomat could not speak freely in public. He feared, 'The obscurity in which diplomatic transactions are necessarily shrouded will probably conceal from the public eye the circumstances upon which his justification rests ... Lord Castlereagh was not the man to jeopardise the meanest English interest for the sake of refuting some calumniator of his own good name.' (*QR* 1862: cxi, 202–3, 213.)

Having in 1862 almost identified himself with Castlereagh in an article which, for a man who had not yet held office, showed considerable insight into the difficulties of a Foreign Secretary, three years later he roundly condemned the policy of Palmerston and Russell, which he stigmatised as both bullying and dishonourable. They had unmercifully bullied Brazil and Japan. The references are to two, almost forgotten but violent, events. Some Brazilian 'wreckers' were accused, on rather slight evidence, of plundering a British ship and three British naval officers, possibly drunk, had become embroiled in an entirely separate incident with a Brazilian sentry. Russell demanded compensation and some ships were seized off Rio. The Brazilian government gave in. About the same time a British subject was murdered in Japan, on the road outside Yokohama. As Salisbury pointed out, 'If a Frenchman got his throat cut in St. Giles, or a German emigrant was shot by a bushranger in Australia', the British Foreign Office would not expect to be held responsible. But, the Japanese government having failed to deliver up the criminal, the British navy bombarded Kagosima, the headquarters of the feudal lord whose retainers were suspected, rightly or wrongly, of the crime until, in the words of the British Admiral, 'The fire, which is still raging, affords reasonable ground for believing that the entire town of Kagosima is now a mass of ruins.' (*QR* 1865: cxv, 485–500.)

This bullying of weaker powers contrasted unpleasantly with Britain's ineffectiveness in Europe. She had been able to do nothing to help Poland. Russia had even secured a humiliating retraction of part of the British protest (*ibid.*: 512–13). But the worst betrayal of all had been that of Denmark over the Duchies. He concluded, '[Britain's] pledges and threats are gone with last year's snow, and she is content to watch with cynical philosophy the destruction of those who trusted to the one, and the triumph of those who were wise enough to spurn the other.' (*ibid.*: 529.)

Salisbury had nailed his colours to the mast long before he actually came to office. The first major foreign policy issue on which he had to take a public position (although he had spoken on China in 1859) was the American Civil War. The English upper classes generally inclined to the South but Salisbury went further than most. Smith speaks of his 'passionate identification with the Confederate cause' (Smith 1972: 11) which he equated with the holding back of advancing democracy at home, and Lady Gwendoline Cecil told of his sleep-walking in which he prepared 'to resist forcibly some dreamt-of intrusion of enemies – presumably Federal soldiers or revolutionary mob leaders', until his wife began to entertain serious fears for his sanity (Cecil 1921: vol. 1, 169–70).

When Derby formed his government in July 1866 he invited Salisbury to become Secretary of State for India and Salisbury returned to that office in 1874. Like the young Palmerston, he showed remarkable industry and attention to detail in mastering the technicalities of his office. Like Palmerston too, he always preferred to conduct policy himself without too much reliance on either colleagues or officials. So far as India itself was concerned his policy was essentially conservative. He had little sympathy for Indian aspirations to have more say in the government of their own country, although he did feel that there might be room for Indian initiatives in the Princely States, as distinct from those parts of India under direct British rule. He was also irritated by parliamentary 'interference' in Indian questions, which he regarded as a matter for the executive branch of government.

His experience at the India Office inevitably influenced his perspective on foreign affairs (just as it did that of Lord Hartington, Gladstone's Secretary for India in the early 1880s). There is no evidence that India stirred Salisbury's imagination in the way in which it did Disraeli's but much of his policy was concentrated on safeguarding India against foreign attack. As imperial possessions once again came to be regarded as the hallmark of a Great Power, it was accepted without question that the loss of India would be an insupportable blow to Britain's prosperity and prestige. To keep India the 'Great Game' must be played, not only in central Asia but in the decaying Ottoman empire and perhaps in Africa as well. And, since Europe was increasingly coming to dominate the world, it must be played in Europe too.

For all his belief in non-intervention, Salisbury was irritated by the supineness of Lord Stanley, later the Fifteenth Earl of Derby, who was Foreign Secretary 1866–68 and 1874–78. Anxious to avoid Russell's mistakes over Schleswig-Holstein, Stanley had pursued a near-isolationist policy in Europe from 1866 to 1868. In 1878 he resigned rather than take a strong line with Russia over the Eastern Question. Even before Derby resigned, it was Salisbury who had gone to the Constantinople Conference in the winter of 1876–77. He accompanied Disraeli to Berlin in the summer of 1878. Salisbury emerged feeling, as Aberdeen had done in an earlier generation, that he was the expert on Near Eastern affairs. He never acquired either the same interest, or the same expertise, in Far Eastern affairs which were to dominate international politics at the end of the century.

So far as the Ottoman empire was concerned, Salisbury was forced to the same conclusions as Aberdeen and Gladstone had reached. It could not be sustained indefinitely. As early as 1876, he made it clear to Disraeli that he did not believe that 'the pure Palmerstonian tradition' would serve any longer (Cecil 1921: vol. 2, 86). He had already told Sir Louis Mallet, 'Peace ... would be in no particular danger if only Turkey could be persuaded to stop crumbling to pieces ... It cannot be left as a no-man's-land. But the division of that kind of jetsam is peculiarly difficult. If the Powers quarrel over it, the calamities of a gigantic war must be undergone. If they agree, people call it a partition and denounce it as immoral.' (*ibid*.: 80.) If there was a partition, Britain must secure control of Egypt and the Suez Canal. He wrote to Lytton in September 1876, 'I do not despair of being told to write to you for your best civilian [i.e. civil servant] to govern the new British province of Egypt.' He would have liked to have seen Cyprus placed under the India Office, rather than the Colonial Office (*ibid.*: 83).

Ironically, it was Gladstone's government which moved into the occupation of Egypt in 1882 and which confronted the major crisis in Central Asia in 1885. In 1874 Salisbury had expressed the view that the Russians must advance to Merv eventually but they should not be allowed to take Herat (Cecil 1821: vol. 2, 70). When the crisis came in the spring of 1885 the Gladstone government took much the same view. They had reluctantly accepted the Russian annexation of Merv the previous year but, when the Russian advance continued and they clashed with a small Afghan force at Penjdeh on the disputed border, they reacted with unusual force. They asked for a substantial Vote of Credit from Parliament. It was in fact the Conservatives who, a few months later, finally negotiated the compromise that the Liberals had suggested which, while leaving the Russians in control of Penjdeh, kept them from more important strategic points. But Central Asia was far from stabilised.

The partition of Africa had begun during the second Gladstone administration. No one supposed that it was a development that the government actively desired. Gladstone grumbling about the 'mountain with the unrememberable name' (Mount Kilimanjaro) seemed to typify the ministry's attitude. But in the face of obvious signs of French and German interest, traders bombarded the Foreign Office with petitions and the government reluctantly conceded that the defence of British trade had always been a national concern (see for example Memorandum by P. Anderson and T. V. Lister, 27 Feb. 1884, FO 84/1862 and discussion in FO Confidential Print 5004). The partition seemed to have an inexorable momentum of its own. It occasioned a serious quarrel with Germany over what became German South West Africa (the modern Namibia) in 1884. The Germans snatched the Cameroons, where Britain had established interests. The British staked their claim in Nigeria, Uganda and Kenya. The Germans took Tanganyika.

Salisbury, like Disraeli and unlike Gladstone, came to be regarded as an active imperialist. In fact, like Disraeli, he had virtually no interest in Africa for its own sake. But, by the late 1880s, the pattern was becoming a good deal clearer. It was possible to make calculated decisions about which areas it was worth acquiring and what bargains should be struck. Salisbury was able to incorporate Africa into his general diplomatic strategy in a way in which Gladstone had not. The chronology, the simple fact that Salisbury's ministry succeeded Gladstone's in office, accounts for something. So does the different, and more *realpolitik* approach of Salisbury to foreign affairs in general. But Salisbury's 'picking up the broken china' in Africa (as he said he had done over the

Eastern Question when Derby left office in 1878) has perhaps misled some historians into seeing the partition primarily in terms of an exercise in international politics and diplomacy, well under government control. It had become that by the 1890s but it should not be forgotten that it started in a much more muddled way in the early 1880s, when Gladstone's government seemed at the mercy of forces it did not understand.

One of the most important decisions of the Salisbury government was to grant Cecil Rhodes his British South Africa Company Charter in 1889, which enabled him to open up and administer the areas which became Northern and Southern Rhodesia (the modern Zambia and Zimbabwe). The initiative came from Rhodes himself and the government's decision in his favour was rather surprising. Rhodes had many enemies in London, ranging from missionary to business interests. His relations with the Cape Boers were, at that time, cordial and his hostility to the 'imperial factor', that is British interference in Cape affairs, well known. But the need to stake a British claim in a sensitive area, where the Portuguese, the Germans and the Boers of the Republics were showing interest over-rode suspicions of Rhodes.

After the failure of the Wolff mission in 1887, it became clear that Britain was not going to be able to extricate herself, on any acceptable terms, from Egypt. The security of Egypt now became almost as important to British prestige as India itself. The Sudan was no longer under Egyptian control. Fears, probably exaggerated, began to be expressed about the control of the head-waters of the Nile right back to its source in Lake Victoria. The Imperial British East Africa Company, which had been chartered in 1888, was always under-capitalised and not ready to move into any effective control of Uganda. The Company insisted that it must have a government guarantee to raise capital for a railway between Mombasa and Lake Victoria, which was a pre-requisite to opening up the region. Salisbury himself was well disposed but all he could secure before leaving office in 1892 was a small sum to finance a preliminary survey.

Two years earlier he had concluded a treaty with Germany, by which the Germans agreed to Britain acquiring the commercially and strategically important island of Zanzibar, in return for the cession of Heligoland, which Britain had held since the Napoleonic wars, but which the Germans now wanted to cover the eastern access to the new Kiel canal.

The Heligoland Treaty, although useful to both parties, was, however, only the remnant of what it had been hoped would be a much more comprehensive arrangement between Britain and Germany. Despite Disraeli's brave words in 1866 that Britain was no longer a 'mere' European power, Salisbury had no intention of allowing Britain to remain friendless in Europe. Russia and France were still the powers with whom it seemed most likely that she would quarrel and this dictated his policy of, in his own words, 'leaning' towards the powers of the Triple Alliance, that is Germany, Austria and Italy (HH 3M A/122/6 Salisbury to Lascelles, 10 March 1896). The Triple Alliance, essentially a defensive alliance although its actual terms were a remarkably well-kept secret, was first concluded in 1882 and regularly renewed up to the outbreak of the First World War.

In the summer of 1885 Salisbury used his private secretary, Philip Currie, 'holidaying' in Germany, to make unofficial contact first with Herbert Bismarck and then with Prince Bismarck himself. Currie first broached the possibility of German mediation to resolve Anglo-Russian disputes in Central Asia. He then hinted at something much more far-reaching. 'The present Prime Mininster of England,' he told Herbert

> is known to be favourable to [such] an alliance in the fullest sense of the term, and once established, the English people who have the strongest leaning towards their old Protestant ally, would not allow their Government (from whatever party it might be taken) to swerve from it. A close union between the greatest military power and the greatest naval power could produce a combination that would not only secure the peace of the world, but would also be in the highest degree advantageous to the interests of the two Countries. (HH M3, E/51/60–61, Currie to Salisbury, 4 August 1885 and Copy of paper shown to Ct. Herbert Bismarck, 3 August 1885.)

In particular, it would guarantee the security of the German colonies and of British India. Bismarck replied courteously and at length. He expressed the hope that the Conservatives would win the election because 'Mr. Gladstone knew nothing of foreign affairs and was impossible to do business with' (HH M3, E/51/96, Currie 'Notes on my visit to Friedrichsruhe, September 1885, Secret', summarised in Cecil 1931: vol. 3, 257–61). But he did not commit himself. He was always unconvinced that the Liberals would abide by any agreements if they returned to office. But the main reasons for his caution were his belief that England needed German friendship more than Germany needed England and his fear of being trapped into paying too high a price, particularly in terms of incurring Russian enmity.

A new international crisis once again centred on the Balkans. While Salisbury was Prime Minister for the first time, Eastern Roumelia, the area south of the Balkan Mountains, which Turkey had been allowed to retain in 1878 as a barrier on the way to Constantinople, revolted and opted to rejoin Bulgaria. Salisbury's first reaction was to insist on the upholding of the Berlin settlement but, as the possible international complications multiplied and as it became apparent that the Roumelians were firm in their wish to join Bulgaria, whose prince, Alexander of Battenberg, was pursuing a stoutly independent policy, Salisbury changed his mind. A large and independent Bulgaria would be the best check to Russian ambitions although, at the same time, Salisbury was prepared to move firmly to prevent Serbia and Greece from causing a further deterioration in the situation by using military force to press their own claims. Unfortunately, further trouble occurred in 1887 when Alexander, in a strange Ruritanian episode, was first kidnapped and then abdicated. Bulgaria in fact managed to retain its independence from Russia with the election of Ferdinand of Saxe-Coburg as Alexander's successor.

But the Balkans were plainly a possible flash-point and Salisbury was receptive to Bismarckian attempts to commit Britain to the upholding of the status quo there. The result was the Mediterranean Agreements of 1887. In February and March Britain and Italy, joined by Austria, agreed to co-operate to maintain the status quo in the eastern Mediterranean and adjacent areas. The agreement was vague, even ambiguous, and potentially directed at France as much as Russia. The second agreement, that of December, was more specific and clearly related to the Russian threat in the Near East. The three powers agreed to uphold the independence of Turkey, including the freedom of the Straits, and the status quo as defined by existing treaties, in particular the position of Bulgaria. The agreements were not treaties but were embodied in notes exchanged between the powers (for text of notes see Lowe: 1967: vol. 2, 56–7, 61–2). They were kept strictly secret and not laid before Parliament. The Cabinet was uneasy. It was, as Taylor puts it, 'more nearly an alliance with a group of Great Powers than any Great Britain had ever made in time of peace' or was to make with France or Russia twenty years later (Taylor 1954: 321).

Two years later in 1889 it was Bismarck who suggested to Britain a defensive alliance against France for a term of years and similar to the arrangements he already had with Italy and Austria. France and Russia seemed to be drawing closer together, despite Bismarck's negotiation of the Reinsurance treaty with Russia. Germany felt compelled to take General Boulanger and the new French demand for 'revenge' seriously. Britain was becoming acutely conscious of her own military weakness (see documents in Lowe 1967: vol. 2, 71–91). Nevertheless, Salisbury rejected Bismarck's overtures. This was partly because of his underlying distrust of Bismarck and his fear that Bismarck might be using him as a cat's paw against France, just as Bismarck feared he was being used against Russia. But, interestingly, Salisbury's caution was also dictated by domestic circumstances. He led a minority government, dependent on the support of the Liberal-Unionists, who were not yet in formal coalition with the Conservatives. He could not count on the support of the Commons for an unpopular policy such as a continental military alliance or even for money, although the House did pass the Naval Defence Act in 1889, providing an additional £20 million to maintain the 'two powers' standard (that is the British fleet must be as strong as the next two most powerful navies, discounting the United States) (Kennedy 1983: 178–9). But behind these practical difficulties of controlling Parliament seemed to lie an even deeper pessimism. Britain was split, in a way she had not been in modern times, by the Irish issue. Salisbury wrote to the Queen, 'Torn in two by a controversy which almost threatens her existence [Britain] cannot in the present state of public opinion interfere with any decisive action abroad.' (For full discussion of this question see Kennedy 1982: 188–98.)

The only outcome was the Heligoland Treaty. Anglo-German relations were to begin to change the same year, 1890, with the accession of William II and the fall of Bismarck. William was a strange and contradictory character (for an exploration of that character see Röhl 1982). Although he was the son of Queen Victoria's favourite daughter, Vicky, his attitude to Britain was always ambiguous. Where Bismarck, despite his brief excursion into a colonial policy in 1884–86, had always thought in continental terms, William wished to pursue a 'world' policy. It was difficult to see how this could avoid bringing Germany into conflict with Britain's world-wide interests, especially when the Germans were conscious of being late arrivals on the colonial scene and still believed, on the whole exaggeratedly, that Britain was hostile to their aspirations. Nevertheless, Anglo-German hostility was slow and complex in its development, long tempered by the continued British belief that the main challenges were likely to come from Russia or France and countered by the now fashionable theories that 'race' was of fundamental importance in world history and that the British and the Germans, like the British and the Americans, were of the same stock and therefore natural allies.

The Liberals returned to power in 1892 but this time British foreign policy did not change. Gladstone himself was absorbed by the Irish question. Lord Rosebery, who became his Foreign Secretary, as he had done during the short 1886 administration, was a more committed imperialist than Salisbury. He believed too that continuity in foreign policy would place it above party politics. The Foreign Secretary, he said, should speak 'with the united voice of the English nation without distinction of party' (Martel 1986: 31, 152).

So far as there was a contest about colonial expansion it was within the Liberal Party between Rosebery and Harcourt. Harcourt, as Chancellor of the Exchequer, disliked the additional expenditure on imperial projects. The question of the retention of Uganda became the key issue between them. Harcourt wrote to Rosebery that in his opinion, the empire was already large enough. 'It is said,' he wrote, ' "We have India and Canada and Australia, why not Africa?" That is like a landowner who, having secured many great estates which he can with difficulty manage, thinks it an argument for buying more and mortgaging those which he has for the purchase. That can only end in bankruptcy.' Rosebery replied publicly at a banquet at the Royal Colonial Institute the following year, 1893. 'It is said,' he remarked, 'that our Empire is already large enough and does not need extension. That would be true enough if the world were elastic, but, unfortunately, it is not elastic, and we are engaged at the present moment in the language of mining in "pegging out claims for the future." We have to consider not what we want now, but what we shall want in the future.' (Bennett 1962: 309–10.) The idea of the pre-emptive strike against potential rivals was very close to the heart of the new imperialist movement. Rosebery won, with the help of both religious and business pressure groups. Uganda was retained. It also showed Rosebery to be the strong man of the cabinet and it was Rosebery, not Harcourt who had long been regarded as Gladstone's successor, who took Gladstone's place as Prime Minister in 1894.

If Rosebery was a more committed ideological imperialist than Salisbury, he was also more committed to a policy of friendship with Germany. He was on terms of personal friendship with the Bismarck family and had been very indiscreet in his communications with them in the early 1880s on the shortcomings of Gladstone's previous Foreign Secretary, Lord Granville. (For interesting revelations on this see RP MSS 10004 and 10005.) But basically Rosebery, like Salisbury, wished to maintain the balance of power in Europe, both because it seemed to promise the preservation of the existing world order, on which his own comfortable position depended, and because it was necessary to restrain Britain's potential antagonists and ensure the safety of the empire (Martel 1986: x, 232).

When Salisbury returned to power in 1895, he was in a stronger domestic position. He now had a clear parliamentary majority and a formal coalition with the Liberal Unionists. It was accepted as a sign of the times that the leader of the Liberal Unionists, Joseph Chamberlain, opted to take the Colonial Office, previously regarded as a comparatively junior office, rather than the Chancellorship of the Exchequer. Although Chamberlain had expressed interest in the Colonial Office in 1886, it is probably more correct to regard Chamberlain as a younger man as a Palmerstonian, rather than an imperialist (see contrasting views of Garvin 1932: vol. I, 443; vol. II, 447 and Frazer 1966: xiv).

Over much of the empire Chamberlain's work was to be that of practical consolidation, trying to attract investment and putting in what would today be called the infrastructure of railways, roads and harbours. He too used the metaphor of a landlord and his estates, in this case 'undeveloped estates'. But there also comes over very starkly in Chamberlain his belief that an empire was necessary to solve the 'social question' at home. He told an audience in Walsall in 1895,

> Whatever the cause of bad trade may be, we have to look for remedies ... to my mind the cause of bad trade, of want of employment, is clear. It is the continual growth of our population at the same time that our trade and industry does not grow in proportion, and if we want our trade and industry to grow we must find new markets for it. Old markets are getting exhausted, some of them are being closed to us by hostile tariffs, and unless we can find new countries which will be free to take our goods you

> may be quite satisfied that lack of employment will continue to be one of the greatest of social evils. (Bennett 1962: 313–14.)

Britain was beginning to feel increasingly beleaguered in an economically hostile world. Chamberlain himself was to move to the next logical position and demand a return to limited protection in the form of imperial preference. But his colleagues were not ready for it. Free trade was still indissolubly identified with national prosperity. The only result was to spit the Conservative party in 1904.

When the Conservatives returned to power in 1895, the Scramble for Africa was entering its last phase. France still seemed to be the most likely opponent. There were two potential flash-points; the Nile and the upper Niger. Chamberlain took a particular interest in the Niger but for Salisbury the Nile had priority. A compromise was reached on the Niger boundary in June 1898 but, almost immediately, a new crisis developed at the obscure village of Fashoda on the upper Nile. (For the latest study of the affair see Bates 1984.) In 1895 Sir Edward Grey, as Under-Secretary at the Foreign Office, had warned the French that any encroachment in the region would be regarded as an 'unfriendly act'. Despite this the French despatched a mission, eventually led by Captain Marchand, from Brazzaville. After an epic journey across Africa he arrived at Fashoda, just before Kitchener's victorious army. The status of the Sudan in international law had been unclear since the Anglo-Egyptian withdrawal in 1885. In 1896 Salisbury decided to re-occupy it, nominally on behalf of Egypt. Kitchener, who was chosen to command the expedition, advanced very carefully. Only in September 1898 did he finally defeat the Dervish power at the battle of Omdurman. Kitchener and Marchand treated one another with formal courtesy and left their governments to work out the problem.

The press in both countries became violent in their denunciations and it was at least popularly believed that war was very near. But France was torn apart by the Dreyfus affair. She had budgetary problems and her navy was not ready. Salisbury was confident that the French would not fight and he drove a hard bargain. The French were compelled to accept the watershed of the Congo and the Nile as the boundary of the Sudan, now under British control, and Salisbury firmly refused any more extensive settlement of colonial disputes which would have enabled the French government to save face. The French Foreign Minister, Delcassé, subsequently maintained that British intransigence delayed the improvement of relations between the two countries he desired. But Britain at this time still felt a great deal more in common with the Triple Alliance than with the new Dual Alliance of France and Russia.

The great issue which was now looming was the fate of China. The westerners had forced their way into Chinese trade by the Opium War of 1839–42 and the 'Arrow' war of 1856–60. The Manchu dynasty was beginning to lose control of the country and their power had been seriously undermined by the Taiping rebellion in the 1850s and 60s. They had turned to a westerner, General Charles Gordon, to help them suppress the rebels and the Chinese finances were also passing into the hands of western 'experts'. All the classic symptoms of decay seemed to be present. The world began to expect the partition of China to follow that of Africa. Britain, France, Germany and even Italy all had interests. (The British interests were mainly in the Yangtse basin.) But there were two important additional players who had taken only a very minor part in the Scramble for Africa, Russia and the United States.

Salisbury was clear in his view that Britain did not want additional formal commitments in China. In 1896 he repeated with approval Disraeli's words 'in Asia there is room for us all', making clear that he meant 'room to trade' (Grenville 1964: 136). He was happy enough to support the American Open Door policy. There was, however, as in Africa and the Ottoman empire, the ever-present possibility that events would outrun British wishes and Britain was not well placed, with no firm allies, to assert her interests. The dangers of being isolated in any carve-up of China were an unspoken background to British policy at the turn of the century.

The first startling revelation of Chinese weakness came in 1895 when Japan, which had successfully modernised in a way in which China had not, so easily defeated her. The 'Triplice', Russia, Germany and France, moved in to prevent Japan from securing the spoils of war. The loans which China needed to pay off the war indemnities gave other powers, especially Russia, a firmer grasp of her finances. In 1898 Russia gained control of Port Arthur and Germany of Kiaochow. Britain could only respond by taking the not very important station of Wei-hai-wei. Negotiations for railway concessions, which seemed likely to turn into 'spheres of influence' were proceeding fast. Salisbury's preferred policy was to try to secure bilateral agreements with other powers to persuade them to accept the principle of no territorial concessions but he failed to clinch such an agreement with Russia just before the Russian move on Port Arthur.

Britain's diplomatic isolation was becoming apparent in other parts of the world too. There were several quite serious quarrels with the United States. The most spectacular was that of December 1895 when President Cleveland announced, mainly for reasons of domestic politics, that he would impose a settlement, by force if necessary, in the current boundary dispute between Venezuela and British Guiana in the name of the Monroe Doctrine. Britain backed down on that and on other disputes in the American hemisphere (Campbell 1960). The reason was partly that, as in the 1840s, America cared more about the disputed matters than Britain did, but the government was also clear that it could not risk a war with the United States in its uncertain position in Europe.

The precariousness of that position became even more apparent during the Boer War. The first shock had been administered in January

1896 when the Kaiser sent his notorious telegram to President Kruger of the Transvaal, congratulating him on repelling Dr Jameson's filibustering raid without having to call on the help of friendly powers. The implications were obvious, more particularly as it was well known that there were pressure groups in Germany anxious to use the Boer republics as the nucleus of German colonies of settlement – although the Boers, who only wanted to be left alone, had been unresponsive (Butler 1967). The furore diverted the attention of the public from the question of how much the British government had known about Jameson's illegal attempt to overthrow Kruger.

Between 1896 and 1899 the Germans supplied the Boers with armaments, particularly Krupp guns, which certainly made Kruger more intransigent in the negotiations in 1899 and helped the Boers to put up such formidable resistance to the ultimately stronger British forces. But when the war came, the Germans maintained a very correct position of neutrality, even when they were subjected to serious provocation in the arrest of the mail steamer, the *Bundesrath*, and other German ships. It was the French and Russian governments which talked about the possibility of a 'continental coalition' against Britain, and Russia actually moved troops in Central Asia.

In these circumstances it is not surprising that despite the quarrels with Germany and the United States, there were still those in Britain who looked on them as Britain's 'natural allies'. Some of Salisbury's cabinet were becoming seriously concerned by Britain's isolation and found a lead in Joseph Chamberlain. Chamberlain made two overtures to Germany, one in 1898, the other in 1899. The evidence does not suggest that he was pursuing an 'independent' foreign policy, still less that Salisbury and Salisbury's nephew, A. J. Balfour, who was to succeed Salisbury as Prime Minister in 1902 and was already assuming some responsibility for foreign affairs, wished Chamberlain to damage himself in this enterprise for domestic reasons. From their point of view it was a convenient kite-flying exercise that did not officially involve the Foreign Office.

They were to have to break cover in 1901 after Lord Lansdowne became Foreign Secretary and opened official negotiations with Germany. All three attempts failed. The old stumbling block remained – the Germans did not want to have to defend Britain's interests against Russia. It was during these negotiations that Salisbury wrote his famous memorandum of 29 May which used to be held to prove that 'the old statesman was still wedded to the idea of splendid isolation' (Langer 1951: 734). Modern research puts a different interpretation on it (Howard 1967; Grenville 1964: 353–4). Salisbury had always distrusted 'entangling alliances', although he had consented to the Mediterranean Agreements, but it was this particular alliance and the German ambassador, Hatzfeldt's, arguments in favour of it, which he was combating. Unlike Hatzfeldt he believed the obligations would be 'unequal' in that Britain was promising more to the Triple Alliance than they were to her. The inability of the continental powers in fact to combine against her during the Boer war showed that she was not in such a weak bargaining position as Germany supposed.

But, interestingly, Salisbury introduced another argument too. The making of treaties in Britain (unlike the United States) has always fallen entirely within the prerogative of the executive, that is, the Crown, or in modern times in practice, the government. They do not need to be brought before Parliament. But Salisbury chose to argue that no British government could any longer guarantee the fulfilment of a treaty unless it was backed by public opinion. He may, like Canning on occasions, have been conjuring up public opinion as an excuse for not doing what he did not wish to do but it remains a remarkable statement from a man who at the beginning of his career had praised Castlereagh for taking no account of public opinion. Whether or not Salisbury was right in his assessment of public reaction on this occasion it is an unexpected acknowledgement that the forces determining diplomacy were changing (*BD* 1927: vol. 2, 68).

The Chinese question had become more acute with the Boxer rebellion and the siege of the foreign legations in Peking. The joint expedition to relieve the legations mounted by the leading European powers together with the United States and Japan went smoothly but the diplomatic legacy was tangled. The powers had renounced territorial gains in advance and in October 1900 Britain and Germany (joined by Japan) signed an agreement promising to uphold the territorial integrity of China. When the Russians showed every sign of remaining in Manchuria after the intervention, the British appealed to the Germans to join them in exerting diplomatic pressure. The Germans declined, arguing that the Agreement had never applied to Manchuria, indeed calling it the 'Yangtse Agreement'. The refusal of the Germans to, as the British saw it, honour the 1900 Agreement did as much as anything to turn official, as distinct from public, opinion against any idea of an Anglo-German alliance.

The Germans on their side were irritated by what they regarded as a parallel act of British bad faith. In 1898 Britain and Germany, while guaranteeing a loan to Portugal on the security of her colonies, reached agreement between themselves as to which power should take what if, as seemed likely, the Portuguese empire did break up. In 1900 Britain renewed her ancient undertakings to uphold the integrity of the Portuguese territories. They could argue that the two undertakings were not incompatible. The Anglo-German agreement was a contingency one but it re-inforced German distrust of Britain.

For the first time British sympathies were moving away from the Central Powers, Germany and Austria, and setting towards France and even Russia. The estrangement from Germany worked at many levels (see Kennedy 1982). The most obvious was the new naval rivalry, consequent upon the German Navy Laws. It is only a slight exaggeration to say that the German navy 'was floated on a tide of Anglophobia'. If a, sometimes reluctant, Reichstag was to be persuaded to find the money, it had to be convinced that there was an enemy against whom the navy might be needed. Who could that be but Britain? The British asked the same question. A German navy, backed by the powerful German army, could only be intended as a threat to the British empire and to the British homeland. Invasion scares now centred on Germany, not France. Erskine Childer's *The Riddle of the Sands* was a best-seller and even forced a government response (Kennedy 1982: 252).

Trade rivalry is more difficult to assess. Germany had certainly become a major British competitor and, with the development of railways, had displaced British trade in a number of vital areas, notably the Balkans. The railways also aided the spread of German influence in Turkey. It was not coincidental that a major Anglo-German dispute arose over the Berlin–Baghdad railway project. At the same time Britain and Germany were important trading partners. The First World War was in no sense a simple 'trade war'. The business communities in both countries were generally horrified at the prospect of war. Yet the trade rivalry did have subtle and profound effects on public feeling and particularly the growth of patriotic fervour (see the views of Hoffman 1964; and Kennedy 1982: 291–305).

In 1901 Britain began wide-ranging discussions with Russia, which encompassed the Straits, Central Asia and the Far East. There has always been some dispute about Salisbury's attitude to the Straits question. Discussing the whole question of the Near East with the Tsar at Balmoral in the autumn of 1896, Salisbury made what Grenville calls an 'unwise and indiscreet' statement (Grenville 1964: 79) in which he implied that Britain no longer had much interest in the Straits question. 'I admitted', Salisbury wrote in a memorandum of the conversations 'that the theory that Turkish rule at Constantinople was a bulwark to our Indian Empire could not be maintained.' Britain's only remaining interest was to see that Austria's position was properly safeguarded.

The Near East could not be ignored. In the mid 1890s the terrible massacres of the Armenians by the Turks (the worst, or at least the most public, occurred in Constantinople itself in August 1896) horrified the world. The rising in Crete in 1897 led to the war between Greece and Turkey, which threatened to set the whole area ablaze. Salisbury was driven to adopt an almost Gladstonian policy of trying to settle these questions by the Concert of Europe.

Attempts to get direct agreements with Russia were overtaken by the Russo-Japanese war in 1904. Prior to 1902 both Britain and Japan had tried to ensure stability in the Far East by deals with Russia. When both powers were finally convinced that such deals were not at that time possible, they joined together in the Anglo-Japanese alliance. From the British point of view, an important attraction was that the Japanese navy could 'hold the ring' in the Pacific in the early stages of a crisis and Britain could afford to transfer part of the Pacific fleet to home waters to meet any threat from Germany. The Anglo-Japanese alliance was a formal commitment of the kind successive British governments had tried to avoid but it may be true that it was seen as an alternative to an 'entangling alliance' in Europe, rather than the inauguration of a new policy (Taylor 1954: 425–6).

The alliance was meant, certainly by Britain, to be entirely defensive but it played its part in persuading the Japanese to risk a war against Russia before the completion of the Trans-Siberian railway gave Russia overwhelming force in the Far East. The war endangered the peace of Europe, even without the Dogger Bank incident when the Russian Baltic fleet en route for the Pacific to replace the fleet already sunk by the Japanese attacked a British fishing fleet, apparently supposing it to be a force of Japanese torpedo boats. France was allied with Russia, Britain with Japan. Neither alliance in itself demanded participation in the Russo-Japanese war but, if more powers were drawn in, the situation would alter.

The French became very anxious to improve their relations with Britain. Tentative discussions had begun as early as 1902. Edward VII's state visit to Paris and the cordiality of his welcome did act as a catalyst, even if his influence on foreign affairs in other ways has been exaggerated. The implacable hostility of the two countries towards each other, evident at the time of Fashoda, no longer seemed to exist.

The Anglo-French agreements of April 1904 were a series of bargains, settling outstanding colonial disputes. The most important related to Egypt and Morocco. Lord Cromer warned the British government from Cairo that the administration of Egypt would break down unless international consent could be secured for financial changes. In order to secure French consent, which meant France abandoning her long-established hostility to the British position in Egypt, Britain was prepared to withdraw her opposition to France acquiring Morocco, which the French colonial party now regarded as the 'missing piece' in their African empire. By other agreements France relinquished irritating fishery rights on the Newfoundland coast in exchange for boundary changes in West Africa and Britain and France agreed on 'spheres of influence' in Siam. Only maladroit German policy turned these colonial bargains into an *entente*, which eventually became almost a quasi-alliance.

Chapter 11

THE COMING OF WAR

The first years of the twentieth century saw an apparent revolution in Britain's foreign policy, and a switch from her traditional policy of supporting the Germanic powers and expecting hostility from France and Russia to cordiality to France and Russia and growing estrangement from Germany. How far was this change of policy deliberate and could it have been reversed? Immediately after 1945, when Britain had fought alongside France and Russia against the Germanic powers in two World Wars (and against Italy in the second), the alignments of the Triple Alliance against the Triple Entente looked natural. After the Cold War and French opposition to Britain joining the European Economic Community, they looked less natural. In fact, in the perspective of the nineteenth century as a whole, they were unusual and at no point between 1904 and 1914 were they regarded as immutable.

The Germans over-reacted to the Anglo-French agreements of 1904. Unlike the Anglo-Japanese alliance, which they welcomed, they saw it as a threat to their interests. They tried to counter it, first, by attempting to strike a similar colonial bargain with Britain. Ironically, this came to nothing because, at this time, there were few outstanding disputes between them. They, or at least the Kaiser, then tried to abort the possibility of an Anglo-French-Russian link by drawing closer to Russia and renewing the policy of the Reinsurance Treaty. But the Kaiser's advisers were still in favour of a 'simpler' foreign policy, which would not try to emulate Bismarck's brilliant but dangerous policy of what Bismarck's successor, Caprivi, had called 'keeping five balls in the air at once'. The German government was thus driven back on the risky policy of mounting a direct challenge to the Anglo-French agreement on Morocco, one of the only two points upon which there was a secret agreement by each power to support the other diplomatically.

In January 1905 a French mission went to Fez to negotiate with the Sultan. Two months later the Kaiser visited Tangiers and publicly proclaimed his belief in the Sultan's total independence. He also made clear that Germany had interests in Morocco and must be consulted in any settlement. In the summer the screw was turned further. The Germans intimated to the French that they wanted the resignation of Delcassé, who had negotiated the Anglo-French agreements, and an international conference on Morocco. The French yielded on both points. The Germans calculated that the British would be glad to get out of the deal on Morocco, which they believed must be unwelcome to them. The international conference met at Algeciras in Spain in January 1906.

Just before it met, the British government changed. Balfour resigned in December 1905 and the general election of January 1906 returned a Liberal administration with an overwhelming majority of 399 MPs (plus the general support of 29 Labour members) against 156 Conservatives. The Liberal landslide was, in part, a verdict on ten years of Conservative inertia in social policy, while the evidence mounted of the need to remedy intolerable conditions. Impressive studies by men such as Charles Booth and Seebohm Rowntree had shown that a third of the population was living at, or below, subsistence level. It was also due, in part, to the split in the Conservative party on the question of imperial preference but it could be argued that this was essentially part of the same question. How should Britain respond to the new industrial challenges? Could her empire save her?

In some quarters there was a sense of euphoria at the Liberal victory and a belief that it heralded a new dawn in foreign, as in domestic, policy. In fact, for all Salisbury's fears that the nature of British parliamentary government meant that a ministry could not bind its successors, foreign policy was more bipartisan in the decades before the First World War than it had been a generation earlier. Such dissent as there was arose within the large Liberal majority (Taylor 1957: 95–131; Morris 1972).

The new British Foreign Secretary, Sir Edward Grey, had no intention of changing the policy of his predecessor, Lord Lansdowne, particularly so far as the engagements to France were concerned. He had made his views clear in a speech in October 1905, for which he had deliberately sought publicity. He told Stephen Spender of the *Westminster Gazette*, 'I think we are running a real risk of losing France and not gaining Germany who won't want us, if she can detach France from us.' In his speech he stressed that the Liberal party would continue the policies of friendship with the United States, the alliance with Japan and the agreements with France. He also hinted at the possibility of reconciliation with Russia and recognised the depth of hostility between Britain and Germany, which was developing at the popular level (Robbins 1971: 132–3).

Grey was the only British Foreign Secretary of the nineteenth or early twentieth century who left a completed political autobiography. But his *Twenty-Five Years* (1925) must be balanced against the fact that he is the only important Foreign Secretary of the period whose private papers seem not to have survived in any quantity. He came from a political family. It was frequently recalled that he was the great-great-nephew of Lord Grey of the Reform Bill and his grandfather was Sir George Grey, who held cabinet posts in all Liberal governments from 1841 to 1866. Edward Grey entered parliament in 1885. But, according to his own account, he had had little interest in politics as a boy or even as an undergraduate at Balliol; his sympathies were only engaged when the Lords rejected Gladstone's proposal in 1884 to extend the franchise to the counties on the same terms as the boroughs (Grey 1925: vol. I, xxii–xxvi). So far his credentials were impeccably Liberal. But he found his métier in foreign affairs and here Liberalism was undergoing a strange evolution (Matthew 1973).

The Boer War had split the Liberal party. The fissure never really healed and, despite the great electoral victory of 1906, some historians have seen the war as marking the beginning of the end for the party. Some, like Lloyd George, espoused the Boer cause. Others, including Asquith, Haldane and Grey himself, supported the British government. Both sides argued about the respective rights of British and Boers. It was still a white man's world. The role of the black African passed almost unnoticed. Among other things, the Boer War revealed what a woefully large proportion of potential army recruits was medically unfit. There began a drive for 'national efficiency', which would culminate in the establishment of school medical services and the provision of free school meals for 'necessitous schoolchildren' under the Liberal government. Grey came to be counted among the Liberal Imperialists, for whom the empire was an integral part of the national efficiency strategy which would regenerate the nation. He owed this identification to his attitude to the Boer War, his association with Lord Rosebery and to the fact that in 1902 he joined the Co-Efficients, the exclusive dining club which included Conservatives, Liberals and Fabians, committed to this policy. His own views were, however, not quite those of a typical Liberal Imperialist. He had little interest in the colonies of settlement and did not want further expansion. He wrote to Herbert Samuel, a fellow Liberal politician, in 1902, 'I hope that Africa is now so divided up that neither philanthropic nor political reasons will lead to our taking more of it.' He was, if anything, a consolidationist. 'Our business', he told Samuel 'is to develop what we have got, wisely and with discrimination.' (Robbins 1971: 135).

Grey remains the most enigmatic of British Foreign Secretaries. To some he was the last of the 'gentleman politicians', who took office from 'a sense of duty to his country and obligations to his party', a man of principle with 'a certain liberal moral view of the world' but handicapped, at least at first by 'his lack of experience and his scanty acquaintance with European history and statesmen'. On this view, he was never comfortable in politics and would have done better to stick to his fishing and birdwatching. To others, especially to German politicians of the revisionist school just after the First World War, this was all so much camouflage and Grey was a politician of exceptional machiavellianism. Later German historians, more critical of their own former leaders, have 'resurrected Grey as the model of simple-minded rectitude in politics' (Williamson 1969: 63; Robbins 1971: xiii–xv).

Although Grey had travelled little outside Britain (and that within the British empire, to India and the West Indies) and although his command of French (still the language of diplomacy) was poor (Trevelyan 1937: 69) he did not come to the Foreign Office in December 1905 with no experience. He had been Parliamentary Under-Secretary (an office rather like a modern Minister of State) there under Rosebery in 1892–95. Grey regarded Rosebery as his mentor in foreign affairs but Rosebery had always been pro-German and Grey had begun to distance himself from him when he welcomed the 1904 agreements with France, of which Rosebery was critical.

Grey had a comparatively easy ride in the Commons. In spite of, or perhaps because of, the widening of the franchise, parliamentary control of foreign affairs was diminishing. It was partly a question of expert knowledge. In the previous century it was not uncommon for men to switch between parliamentary and diplomatic careers. This practice had now almost ceased, although such expertise could occasionally be found in the Lords. But even more important was the tighter party organisation and the pervasive power of the party whips. On foreign, as on domestic, questions the party in power could count on an almost automatic majority in any important division.

Nevertheless, Grey's policy did attract severe criticism. The radical wing of the party had disliked his speech in October 1905, stressing the essential continuity of foreign policy and it was not only radicals who felt that the Liberals should have a distinctive foreign policy. Some welcomed the support he gave to France. There was still a Francophile tradition within the party but it was harder to reconcile themselves to co-operation with Russia, even a Russia which since 1905 had made some constitutional progress with the summoning of the Duma. Anti-war groups within the party were dissatisfied with what they saw as Grey's surrender to power politics and militarism (A. J. A. Morris 1972). The critics became organised, after the Agadir crisis, in the Foreign Affairs Group in parliament and the Foreign Policy Committee outside, a process culminating after the outbreak of the First World War in the establishment of the Union of Democratic Control. But Grey's policy was more inhibited by the fact that many of his critics were within the Cabinet. Wilson contends that 'there were never more than five ministers with the same outlook as Grey'. As a result Grey resorted to concealing matters, some important, from his colleagues (Wilson 1987: 188–9). Most early nineteenth-century Foreign Secretaries had done the same thing but there is no doubt that it would, if known, have been considered more heinous in 1912 than in the 1820s and 1830s.

One of the charges brought against Grey by his critics was that he was 'a puppet of his permanent officials ... a weak man' (E. D. Morel quoted Taylor 1957: 97). It was, of course, an absurd exaggeration but it represented a correct appreciation that Foreign Office officials, the 'experts', were beginning to play a much more active role in shaping policy than ever before. This was partly because of the sheer volume of business and the greater sophistication of techniques required to process it. But the development of Foreign Office influence had been held back by the strength and personality of their political chiefs. Salisbury in particular continued to regard even senior officials as essentially 'clerks'. As Salisbury declined in his last years, they became more powerful. Lansdowne did not arrest this process and, under Grey, it accelerated.

This growing influence was all the more important because it coincided with a shift of sympathy within the Foreign Office (Steiner 1963, 1965, 1969). This is traditionally symbolised by Eyre Crowe's memorandum of January 1907, in which he developed the argument that Germany had been hostile to Britain since the 1880s and was currently a serious threat to her, especially at sea. Although Crowe was still a comparatively junior official (he did not become Permanent Under-Secretary until 1920), the memorandum attracted the attention of Grey, who wrote on it, 'This Memorandum by Mr Crowe is most valuable' and directed that it should go to the Prime Minister and other senior Cabinet colleagues. It provoked a strong reply from the then Permanent Under-Secretary, Sir Thomas Sanderson, in which he argued that, although Germany was naturally pursuing her own interests as a great power, there was no consistent hostility to Britain in German policy (*BD* 1928: vol. III, 397–431). The Crowe-Sanderson clash did fairly reflect the divergence of opinion between the older generation, such as Sanderson, and the younger men, like Crowe or Sir Francis Bertie, Monson's successor, who distrusted Germany and were prepared to seek closer relations with France.

Sanderson himself was about to retire and was succeeded by Charles Hardinge. Hardinge had a long experience in the diplomatic service. He also had excellent contacts in Whitehall and was on terms of friendship with the king, Edward VII. He wanted, and expected, to play an active rôle in policy making, in particular, he was an advocate, not only of friendship with France, but still more of reconciliation with Russia. His relations with Grey were excellent and, especially in the early days, Grey leaned heavily on his advice. Steiner concluded, 'The relationship between Grey and Hardinge was more one of peers than any previous partnership between a foreign secretary and his permanent under-secretary.' (1969: 92–5.) At the same time there was probably coincidence of views, rather than the 'undue influence' at which radical critics hinted. Grey had expressed support for France and doubts about Germany before he came into office. For both Grey and the Foreign

Office officials, new attitudes arose in large part from the logic of a new situation.

Grey took office in the middle of a crisis. In January 1906 the French ambassador, Paul Cambon, asked what Britain would do if Germany attacked France as a result of the Moroccan dispute. Grey was in no position to give Cambon the assurances he sought. No alliance existed and Britain was in the throes of a general election. Grey could only promise 'benevolent neutrality' and express the opinion that 'public opinion would be strongly moved in favour of France' in such an eventuality (Grey 1925: vol. I, 72–4; Trevelyan 1937: 126–33). At the same time he warned the German ambassador, Count Metternich, that Britain was likely to support France. He also authorised the continuation of the 'military conversations', which, he always maintained, had begun under Lansdowne (Monger 1963: 243–4).

The 'military conversations' have always formed the centre-piece of charges of Grey's machiavellian cleverness. The conversations were a rather untidy series of discussions involving, at different stages, various members of the Committee of Imperial Defence, Sir George Clarke, Viscount Esher and Admiral Sir John Fisher, Sir John Grierson, the Director of Military Intelligence, Major Huguet, the French Military Attaché, and others. A parallel series of discussions took place with Belgium. It is unclear when Grey first learnt of them but he probably knew by 9 January. The full Cabinet was never told of them. Apart from Grey, only Campbell-Bannerman, Lord Ripon, the Lord Privy Seal, Haldane, the Secretary for War, Lord Tweedmouth, the First Lord of the Admiralty, and possibly Asquith, then Chancellor of the Exchequer, knew. The excuses subsequently offered for keeping the Cabinet in the dark, the distractions of the election, the shock of the sudden death of Grey's wife, were transparently inadequate. The inner group may have feared leaks but the most probable reason was that they knew there would be dissension. (The fullest discussion is in Monger 1963: 236–56.) The argument that the conversations were simply contingency planning of the kind that must always go on has more substance to it but the mere discussion of the possibility of Britain aiding France against Germany represented a major shift in British strategic thinking. In 1907, for the first time, Britain's summer manoeuvres were conducted on the assumption that Germany, not France, was the enemy.

When the Algeciras conference met, the Germans found that they had miscalculated badly. They had expected France to be isolated and Britain glad to have an excuse to drop her engagements. In fact Britain stood by France. Italy and Spain also had prior agreements with her. Russia could not afford to offend the ally on whom, since the Russo-Japanese war and her internal troubles of 1905, she was ever more financially dependent. On paper, Germany did not do badly at Algeciras. Morocco was formally recognised as an international problem. Some international control of both the Moroccan Bank and the policing of the ports remained. The way was not yet clear for France to assume a protectorate. But, for all that, Algeciras was universally recognised as a major diplomatic defeat for Germany, which revealed that her position in Europe was by no means as secure as it had been and helped to foster German fears of 'encirclement' by potentially hostile powers.

The following year German fears were apparently realised by the conclusion of an Anglo-Russian *entente*. As in the case of the Anglo-French agreements of 1904, there was no question of an alliance, simply of a series of bargains to settle outstanding disputes. Here again the Liberal government was taking up an initiative left by their predecessors. The tentative negotiations of 1901 had been suspended by the Anglo-Japanese alliance and the Russo-Japanese war. On the face of it, agreement with Russia was a surprising policy for a Liberal government and it certainly attracted criticism from the radicals. But it was something that Grey, assisted by Hardinge and the able new ambassador to St Petersburg, Arthur Nicolson (later Lord Carnock), was determined to bring about. It had in fact been Liberal Imperialist policy since the mid 1890s and there was now the additional motive of balancing German power. Grey wrote in January 1906, 'An *entente* between Russia, France and ourselves would be absolutely secure. If it is necessary to check Germany it could then be done.' (Kennedy 1982: 284; *cf.* Monger 1963: 281–3 and Wilson 1987: 177–84.)

Two areas which had been discussed in 1901, the Straits and the Far East, had been settled by events. Russia had retreated from Manchuria as a result of the Japanese war, although it is often forgotten that, in 1907, Russia and Japan concluded a new agreement that left Russian influence dominant in northern Manchuria and Japan dominant in the south – roughly the settlement the two powers had discussed prior to the war. The Straits question was also affected, although less directly, by the war. In 1901 Britain had seemed to be on the point of relinquishing her old objections to the opening of the Straits but, in 1904–05, one of the few ways in which Britain could demonstrate her 'benevolent neutrality' towards Japan was to insist on the strict enforcement of the Straits treaty, which kept the Russian Black Sea fleet bottled up and unable to join the Baltic fleet on its way to the Far East.

The Anglo-Russian agreements of 1907 therefore concerned only Tibet, Afghanistan and Persia. Tibet was an outlying province of the Manchu empire over which China had almost lost control by 1900. In 1904 the Younghusband mission compelled the Tibetans to open up trading relations with Britain but Younghusband exceeded his instructions and the British government was content in 1907 to restore Tibet to a neutral rôle by agreeing that neither Britain nor Russia would have any relations with Tibet except through China, which re-asserted its control in 1910. Since the death of Abdur Rhaman in 1901 there had been fears that Afghanistan would drift into the Russian sphere. Britain was therefore well satisfied with a settlement by which Russia recognised Britain's special interests there and agreed not to have direct relations with the Amir.

Persia was the most critical issue. It was agreed that the country should be divided into three areas, a Russian sphere in the north, a British sphere in the south and a large 'neutral' area in between. On the face of it, Russia got the better deal. Her sphere included the capital, Teheran, and most of the other major cities and trading centres. But the British were content with an arrangement which left the whole coast of the Persian Gulf in their sphere. Interest in Persia was still determined by strategic concern for the defence of India. Although an Englishman, William Knox D'Arcy, had been looking for oil in the region since 1901, with some encouragement from the Admiralty where Admiral Fisher had realised that in the future ships would be fired by oil, not coal, the first important strike was not made until 1908. The Anglo-Persian Oil Company was established in 1912 and on the eve of the First World War, the British government took a controlling interest in it.

Persia in fact remained a bone of contention between Britain and Russia despite the 1907 agreement. The most serious crisis occurred in 1911 and the British position was further weakened by the fact that the Russians had secured a separate agreement with Germany. In 1909 there was a revolution in Persia which led to the setting up of a parliamentary form of government. The American President Taft nominated an American citizen, W. Morgan Shuster, to advise the Persian government on financial matters. Shuster ignored, and recommended the Persians to ignore, what he regarded as the thoroughly immoral Anglo-Russian arrangement of 1907. The Russians demanded his removal and followed up the demand with the despatch of troops to northern Persia. The matter was settled by negotiation but it led to a major parliamentary attack on Grey's policy (Robbins 1971: 253).

A modern critic has argued (Wilson 1987: 172–93) that Grey allowed his policy to become fatally dependent on his conception of the necessity of the Anglo-Russian *entente* and so disastrously weakened his ability to manoeuvre and, in particular, to restore relations with Germany. In fact all did not seem to be lost even during the period which Kennedy has called 'the flowering of the antagonism' (Kennedy 1982: 251–88). The continued growth of the German navy and technical developments, such as the building of the *Dreadnought*, which, far from safeguarding the British position, seemed to make it likely that another power could overhaul her previously secure lead, certainly alarmed Britain. It culminated in the McKenna programme of 1909, which resulted in the building of eight Dreadnoughts immediately and ten more over the next two years. The increased naval expenditure so upset the financial estimates that it was a direct cause of Lloyd George's 1909 Budget and the constitutional clash with the House of Lords.

At the same time the Kaiser, William II, was totally unpredictable. In

171

October 1908 came the slightly ridiculous *Daily Telegraph* affair, when he boasted to that paper that he had always really been the friend of England, provoking an unexpected outcry in Germany. But his visit to Britain for the funeral of Edward VII in 1910 left a genuinely good impression. Tentative discussions for naval limitations took place in 1909–10 and some surprisingly modern-sounding proposals were put forward for exchange of information and even mutual inspection of dockyards. But progress was slow and was overtaken by a new Moroccan crisis in 1911.

The French intervened in the civil war which broke out there in the spring and a French force went to Fez in May. It soon became apparent that the French were likely to stay and establish a protectorate. On 1 July Germany sent a gunboat, the *Panther*, to Agadir on Morocco's Atlantic coast. The Germans were not unwilling to let France have Morocco so long as they got compensation elsewhere. The *Panther's* mission was an over-strong opening gambit in these intended negotiations. It happened that on 21 July the Chancellor of the Exchequer, Lloyd George, was due to speak at a Mansion House dinner. Lloyd George was generally regarded as both pacific and pro-German in his sympathies. It therefore caused a sensation when he said that, although he would make sacrifices for peace, if Britain were to be treated as of 'no account in the Cabinet of Nations', where 'her interests were vitally affected', it would be an intolerable humiliation. Grey had approved the speech. At the time, it was interpreted as a warning to Germany. Historians have differed somewhat in their interpretations. Some have seen it as a warning to both France and Germany that they should not do a deal without consulting Britain too. Certainly, there seems to have been something approaching war fever in London but the crisis also revealed deep divisions within the British Cabinet (Robbins 1971: 239–44).

The crisis between France and Germany was settled by negotiation. Germany received 'compensation' in central Africa and raised no objection to the proclamation of a French Protectorate over Morocco the following year. But it had also led to even closer military co-operation between Britain and France. During the excitement of the summer, contingency planning went on apace among the service chiefs. Grey himself had always been regarded as a 'blue water' man, who believed that Britain's security essentially depended upon her navy but the issue was now the despatch of an expeditionary force in 'the initial stages of a war between France and Germany'. Kennedy sees this as a vital (and disastrous) change of strategy, marking for all practical purposes the end of the *Pax Britannica* (Kennedy 1983: 234–7).

Things had gone too far to be kept from the Cabinet any longer. The session of 1 November when matters were revealed to them was a stormy one. They were assured that all political (as distinct from technical) decisions remained with the Cabinet. They then insisted that this principle should be firmly stated in an exchange of notes with the French. It is arguable that this very exchange of notes gave some official status to arrangements, which had previously had no standing at all. But matters went even further than this. Since 1904 the Admiralty had been transferring British ships from the Mediterranean to the Channel and North Sea in recognition of the fact that Germany, not France, was now the likely enemy. As the military discussions continued the logical decision was taken that France should concentrate her forces in the Mediterranean, Britain hers in the North Sea. These arrangements were specifically mentioned in the 1912 notes and it was laid down that they were not 'based upon an engagement to co-operate in war'. It was, however, agreed that, if war threatened, the two governments would consult. This in itself was a considerable extension of the *entente* of 1904 but it slid over the fact that a moral, if not legal, obligation had been created. Could Britain allow Germany to attack France's Channel ports with impunity if the French fleet was in the Mediterranean by arrangement with Britain?

In 1912 the main focus of interest switched to the Balkans. In 1897 Russia and Austria had reached an agreement which established the situation there for some years but the check which Russian policy had received in the Far East as a result of the Russo-Japanese war and shifts in power within Russia brought the Panslavists into influential positions and their ambitions were centred on the Balkans. Already, in 1903, Russia had entered into an alliance with the strongest independent Slav state there, Serbia. In 1908 Austria annexed Bosnia and Herzegovina, the two provinces over which she had had a protectorate since 1878. Russia would have acquiesced in this in return for the opening of the Dardanelles but the deal had fallen through. Instead she supported Serbian protests. Serbia objected to the annexation both because she had ambitions to incorporate the provinces in an enlarged Slav state and because she feared, with some reason, that the Austrian action was the prelude to an attack on Serbia itself. The 'first strike' doctrine, the belief that Austria would only be able to hold her multi-national empire together by a preventive war against her Slav neighbours, was beginning to gain the ascendancy among the Austrian military. In January 1909 the Germans made the promise to Austria, which Bismarck had always avoided, namely, that they would support Austria in such a preventive war if she felt compelled to resort to it, as well as in the case envisaged in the Triple Alliance, of a direct military attack. The Germans, by this time, had interests of their own in the Balkans, and they were rapidly gaining influence in Turkey, both commercially and through military advisers. A forward Russian move in the Balkans would place an unacceptable stumbling block in their way. In fact Russia was in no state to make a forward move in 1908 and was humiliated by her inability to bring effective aid to Serbia. The Russian determination not to accept a second similar humiliation certainly played its part in her decision in 1914.

There was little Britain could do. Grey took his stand on treaty obligations and suggested that the Bosnian crisis, like the Russian abrogation of the Black Sea clauses in 1870, must be referred to an international conference of all the original signatories. Austria, backed by Germany, refused. The result was the ending of the old, always informal but powerful, co-operation between Britain and Austria to stabilise central Europe and check Russia. Instead, despite the strains which were beginning to show in Persia, the Anglo-Russian alignment was strengthened.

Just before the Austrian annexation – and to some extent the cause of it – there had been a revolution in Turkey. The Young Turks, intent on modernising their country, had forced the Sultan to grant a constitution. In the end the Young Turks achieved what the European powers and particularly Britain, with Palmerston at the Foreign Office, had tried in vain to do, reform their country and make it into a modern state. But, in the short run, it was a further destabilising factor. Late in 1911 Italy took advantage of Turkey's weakness to seize Tripoli. The Albanians rebelled and, in July 1912, the Young Turk leaders resigned.

Both the Young Turks and the Moslem Albanians seemed to pose an entirely new threat to the small Christian states of the Balkans and, under the stress of these events, they finally concluded treaties among themselves, which had actually been secretly discussed for some time. Essentially, they aimed at expelling the Turks and partitioning the Balkans between them. In October 1912 Bulgaria, Serbia, Greece and Montenegro declared war on Turkey and quickly won a series of major victories.

Grey's original hope had been that Britain could keep out of the matter but the extent of the Balkan League's success was such that it seemed likely to raise international questions, including even the fate of the Straits and Constantinople. Grey persuaded Germany, Austria, Italy and France to join in an ambassadorial conference under his chairmanship in London. This seemed to be a clear reversion to Gladstonian, or even older, policies which recognised the Near East as a matter of international concern and Concert diplomacy as the best means of dealing with it. All except Grey's severest critics have seen this as a genuine triumph. It certainly enhanced Grey's prestige at the time, although it attracted criticism from the most pro-Russian men in the Foreign Office, including Arthur Nicolson (Robbins 1971: 267). The Balkan situation became ever more complicated with Bulgaria going to war with her former allies over the spoils. Nevertheless, this extremely dangerous crisis in one of the most sensitive areas in Europe was finally brought to a peaceful conclusion (however dissatisfied Bulgaria might be) by the Treaty of Bucharest in August 1913.

Other evidence suggests that, despite recent criticism (e.g. Wilson 1987), Grey was still trying to keep his options open and had by no means become a prisoner of a pro-Russian policy. Negotiations were begun with Germany both about arms limitation and colonial questions. Haldane's mission to Berlin in 1912 did not achieve much on the first point. The British were not prepared to give the pledge of unqualified neutrality the Germans sought and the failure of these very unofficial negotiations helped the more militaristic party to gain the ascendancy in the German capital. Colonial discussions made more progress. In the early months of 1914 a bargain was struck on the vexed question of the Portuguese colonies and Britain finally withdrew her objections to the Berlin–Baghdad railway project. In many ways relations between Britain and Germany were more cordial in 1914 than they had been for a decade.

In the end it was the Eastern Question which brought Europe to disaster, as diplomats had expected for a century. Franz Ferdinand, the heir to the Austrian throne, went to Sarajevo, the capital of Bosnia, on 28 June, the Serbs' national day. He was assassinated in a bungled and amateurish plot by a group of young Serb conspirators. Within six weeks Europe was engaged in a war which brought down the Hapsburg, Romanov and Hohenzollern dynasties. Many historians would contend that the First World War led directly to the Second and that the years 1919–39 were merely a 'twenty year truce'. The two wars between them totally destroyed the old order.

The first question which naturally arises is – could any action on Britain's part have averted the war? Some continental historians (e.g. Albertini 1957: vol. 3, 523–5) have blamed Grey severely, believing that, if Britain had made her position clear from the beginning, Germany would have withdrawn her support for Austria. There are two objections to this. First, Grey, even if he had wished, did not have a free hand to warn Germany or threaten war. Grey was the Foreign Secretary of a constitutional state. He had to carry the Cabinet, Parliament and, ultimately, the public with him. The public was taken completely by surprise. If they expected any war in the summer of 1914, it was civil war in Ireland. (In fact, the Kaiser believed that the imminence of such a civil war would in itself prevent any British intervention.) But ultimately the public was to respond to the war with almost universal enthusiasm (although there were exceptions, notably on Clydeside), which was reminiscent in some ways of the excitement about the Crimean War. They took little persuading that Germany was an evil force that must be defeated.

The Cabinet was a different question. Here Grey's relations with his colleagues become of central importance. In some ways he had been given a remarkably free hand in carrying on his foreign policy but there had always been a substantial part of the Cabinet which had not shared his preconceptions. It was difficult to persuade them that there was sufficient reason for Britain to enter the war on the side of France and Russia against Germany and Austria. (Italy did not come to the aid of her Triple Alliance partners on the grounds that Austria had not been attacked.) It was for this reason that Grey proposed making Belgian neutrality the test. He had a good precedent in 1870. He also knew that it was a loaded question. Since 1905 the French had known that the German war plans, originally drawn up by their chief of staff, General Schlieffen, involved passing through southern Belgium. The British now knew it too. In vain the Germans argued that the original treaty, that of 1839, had been directed against French aggrandisement and that plenty of other treaties had been ignored over the previous century. Belgium seemed to present a nice clear moral issue. Even so, Grey failed to carry all the British Cabinet with him. The veteran radical, John Morley, and the Lib–Lab MP, John Burns, resigned. As late as 2 August, Morley thought that Earl Beauchamp, Sir John Simon, Lloyd George, Lewis Harcourt, Sir Herbert Samuel, J. A. Pease, McKinnon Wood and perhaps Walter Runciman would go too. In the event Simon and Beauchamp did resign but were persuaded to return. If all the dissidents had gone, the government could not have survived.

The second objection is that the evidence suggests that, although the Germans would certainly have preferred Britain to remain neutral, and hoped up to a late stage that she might do so, they had determined to go ahead in any case (for discussion see Fischer 1967: 50–92; Joll 1984: 9–33; Koch (ed.) 1984: 30–188). Immediately after the assassination in Sarajevo, the Austrians decided to use the opportunity to deal with Serbia once and for all. On 5 July the Germans told them that they would support them even if Russia intervened. On 23 July the Austrians delivered the ultimatum to Serbia which was intended to be rejected. On 26 July Grey invited Italy, Germany and France to join in an ambassadorial conference to try to find a peaceful solution. France and Italy accepted. Germany refused. The same day Russia ordered partial mobilisation. A new factor now came into the situation. It was the received wisdom of all military staffs that Prussia had beaten Austria in 1866 and France in 1871 because of the speed of her mobilisation. It was assumed that all modern wars would be short ones (how ironic that was to come to seem by the end of 1914) and that the first strike was all important. On 18 July Austria declared war on Serbia. As Joll puts it, 'Between 28 and 31 July, events were moving too fast for the diplomats because the decisions were now more and more being taken by the soldiers.' (Joll 1984: 18). One after the other, Russia, Austria, France and Germany moved to full mobilisation. When the Kaiser realised on 1 August that Britain was unlikely to remain neutral if France were invaded, he asked Moltke, the chief of staff, if it was possible to stop the troop movements in the west and concentrate the German army against Russia. He was told it was impossible. The orderly mobilisation procedure, on which the outcome of the war depended, would be reduced to a rabble. William acquiesced.

Germany declared war on Russia on 1 August and on France on 3 August. Nothing could now stop a great European war, the first since

1815. On the afternoon of 3 August, Grey spoke to Parliament. An eye-witness described his speech as 'wholly unadorned, precise, simple, accurate, austerely dignified' (quoted Robbins 1971: 296). But he carried the House with him. The Conservative leader, Bonar Law, gave him his support. So, more unexpectedly, did the Irish leader, John Redmond. At 11 p.m. on 4 August, the Germans having failed to pledge that they would respect Belgian neutrality, Britain too entered the war.

The reasons for the catastrophe are still the matter of hot political, as well as scholarly, debate. Although the variations of detail are almost infinite, the interpretations divide into two main categories. There are those who believe that the outbreak of war in the summer of 1914 was the result of a sudden breakdown in the European diplomatic system, which had served the continent very well for several generations. The reasons are identifiable, sometimes accidental, the result of the bad luck or the bad judgement of individual politicians. There was nothing at all inevitable about the process. As Remak put it, 'World War I was a modern diplomatic crisis gone wrong, the one gamble that did not work out, the one deterrent that did not deter.' (Remak 1971: 366.)

The opposite school is represented by those who believe that the causes were much deeper, that they were the result of what is sometimes called a 'structural failure' of European society. At its simplest level, this could mean that the fault lay in the system, in secret diplomacy, tight alliances, militarism or the arms race, rather than in individuals, or even individual nations. This view was very common among 'revisionist' historians, who wrote between the wars. Nowadays, it more often takes the form of the proposition that the structural failure was due to the attempts of the old social order to survive in the face of profound economic changes which must ultimately doom it. This is usually linked with the so-called 'primacy of domestic policy', that is the belief that foreign policy decisions were dictated by domestic considerations.

The 'primacy of domestic policy' has been rejected by some distinguished modern writers. Zara Steiner, for example, in one of the best studies of this period, *Britain and the origins of the First World War* (1977) states categorically that her argument is based on the '*Primat der Aussenpolitik* [the primacy of foreign policy] in any understanding of British diplomacy' (p. 248). Diplomatic decisions were a response to outward events and external situations. 'Foreign policy not only remained the preserve of a small élite recruited from the traditional ruling class, but continued to be conducted in isolation from the democratic currents of the day.' (*ibid.*)

The fact that the German terms 'Primat der Aussenpolitik' (or 'Innenpolitik') are habitually used is a clue to the fact that the argument began in Germany. In the case of Austria, it is difficult for any writer to dispute that 'domestic politics', in the sense of the urgent need to hold the empire together, was what determined Austrian foreign policy. A powerful case has been argued for applying the same considerations to

Germany by Fritz Fischer (1967), H.-U. Wehler (1969 and 1985) and V. R. Berghahn (1973). Can it also be applied to Britain?

For Marxists, of course, the idea of structural failure and the attempt of the established classes to avert it, is one of the 'inherent contradictions' of capitalism. It is not, however, a purely Marxist idea. It was assumed as more or less self-evident by a very eminent British historian, R. C. K. Ensor, in his volume in the *Oxford history of England* series (1936). Although a strong critic of Grey before 1914, Ensor was certainly not a Marxist but, discussing the constitutional crisis which arose when the Lords opposed the elected majority in the Commons after 1906 he wrote,

> In the light of post-war democracy no student can avoid asking, how practical men like Balfour and Lansdowne ... could be so short-sighted. The psychology of it was that both were aristocrats born into the purple. They belonged to, they led in, and they felt themselves charged with the fortunes of, a small privileged class; which for centuries had exercised a sort of collective kingship, and at the bottom of its thinking instinctively believed that it had a divine right to do so. Passionately devoted to the greatness of England, these men were convinced that she owed it to patrician rule. (p. 387)

From the time of Disraeli the Conservative party managed to annex to itself the title of the 'strong' party in foreign affairs, as well as the party which wished to preserve England's traditional institutions. It may be objected that it was the Liberal party which was in office in 1914 but the problem is complicated by the fact that the policy of the Liberal Imperialists approximated in many ways to that of the Conservatives. Grey himself was severely criticised from within his own party for his bipartisan policy. Some writers would regard the explanation for this new bipartisan policy as lying much deeper than any idiosyncratic choice by Grey. Koch, for example, contends:

> The Industrial Revolution in Europe had not only created a new middle class, but also a growing urban proletariat, which in time began to formulate its own political and social demands. *Vis-à-vis* this new working class, liberals began to defend the political and social *status quo* and consequently were bound to appear as conservatives and reactionaries. Political positions changed; liberalism transformed itself from a middle-class reform movement to a bastion of defence of the existing political, economic and social order. (1984: 322)

This too is a point which Steiner rejects, believing that the Liberals still had plenty of room for manoeuvre in the decade before the First World War and dismissing, for example, George Dangerfield's (1970) 'portrait of a volcanic age' as ignoring 'the solid and still stable base of Edwardian society' although she concedes that 'the political and social tensions of the period shaped the views of those in power and affected their vision of the world overseas' (Steiner 1977: 249).

Whether or not the Edwardian age was (or was perceived by contemporaries as) a stable age or as a cauldron, always on the verge of boiling over, is itself controversial. Certainly, there was much to worry the thoughtful politician, not only the constitutional crisis about the authority of the House of Lords but also the grave industrial unrest of 1911 and the (for those who wished to keep society unchanged, still more alarming) activities of the women's suffrage movement.

For Britain, as for Germany, imperialism, the assertion of her rôle as a world power might seem the only possible safety-valve for such pressures. In the simplest sense the First World War cannot be regarded as an 'imperialist' war. The last Great Power clash over colonial possessions had been the Agadir crisis in 1911 and that had been peacefully resolved. It is, however, arguable that the battle for the legacy of the Ottoman empire in the Balkans, particularly when its importance for both German and Russian expansion is considered, is essentially part of the same process.

It is, however, also probably true that the collapse of the Ottoman empire caused a major European war, where the scramble for Africa or the abortive scramble for China had not, because the contest lay within Europe itself. The balance of power (a concept which Europe has never really renounced even in the ideological upheavals after the First World War and which has probably done more than any other to prevent war) was at stake. It can plausibly be argued that Britain could not afford to see Germany defeat France again, even if there had been no *entente* and if the Belgian question had not come into it. It has been vigorously contended (Schroeder 1972: 336–45; it is more soberly discussed by Bridge 1972) that, if Britain had really wanted to uphold the balance of power, the country she should have supported in the decade before 1914 was Austria because Austria was vital to the European balance and it was the collapse of the Austrian, as much as the Ottoman, empire, which was fatal to European peace. It is an argument which would have been thoroughly appreciated by British Foreign Secretaries of the early nineteenth century. Grey himself would probably have dismissed it as he dismissed much theoretical advice, 'A Minister beset with the administrative work of a great Office must often be astounded to read of the carefully laid plans, the deep, unrevealed motives that critics or admirers attribute to him. Onlookers ... have time to invent.' (Grey 1925: vol. 1, 6).

He went on to say, 'critics may find many mistakes and short-comings in British foreign policy of the last hundred years, and these may be legitimately exposed, or even derided; but, when all has been said, let them ask, what other nation in Europe can, after a review of the last hundred years, say confidently of its own policy "*Si monumentum requiris, circumspice*"? [If you seek its monument, look around].' He meant it had been 'suited to the development and needs of the Empire' (*ibid.*: 7). The question may attract a different answer today.

CONCLUSION

Britain emerged from the First World War apparently stronger than ever. Despite the horrors of the trenches and tragedies such as Gallipoli, the army was felt to have acquitted itself well. Britain was among the victorious allies who could determine the peace. The British empire actually increased as a result of the war when Britain acquired a number of former German colonies, such as Tanganyika, as mandated territories from the League of Nations. The setting up of the League itself was seen as the fulfilment of the strivings towards international co-operation, which had co-existed even with the rampant nationalism of the last quarter of the nineteenth century.

This optimism did not last long. From the beginning it was clear that the League could do little to curb the ambitions of a recalcitrant Great Power. The world economy began to suffer, first from inflation and then from depression. The weakness of the British economy became more and more apparent. Some of this was due to the war itself, which had eaten up British overseas investments and led her former customers to look elsewhere for supplies, while British iron and coal in particular were diverted to the war effort. But the more perceptive began to realise that Britain had been living on borrowed time for a generation or more. Her long industrial lead of the early nineteenth century had not been maintained. Her major competitors had greater natural resources than she had. Britain had not attempted to adjust by becoming a highly educated or technically advanced nation. That solution had been suggested by those concerned with 'national efficiency' before the First World War. Instead Britain's education system still lagged behind that of France, Germany or the United States and it was in the 'high technology' industries of the time, chemicals or electricity, that Britain was most completely overtaken by the newer industrial nations.

The British were extremely slow to adjust their world picture to accord with reality. Until the eighteenth century Britain had not counted as one of the Great Powers of Europe, although some Britons might have claimed the title earlier. Her industrial lead and her naval power made Victorian Britain a world power of the first rank. This world rôle co-existed with much poverty and misery at home but for the middle and upper classes – in general the articulate classes – it was a period of comfortable prosperity and, usually, complacency. What was really a brief and exceptional situation was happily accepted as the norm for the foreseeable future. Britain was indeed 'top nation' and likely to remain so.

This would have been a strange concept to men whose views were formed in the eighteenth century, Pitt, Castlereagh, Canning, Wellington or Aberdeen. They continued to have a juster appreciation of Britain's long-term rôle in Europe, as one cog, albeit an important one, in a larger machine. It was Palmerston who made the breakthrough, apparently largely accidentally, to the realisation of the picture which his fellow countrymen wished to have of themselves, as a benevolent giant guiding, first fellow Europeans, and later non-Europeans, towards the virtues of constitutional government and free trade. How far Palmerston himself quite believed in the picture is as difficult a problem as how far Otto von Bismarck was a German nationalist and how far he captured and exploited German nationalism. Palmerston was in many ways a generous and impulsive man and he probably was seduced by the vision himself to some extent, but he also saw the usefulness of a strong John Bull stance in uniting the British people and diverting attention from the extension of the franchise and other social changes which he dreaded.

The British do not usually think of themselves as a gullible people. Bonapartism, being carried away by the pursuit of 'la gloire', was for others. But during the late nineteenth century they were not immune from it. The idea of Britain as a great imperial power, fulfilling her destiny, did divert minds from real problems at home. The Marxist belief that what we are really witnessing in nineteenth-century British foreign policy was a bourgeois society defending itself, cannot be lightly shrugged off. The propertied classes, the 'haves' of British society, had no intention of surrendering their position. When challenged by movements which wished to change society they rallied, as they did to Pitt during the French wars. Palmerston's sympathy with con-stitutionalism in 1848 stopped well short of any support for those who would challenge property rights. In the last quarter of the nineteenth century, politicians had to find new ways of managing the now large electorate. Disraeli and Salisbury generally followed in the Palmerston tradition, as did Rosebery. Gladstone tried a much more interesting experiment in appealing to the common morality, rather than the common interest, of the electorate. Grey, as usual, is very hard to interpret. He saw himself as the disciple of Rosebery but he came over to many of the public – although not to his critics in the House – more like the disciple of Gladstone.

This diversion of attention was not, however, crude, except perhaps very occasionally in Disraeli's more flamboyant moments. The working classes probably felt that they had a genuine community of interests with the employers in the maintenance of the empire and especially the retention of markets. The situation is further complicated by the fact that many, Joseph Chamberlain for example, honestly believed that the empire would solve Britain's social problems, and not merely disguise them. That this would be at the expense of other, non-European, peoples did not trouble many consciences at a time when most believed in the inferiority of non-Europeans. For those of more tender conscience there was always the argument, developed a little later in Lord Lugard's *Dual Mandate* (1922), that imperialism was of mutual benefit by advancing those peoples who had been left behind in the forward march of evolution, and at the same time opening the resources of the undeveloped world to Europeans.

This was the argument which J. A. Hobson attacked. He believed that Britain was diverting precious resources to expanding and defending an empire, which could never really be a source of strength, and away from essential investment and growth at home. Hobson can be criticised on a number of points, particularly his apparent belief that the home market was capable of almost infinite expansion and his failure to give due weight to the importance of foreign trade in the British economy, but it is a line of thought to which recent critics have returned (Hobson 1902; Cain 1978).

What of Hobson's other argument – that the British were hypocritical in supposing that their activities had vastly increased the area of free government in the world? If one looks first at Europe, the picture is certainly less impressive than the Victorians liked to believe. European liberals and nationalists looked more to the ideas and precedents of the French political philosophers and the French Revolution than to the rather idiosyncratic British traditions. France played a much larger part in freeing Greece from the Turks or in unifying Italy than did Britain, although this was largely hidden from the British public who accepted with happy insularity the assumption that they had played the major role. Even in Spain and Portugal, France was at least as influential as Britain. German unification owed nothing to Britain and British sympathy achieved nothing for Poland.

Towards the end of this period, however, British eyes were turned towards the empire, rather than Europe. Here obviously there was more influence. Indians and others did look towards the precedents of British constitutional history. The British empire developed differently from those of the continental powers. Pro-consuls with a classical bent, like Lord Cromer, were right in thinking that it resembled the Hellenic, rather than the Roman, empire. Instead of centralisation and assimilation like the French empire, it was marked by devolution of responsibility to the colonies of settlement and 'indirect rule' in many of the colonies of conquest. As a result, it proved remarkably easy to dissolve without any deep shock to the British constitution – quite unlike the experience of France or Portugal.

Does this suggest that, at least in some spheres, there was substance in the optimistic Whig interpretation of history? One of the problems of the working historian is that the facts seldom fit in either with the theories, or with the fashionable demolition of theories. Britain did become a constitutional state with secure representative (although not democratic) government before any of the other European great powers. The articulate, and politically influential, upper and middle classes did have a clear sense of Britain's unique political identity. Astute politicians exploited this but also shared it. If one cannot dismiss the Marxist insights, neither can one entirely dismiss the Whig interpretation. Nostalgia for a largely imaginary past can be unbecoming and even dangerously misleading but one should perhaps also remember the caution Gladstone's biographer, John Morley, left with his readers, to 'take care lest in quenching the spirit of Midlothian, we leave the sovereign mastery of the world to Machiavelli' (Morley 1903: vol. 2, 594).

BRITISH PRIME MINISTERS, 1789–1914

William Pitt	December 1783 – February 1801
Henry Addington	February 1801 – May 1804
William Pitt	May 1804 – January 1806
Lord Grenville	January 1806 – March 1807
Duke of Portland	March 1807 – October 1809
Spencer Perceval	October 1809 – May 1812
Lord Liverpool	June 1812 – March 1827
George Canning	April 1827 – August 1827
Viscount Goderich	September 1827 – January 1828
Duke of Wellington	January 1828 – November 1830
Earl Grey	November 1830 – July 1834
Viscount Melbourne	July 1834 – November 1834
Sir Robert Peel	December 1834 – April 1835
Viscount Melbourne	April 1835 – August 1841
Sir Robert Peel	September 1841 – July 1846
Lord John Russell	July 1846 – February 1852
Earl of Derby	February 1852 – December 1852
Earl of Aberdeen	December 1852 – January 1855
Viscount Palmerston	February 1855 – February 1858
Earl of Derby	February 1858 – June 1859
Viscount Palmerston	June 1859 – October 1865
Lord John Russell	October 1865 – June 1866
Earl of Derby	June 1866 – February 1868
Benjamin Disraeli	February 1868 – December 1868
William Gladstone	December 1868 – February 1874
Benjamin Disraeli	February 1874 – April 1880
William Gladstone	April 1880 – June 1885
Marquess of Salisbury	June 1885 – January 1886
William Gladstone	February 1886 – July 1886
Marquess of Salisbury	August 1886 – August 1892
William Gladstone	August 1892 – March 1894
Earl of Rosebery	March 1894 – June 1895

Marquess of Salisbury	June 1895 – July 1902
A. J. Balfour	July 1902 – December 1905
Sir Henry Campbell–Bannerman	December 1905 – April 1908
H. H. Asquith	April 1908 – December 1916

BRITISH FOREIGN SECRETARIES, 1789–1914

Duke of Leeds	December 1783 – April 1791
Lord Grenville	April 1791 – February 1801
Lord Hawkesbury	February 1804 – May 1804
Lord Harrowby	May 1804 – January 1805
Lord Mulgrave	January 1805 – January 1806
Charles James Fox	January 1806 – September 1806
Viscount Howicke	October 1806 – March 1807
George Canning	March 1807 – October 1809
Earl Bathurst	October 1809 – December 1809
Marquess Wellesley	December 1809 – February 1812
Viscount Castlereagh	February 1812 – August 1822
George Canning	September 1822 – April 1827
Lord Dudley	April 1827 – May 1828
Earl of Aberdeen	May 1828 – November 1830
Viscount Palmerston	November 1830 – November 1834
Duke of Wellington	December 1834 – April 1835
Viscount Palmerston	April 1835 – September 1841
Earl of Aberdeen	September 1841 – July 1846
Viscount Palmerston	July 1846 – February 1852
Earl of Malmesbury	February 1852 – December 1852
Lord John Russell	December 1852 – February 1853
Earl of Clarendon	February 1853 – February 1858
Earl of Malmesbury	February 1858 – June 1859
Lord John Russell	June 1859 – October 1865
Earl of Clarendon	October 1865 – June 1866
Lord Stanley	June 1866 – December 1868
Earl of Clarendon	December 1868 – June 1870
Earl Granville	June 1870 – February 1874
Earl of Derby	February 1874 – April 1878
Marquess of Salisbury	April 1878 – April 1880
Earl Granville	April 1880 – June 1885
Marquess of Salisbury	June 1885 – January 1886

Earl of Rosebery	February 1886 – July 1886
Earl of Iddesleigh	August 1886 – January 1887
Marquess of Salisbury	January 1887 – August 1892
Earl of Rosebery	August 1892 – March 1894
Earl of Kimberley	March 1894 – June 1895
Marquess of Salisbury	June 1895 – October 1900
Lord Lansdowne	October 1900 – December 1905
Sir Edward Grey	December 1905 – December 1916

BIBLIOGRAPHY

PRIMARY SOURCES

The principal manuscript sources are to be found in the following collections:

Royal Archives, Windsor Castle.
These include the Melbourne Papers.

Public Record Office, Kew, London.
The official records of the Foreign, Colonial and War Offices and the
    Admiralty. Also Cabinet Papers and the records of the Committee of
    Imperial Defence.
  Deposited private papers including those of William Pitt the Younger
    (Chatham MSS), Cromer, Crowe, Curzon, Dilke, Granville, Sir Edward
    Grey, Lansdowne, Lord John Russell, Stratford Canning.

Manuscript Department, British Library, London.
Private papers of Aberdeen, Balfour, Campbell-Bannerman, Gladstone,
    Liverpool, Peel.

India Office Library, London.
Curzon, Lansdowne, Northbrook.

National Library of Scotland, Edinburgh.
Haldane, Kimberley, Rosebery.

Northern Ireland Record Office, Belfast.
Castlereagh

Bodleian Library, Oxford.
Asquith, Clarendon, Disraeli, Sir James Graham, Harcourt, Milner, Rhodes.

Cambridge University Library, Cambridge.
C. Hardinge.

Birmingham University Library, Birmingham.
J. Chamberlain.

Durham University Library, Durham.
Second Earl Grey.

Southampton University Library, Southampton.
Palmerston, Wellington.

Leeds City Libraries, Archives Department, Leeds.
Canning (Harewood MSS).

East Suffolk Record Office, Ipswich.
Younger Pitt (Pretyman MSS).

Hatfield House, Hatfield, Herts.
Salisbury.

SELECT SECONDARY SOURCES

(The references in the text are generally to a modern or paperback edition, where these exist, but this can sometimes be misleading. Where appropriate, the date of first publication is also given in brackets.)

Adams, E. D., 1925, *Great Britain and the American Civil War* (2 vols).
Allen, H. C., 1954, *Great Britain and the United States: a History of Anglo-American Relations, 1783–1952*.
Anderson, M. S., 1966, *The Eastern Question, 1774–1923*.
Albertini, L., 1957, *The Origins of the War of 1914* (3 vols) trans. I. M. Massey (1952–57).
Ashley, Evelyn, 1876, *The Life of Henry John Temple, Viscount Palmerston, 1846–1865* (2 vols).
Barnett, C., 1972, *The Collapse of British Power*.
Bartlett, C. J., 1963, *Great Britain and Sea Power, 1815–1853*.
Bartlett, C. J., 1966, *Castlereagh*.
Bartlett, C. J. (ed.), 1969, *Britain Pre-eminent*.
Bates, D., 1984, *The Fashoda Incident of 1898*.
Beales, Derek, 1961, *England and Italy, 1859–60*.
Beasley, W. G., 1951, *Great Britain and the Opening of Japan, 1834–1858*.
Bell, H. C. F., 1936, *Lord Palmerston* (2 vols).
Bemis, S. F., 1955 (1936), *A Diplomatic History of the United States*.
Bennett, G., 1962, *The Concept of Empire: Burke to Attlee, 1774–1947*.
Benson, A. C., 1908, *Letters of Queen Victoria* (3 vols).
Berghahn, V. R., 1973, *Germany and the Approach of War in 1914*.
Bindoff, S. T., *et al.* 1934, *British Diplomatic Representatives, 1789–1852*.

Bindoff, S. T., 1935, 'The unreformed diplomatic service', 1812–1860. *Transactions Royal Historical Society*, 4th series, XVIII (1935), 143–72.

Blake, R., 1966, *Disraeli*.

Blake, R., Cecil H. (eds), 1987, *Salisbury: the man and his policies*.

Bodelsen, C. A., 1924, (re-issued 1960), *Studies in Mid-Victorian imperialism*.

Bolsover, G. H., 1948, 'Nicholas I and the partition of Turkey', *The Slavonic and East European Review*, 27 (1948–9), 115–42.

Bourne, K., 1967, *Britain and the Balance of Power in North America, 1815–1908*.

Bourne, K., 1970, *The Foreign Policy of Victorian England, 1830–1902*.

Bourne, K., 1982, *Palmerston: the Early Years 1784–1841*.

Bourne, K., Watt D. C., 1967, *Studies in International History*.

Brebner, J. B., 1947, *The Atlantic Triangle: the Interplay of Canada, the United States and Great Britain*.

Bridge, F. R., 1972, *Great Britain and Austria-Hungary, 1906–1914: a Diplomatic History*.

Bridge, F. R., Bullen, R., 1980, *The Great Powers and the European System, 1815–1914*.

Bullen, R., 1974, *Palmerston, Guizot and the Collapse of the Entente Cordiale*.

Bulwer, H. L. (Baron Dalling), 1871–4, *The Life of Henry John Temple, Viscount Palmerston* (3 vols).

Butler, I., 1973, *The Eldest Brother: the Marquess Wellesley, 1760–1812*.

Butler, J., 1967, 'The German factor in Anglo-Transvaal relations', in *Britain and Germany in Africa* P. Gifford and W. R. Louis (eds).

Cain, P. J., 1978, 'J. A. Hobson, Cobdenism and the radical theory of economic imperialism', *Economic History Review*, 2nd ser., 31 (1978), 565–84.

Cain, P. J., Hopkins, A. G., 1980, 'The political economy of British expansion overseas, 1750–1914', *Economic History Review*, 2nd ser., 33 (1980), 463–90.

Cain, P. J., Hopkins, A. G., 1986, 'Gentlemanly capitalism and British expansion overseas. I. The old colonial system, 1688–1850', *Economic History Review*, 2nd ser., 39 (1986), 491–525.

Cain, P. J., Hopkins, A. G., 1987, 'Gentlemanly capitalism and British expansion overseas. II. New imperialism, 1850–1945', *Economic History Review*, 2nd ser., 40 (1987), 1–26.

Campbell, A., 1960, *Great Britain and the United States, 1895–1903*.

Carr, W., 1963, *Schleswig-Holstein, 1815–1848*.

Cecil, Lady Gwendoline, 1921–32, *The Life of Robert, Marquis of Salisbury* (4 vols).

Chamberlain, M. E., 1976, 'Sir Charles Dilke and the British intervention in Egypt in 1882: decision-making in a nineteenth-century cabinet', *British Journal of International Studies*, 2 (1976), 231–45.

Chamberlain, M. E., 1981, 'British public opinion and the invasion of Egypt 1882', *Trivium*, XVI (1981), 5–28.

Chamberlain, M. E., 1983, *Lord Aberdeen: a political biography*.

Chamberlain, M. E., 1987, *Lord Palmerston*.

Church, R. A., 1975, *The Great Victorian Boom 1850–1873*.

Cobban, A., 1954, 'British Secret Service in France 1784–1792', *English Historical Review*, LXIX (1954), 226–61.

Cobban, A., 1960, *In Search of Humanity: the rôle of the Enlightenment in History*.

Conacher, J. B., 1968, *The Aberdeen Coalition 1852–1855*.

Conacher, J. B., 1987, *Britain and the Crimea, 1855–6: Problems of War and Peace.*

Connell, B., 1962, *Regina v. Palmerston: the Correspondence between Queen Victoria and her Foreign and Prime Minister, 1837–1865.*

Conwell-Evans, T. P., 1932, *Foreign Policy from a Back Bench, 1904–1918.*

Cookson, J. E., 1982, *The Friends of Peace: Anti-war Liberalism in England, 1793–1815.*

Costin, W., 1968 (1937), *Great Britain and China, 1833–1860.*

Coupland, R., 1930, *The American Revolution and the British Empire.*

Crawley, C. W., 1930, *The Question of Greek Independence: a Study of British Foreign Policy, 1821–1833.*

Crowe, S. E., 1970 (1942), *The Berlin West Africa conference.*

Dakin, D., 1955, *British and American Philhellenes during the War of Greek Independence, 1821–1833.*

Dangerfield, G., 1983 (1970), *The Strange Death of Liberal England.*

Derry, J. W., 1972, *Charles James Fox.*

Derry, J. W., 1976, *Castlereagh.*

Dike, K. O., 1956, *Trade and Politics in the Niger Delta, 1830–1885.*

Dixon, P., 1976, *Canning: Politician and Statesman.*

Duhamel, J., 1951, *Louis Philippe et la première entente cordiale.*

Edwardes, Michael, 1975, *Playing the Great Game: a Victorian Cold War.*

Ehrman, John, 1984 (1969); 1986 (1983), *The Younger Pitt*; vol. 1, *The years of acclaim*; vol. 2, *The reluctant transition.* This is much more than a new biography; it gives a concise summing up of most recent research on the period.

Eldridge, C. C., 1973, *England's Mission: the Imperial Idea in the Age of Gladstone and Disraeli, 1868–1880.*

Eldridge, C. C., 1978, *Victorian Imperialism.*

Eldridge, C. C. (ed.), 1984, *British Imperialism in the Nineteenth Century.*

Ellenborough, Earl of, 1881, *A Political Diary 1828–1830* (2 vols).

Elliott, M., 1982, *Partners in Revolution: United Irishmen and France.*

Ellis, Kenneth, 1958, *The Post Office in the Eighteenth Century.*

Emsley, C., 1979, *British Society and the French Wars, 1793–1815.*

Ensor, R. C. K., 1936, *England, 1870–1914.*

Evans, E. J., 1983, *The Forging of the Modern State: Early Industrial Britain.*

Farwell, B., 1973, *Queen Victoria's Little Wars.*

Fischer, F., 1967 (1961), *Germany's Aims in the First World War.*

Fischer, F., 1975 (1969), *War of Illusions.*

Fitzmaurice, E., 1905, *The Life of Granville George Leveson Gower, Second Earl Granville* (2 vols).

Foot, M. R. D., 1971, *See* Gladstone, W. E.

Fraser, P., 1966, *Joseph Chamberlain.*

Gallagher, J. (ed. A. Seal), 1982, *The Decline, Revival and Fall of the British Empire.*

Gash, N., 1953, *Politics in the Age of Peel.*

Gash, N., 1961, *Mr Secretary Peel.*

Gash, N., 1972, *Sir Robert Peel.*

Garvin, J. L., Amery, J., 1931–69, *Life of Joseph Chamberlain* (6 vols).

Gifford, P., Louis, W. R., (eds), 1967, *Britain and Germany in Africa: Imperial Rivalry and Colonial Rule.*

Gifford, P., Louis, W. R. (eds), 1971, *France and Britain in Africa: Imperial Rivalry and Colonial Rule.*

Gillard, D., 1977, *The Struggle for Asia: a Study in British and Russian Imperialism.*

Gladstone, W. E. (ed. M. R. D. Foot), 1971, *Midlothian Speeches, 1879.*

Gleason, J. H., 1951, *The Genesis of Russophobia in Great Britain.*

Goodwin, A., 1979, *The Friends of Liberty: the English Democratic Movement in the Age of the French Revolution.*

Gordon, Sir Arthur, 1893, *The Earl of Aberdeen.*

Gordon, M., 1974, 'Domestic conflict and the origins of the First World War: the British and German cases', *Journal of Modern History*, XLVI (1974), 191–226.

Graubaud, S. R., 1963, 'Castlereagh and the peace of Europe', *Journal of British Studies*, 3 (1963), 79–87.

Greaves, R., 1959, *Persia and the Defence of India, 1884–1892.*

Gregory, J. S., 1969, *Great Britain and the Taipings.*

Grenville, J. A. S., 1964, *Lord Salisbury and Foreign Policy: the Close of the Nineteenth Century.*

Greville, Charles, (ed. H. Reeve), 1888, *Memoirs* (8 vols).

Grey, Viscount (Grey of Falloden), 1925, *Twenty-five Years, 1892–1916.* (2 vols).

Guedalla, P., 1926, *Palmerston.*

Guedalla, P., 1928, *Gladstone and Palmerston: being the Correspondence of Lord Palmerston and Mr Gladstone 1851–1865.*

Gulick, E. V., 1955, *Europe's Classical Balance of Power.*

Guyot, R., 1926, *La Première Entente cordiale.*

Hammond, J. L., 1938, *Gladstone and the Irish nation.*

Harcourt, F., 1980, 'Disraeli's imperialism, 1866–1868: a question of timing', *Historical Journal*, XXIII (1980), 87–109.

Harlow, V., 1951, 1954, *The Founding of the Second British Empire* (2 vols).

Harvey, A. D., 1981, *English Literature and the Great War with France.*

Helleiner, Karl F., 1965, *The Imperial Loans: a Study in Financial and Diplomatic History.*

Henderson, G. B., 1947, *Crimean War Diplomacy and other Essays.*

Hertslet, Sir Edward, 1875–91, *The Map of Europe by Treaty* (4 vols).

Hinde, Wendy, 1973, *George Canning.*

Hinde, Wendy, 1981, *Castlereagh.*

Hinsley, F. H., 1963, *Power and the Pursuit of Peace.*

Hinsley, F. H. (ed.), 1977, *The Foreign Policy of Sir Edward Grey.*

Hobson, J. A., 1902 (1st ed.), 1938 (3rd ed.), *Imperialism: a Study.*

Hobson, J. A., 1968 (1919), *Richard Cobden: the International Man.*

Hoffman, R. J. S., 1964 (1933), Great Britain and the German Trade Rivalry.

Holbraad, C., 1970, *The Concert of Europe: a Study in German and British International Theory, 1815–1914.*

Horn, D. B., 1967, *Great Britain and Europe in the Eighteenth Century.*

Hoskins, H. L., 1968 (1928), *British Routes to India.*

Howard, C., 1967, *Splendid Isolation.*

Howard, C., 1974, *Britain and the Casus Belli.*

Hutt, M., 1962, 'Spies in France 1793–1808', *History Today*, XII (1962), 158–67.

Hyam, R., 1967 'British imperial expansion in the late eighteenth century', *Historical Journal*, X (1967), 113–24.

Imlah, A. G., 1966, *Britain and Switzerland, 1845–1860.*

Ingle, H. H., 1976, *Nesselrode and the Russian Rapprochement with Britain, 1836–1844.*

Ingram, E., 1981, *Commitment to Empire: Prophecies of the Great Game in Asia, 1797–1801.*

Ingram, E., 1984, *In Defence of British India: Great Britain and the Middle East, 1775–1842.*

James, R. R., 1963, *Rosebery.*

Jarrett, Derek, 1974, *Pitt the Younger.*

Johnson, F., 1962, *Defence by Committee.*

Joll, J., 1984, *Origins of the First World War.*

Jones, Ray, 1971, *The Nineteenth-Century Foreign Office: an Administrative History.*

Jones, R. A., 1983, *The British Diplomatic Service, 1815–1914.*

Jones, W. D., 1958, *Lord Aberdeen and the Americas.*

Kelly, J. B., 1968, *Britain and the Persian Gulf, 1795–1880.*

Kennedy, P. M., 1983 (1976), *The Rise and Fall of British Naval Mastery.*

Kennedy, P. M., 1982 (1980), *The Rise of the Anglo-German Antagonism, 1860–1914.*

Kennedy, P. M., 1981, *The Realities behind Diplomacy: Background Influences on British External Policy, 1865–1980.*

Kennedy, P. M., 1983, *Strategy and Diplomacy, 1870–1945.*

Kerner, R. J., 1937, 'Russia's new policy in the Near East after the Peace of Adrianople', *Cambridge Historical Journal*, V (1937), 280–90.

Kissinger, H., 1957, *A World Restored: Metternich, Castlereagh and the Problems of Peace, 1812–1822.*

Koch, H. W. (ed.), 2nd edn, 1984 (1972), *Origins of the First World War.*

Koebner, R., Schmidt, H. D., 1964, *Imperialism: the Story and Significance of a Political Word, 1840–1960.*

Koss, S. E., 1976, *Asquith.*

Koss, S. E., 1981, *The Rise and Fall of the Political Press in Britain*, vol. 1, *The Nineteenth Century.*

Krein, D. F., 1978, *The Last Palmerston Government.*

Lamb, A., 2nd edn, 1986 (1960), *British India and Tibet, 1766–1910.*

Lambert, S., 1967, Review article of the re-issue of *A Century of British Blue Books*, *Historical Journal*, X (1967), 125–31. A modern criticism.

Lane-Poole, S., 1888, *Life of Stratford Canning* (2 vols).

Langer, W. L., 1950 (1931), *Alliances and Alignments.*

Langer, W. L., 1951 (1935), *Diplomacy of Imperialism.*

Longford, Lady, 1969; 1972, *Wellington*, vol. 1, *The Years of the Sword*; vol. 2, *Pillar of State.*

Louis, W. R., 1966, 'Sir Percy Anderson's grand African strategy, 1883–1896', *English Historical Review*, LXXXI (1966), 292–314.

Lowe, C. J., 1967, *The Reluctant Imperialists* (2 vols).

McIntyre, W. D., 1967, *The Imperial Frontier in the Tropics 1865–1875.*

Mackenzie, J. M., 1984, *Propaganda and Empire: the Manipulation of British Public Opinion, 1880–1960.*

Mackenzie, J. M. (ed.), 1986, *Imperialism and Popular Culture.*

Mackesy, Piers, 1957, *The War in the Mediterranean, 1803–1810.*

Mackesy, Piers, 1974, *Statesmen at War: the Strategy of Overthrow, 1798–1799.*

Mackesy, Piers, 1984, *War without Victory: the Downfall of Pitt, 1799–1802.*

McKnight, T., 1855, [publ. anonymously] *Thirty Years of Foreign Policy.*

Magnus, P., 1963, *Gladstone.*

Malmesbury, Earl of, 1885, *Memoirs of an Ex-Minister.*

Mansergh, N., 1949, *The Coming of the First World War.*

Marlowe, J., 1971, *Perfidious Albion: the Origins of Anglo-French Rivalry in the Levant.*

Marshall, P., 1964, 'The first and second British empires: a question of demarcation', *History*, XLIX (1964), 13–23.

Martel, G., 1986, *Imperial Diplomacy: Rosebery and the Failure of Foreign Policy.*

Martin, B. Kingsley, rev. ed. 1963 (1924), *The Triumph of Lord Palmerston: a Study of Public Opinion in England before the Crimean War.*

Matthew, H. C. G., 1973, *The Liberal Imperialists.*

Maxwell, Sir Herbert, 1913, *The Life and Letters of George William Frederick, Fourth Earl of Clarendon* (2 vols).

Mayer, A. J., 1969, 'Internal causes and purposes of war in Europe, 1870–1956: a research assignment', *Journal of Modern History*, XLI (1969), 291–303.

Medlicott, W. N., 1938, *The Congress of Berlin and after.*

Medlicott, W. N., 1969 (1956), *Bismarck, Gladstone and the Concert of Europe.*

Middleton, C. R., 1977, *The Administration of British Foreign Policy, 1782–1846.*

Mitchell, Harvey, 1965, *The Underground War with Revolutionary France, 1784–1800.*

Monger, G. W., 1963, *The End of Isolation: British Foreign Policy, 1900–1907.*

Monypenny, W. F., Buckle, G. E., 1910–20, *The Life of Benjamin Disraeli, Earl of Beaconsfield* (6 vols).

Morley, John, 1881, *Life of Richard Cobden.*

Morley, John, 1903, *Life of Gladstone* (3 vols).

Morris, A. J. A., 1972, *Radicalism against War.*

Morris, A. J. A., 1984, *The Scaremongers: the Advocacy of War and Rearmament, 1896–1914.*

Morris, D. R., 1966, *The Washing of the Spears.*

Mosse, W. E., 1958, *The European Powers and the German Question 1848–1871.*

Mosse, W. E., 1963, *The Rise and Fall of the Crimean System, 1855–1871.*

Newbury, C. W., 1962, 'Victorians, republicans and the partition of Africa', *Journal of African History*, iii, 493–501.

Nichols, Irby C., 1971., *The European Pentarchy and the Congress of Verona, 1822.*

Nicolson, H., 1961 (1946), *The Congress of Vienna: a Study in Allied Unity, 1812–1822.*

Nicolson, H., 3rd edn, 1954, *Diplomacy.*

Nish, I. H., 1966, *The Anglo-Japanese Alliance: the Diplomacy of Two Island Empires, 1894–1907.*

O'Gorman, F, 1967, *The Whig Party and the French Revolution.*

Owen, R., Sutcliffe, B. (eds), 1972, *Studies in the Theory of Imperialism.*

Pakenham, Thomas, 1979, *The Boer War.*

Parkinson, C. Northcote (ed.), 1948, *The Trade Winds: a Study of British Overseas Trade during the French Wars 1793–1815.*

Parry, E. Jones, 1934 'Under-secretaries of state for foreign affairs, 1782–1855', *English Historical Review*, XLIX (1934), 304–20.

Parry, E. Jones, 1936, *The Spanish Marriages.*

Perkins, Bradford, 1964, *Castlereagh and Adams: England and the United States.*

Perkins, Bradford, 1968, *The Great Rapprochement: England and the United States, 1895–1914.*

Platt, D. C. M., 1968, *Finance, Trade and Politics in British Foreign Policy, 1815–1914.*

Porter, Bernard, 2nd edn, 1984 (1975), *The Lion's Share: a Short History of British Imperialism, 1850–1980.*

Prest, J., 1972, *Lord John Russell.*

Price, R., 1972, *An Imperial War and the British Working Class.*

Puryear, V. J., 1931, *England, Russia and the Straits Question.*

Puryear, V. J., 1935, *International Economics and Diplomacy in the Near East, 1834–53.*

Reese, T. R., 1968, *History of the Royal Commonwealth Society.*

Remak, J., 1971, '1914 – the third Balkan War: origins reconsidered', *Journal of Modern History*, 41 (1971).

Renier, G. J., 1930, *Great Britain and the Establishment of the Kingdom of the Netherlands, 1813–1815: a Study in British Foreign Policy.*

Rich, N., 1985, *Why the Crimean War? A Cautionary Tale.*

Ridley, Jasper, 1970, *Lord Palmerston.*

Robbins, K., 1971, *Sir Edward Grey.*

Robbins, K., 1979, *John Bright.*

Robinson, R. Gallagher, J., 1953, 'The imperialism of free trade', *Economic History Review*, 2nd ser., VI (1953), 1–15.

Robinson, R. Gallagher, J., 2nd edn, 1981, (1961) *Africa and the Victorians: the Official Mind of Imperialism.*

Röhl, J. C. G., 1973, *1914: Delusion or Design?*

Röhl, J. C. G., (ed.), 1982, *Kaiser Wilhelm II: New Interpretations.*

Rolo, P. J. V., 1965, *George Canning: Three Biographical Studies.*

Rose, J. Holland, 1911, *William Pitt and the Great War.*

Russell, J., (Earl), 1859–66, *Memorials and Correspondence of C. J. Fox* (3 vols).

St Clair, William, 1972, *That Greece Might Still be Free.*

Sanderson, G. N., 1965, *England, Europe and the Upper Nile, 1882–1899.*

Schroeder, Paul W., 1972, 'World War I as Galloping Gertie: a Reply to Joachim Remak', *Journal of Modern History*, 44 (1922), 319–45.

Semmel, B., 1986, *Liberalism and Naval Strategy: Ideology, Interest and Sea Power during the Pax Britannica.*

Seton-Watson, R. W., 1935, *Disraeli, Gladstone and the Eastern Question.*

Seton-Watson, R. W., 1945, *Britain in Europe, 1789–1914.*

Shannon, R. T., 1975 (1963), *Gladstone and the Bulgarian Agitation.*

Shannon, R. T., 1976, *The Crisis of Imperialism, 1865–1915.*

Shannon, R. T., 1982, *Gladstone.*

Sherwig, J. M., 1969, *Guineas and Gunpowder: British Foreign Aid in the Wars with France 1793–1815.*

Smith, Paul, (ed.), 1972, *Lord Salisbury on Politics.*

Southgate, Donald, 1966, *'The Most English Minister ...': the Policies and Politics of Palmerston.*

Sproxton, C., 1919, *Palmerston and the Hungarian Revolution.*

Stansky, P., 1964, *Ambitions and Strategies: the Struggle for the Leadership of the Liberal Party in the 1890s.*

Steefel, L., 1932, *The Schleswig-Holstein Question.*

Steiner, Z., 1963, 'The last years of the old Foreign Office 1898–1905', *Historical Journal*, VI (1963), 27–36.

Steiner, Z., 1965, 'Grey, Hardinge and the Foreign Office, 1906–1910', *Historical Journal*, X (1965), 59–90.

Steiner, Z., 1969, *The Foreign Office and Foreign Policy, 1895–1914.*

Steiner, Z., 1977, *Britain and the Origins of the First World War.*

Stembridge, S. R., 1965, 'Disraeli and the millstones', *Journal of British Studies*, V (1965), 122–39.

Stengers, J., 1962, 'L'impérialisme colonial de la fin du XIX siècle: mythe ou réalité?' *Journal of African History*, iii, 469–91.

Swartz, M., 1985, *The Politics of British Foreign Policy in the Era of Disraeli and Gladstone.*

Taylor, A. J. P., 1934, *The Italian Problem in European Diplomacy, 1847–1849.*

Taylor, A. J. P., 1954, *The Struggle for the Mastery in Europe.*

Taylor, A. J. P., 1957, *The Trouble Makers: Dissent over Foreign Policy, 1792–1939.*

Temperley, H. W. V., 1966 (1925), *The Foreign Policy of Canning, 1822–1827: England, the Neo-Holy Alliance and the New World.*

Temperley, H. W. V., 1964 (1936), *England and the Near East: the Crimea.*

Temperley, H. W. V., 1938, 'British secret diplomacy from Canning to Grey', *Cambridge Historical Journal*, VI (1938), 1–32.

Temperley, H. W. V., Penson, L. M., 1966 (1938), *A Century of Diplomatic Blue Books, 1814–1914.*

Temperley, H. W. V., Penson, L. M., 1938, *The Foundations of British Foreign Policy from Pitt (1792) to Salisbury (1902).*

Temperley, H. W. V., 1933, 1934, 'Stratford de Redcliffe and the origins of the Crimean War', *English Historical Review*, XLVIII (1933), 601–21 and XLIX (1934), 265–98.

Thompson, E. P., 1968, *The Making of the English Working Class.*

Thompson, N., 1987, *Wellington after Waterloo.*

Thornton, A. P., 1953, 'Afghanistan in Anglo-Russian Diplomacy, 1869–1873', *Cambridge Historical Journal*, II (1953), 204–18.

Trevelyan, G. M., 1937, *Grey of Falloden.*

Turner, L. C. F., 1970, *Origins of the First World War.*

Watson, J. Steven, 1960, *The Reign of George III.*

Webster, C. K., 1921, *British Diplomacy, 1813–1815.* (Documents)

Webster, C. K., 1925, *The Foreign Policy of Castlereagh, 1815*–1882: Britain and the European Alliance.

Webster, C. K., 1931, *The Foreign Policy of Castlereagh, 1812–1815: Britain and the Reconstruction of Europe.*

Webster, C. K., 1963 (1934), *The Congress of Vienna, 1814–1815.*

Webster, C. K., 1944, *Britain and the Independence of Latin America, 1812–1830.*

Webster, C. K., 1951, *The Foreign Policy of Palmerston, 1830–1841* (2 vols).

Webster, C. K., 1961, *The Art and Practice of Diplomacy.*

Wehler, H.-U., 1969, *Bismarck und der Imperialismus.*

Wehler, H.-U., 1985, *The German Empire, 1871–1918.*

Wells, Roger, 1983, *Insurrection: the British Experience, 1795–1803.*

Williamson, S. R., 1969, *The Politics of Grand Strategy: Britain and France Prepare for War, 1904–1914.*

Wilson, K. M., 1985, *The Policy of Entente: the Determination of British Foreign Policy, 1904–1914.*

Wilson, K. M., 1987, *Empire and Continent: Studies in British Foreign Policy from the 1880s to the First World War.*

Wilson, K. M. (ed.), 1987, *British Foreign Secretaries and Foreign Policy from the Crimean War to the First World War.*

Woodward, E. L., 1938, *The Age of Reform, 1815–1870.*

MAPS

Map 1 Europe in the late eighteenth century

Map 2 Europe under Napoleon

Legend:
- France at the end of 1802
- Acquisitions 1803–05
- Acquisitions 1805–10
- Kingdom of Italy, directly ruled by Napoleon
- Dependent states
- Boundary of France, 1792
- Boundary of Confederation of the Rhine

0 — 300 mls
0 — 300 km

SWEDEN

BALTIC SEA

BORNHOLM

Copenhagen

Danzig (Rep.)

Tilsit

Friedland

PRUSSIA

Berlin

GRAND DUCHY OF WARSAW

Posen

Warsaw

R. Nieman

SAXONY

SILESIA

R. Oder

R. Elbe

Prague

Cracow

BOHEMIA

GALICIA

Austerlitz ×

AUSTRIA

Wagram ×

R. Danube

Pressburg

Vienna

Pesth

HUNGARY

EMPIRE

TRANSYL-VANIA

R. Pruth

MOLDAVIA

R. Dniester

R. Dnieper

RUSSIA

WALLACHIA

BOSNIA

SERBIA

R. Danube

BLACK SEA

MONTE-NEGRO

ADRIATIC SEA

TURKISH

Bosphorus

Constantinople

NAPLES

ALBANIA

Janina

Dardanelles

ASIA MINOR

EMPIRE

Smyrna

ITALY

IONIAN ISLANDS (French)

MOREA

CRETE

MALTA (British)

SEA

Map 3   Europe in 1815

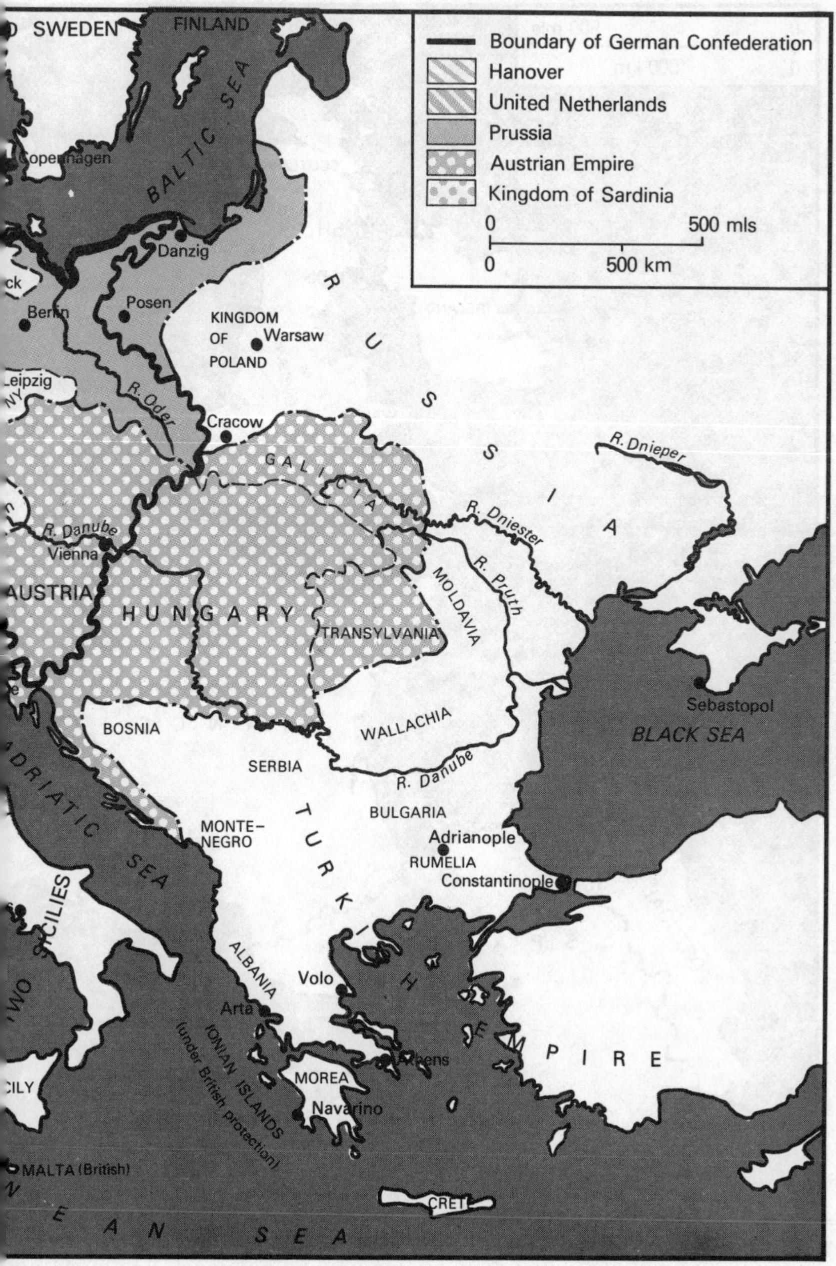
Boundary of German Confederation
Hanover
United Netherlands
Prussia
Austrian Empire
Kingdom of Sardinia
0
500 mls
0
500 km
SWEDEN
FINLAND
BALTIC SEA
Copenhagen
Danzig
Berlin
Posen
KINGDOM OF POLAND
Warsaw
RUSSIA
Leipzig
R. Oder
Cracow
GALICIA
R. Dnieper
R. Dniester
R. Danube
Vienna
AUSTRIA
HUNGARY
TRANSYLVANIA
MOLDAVIA
R. Pruth
Sebastopol
BLACK SEA
BOSNIA
WALLACHIA
SERBIA
R. Danube
BULGARIA
ADRIATIC SEA
MONTE-NEGRO
Adrianople
RUMELIA
Constantinople
TURKISH EMPIRE
ALBANIA
Volo
Arta
IONIAN ISLANDS (under British protection)
Athens
MOREA
Navarino
MALTA (British)
CRETE
SEA

Map 4 Europe in 1871

Map 5 The world in 1878

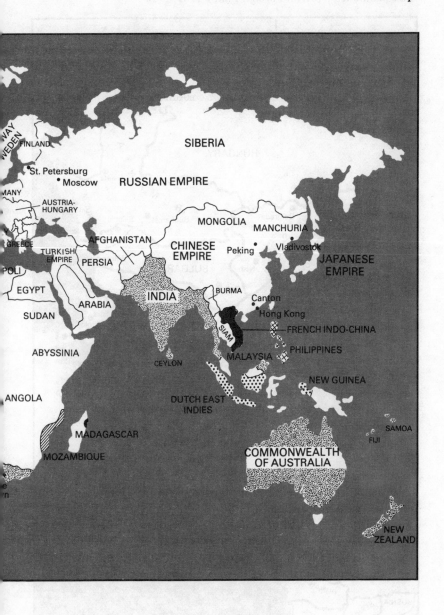

Map 6   The Balkan peninsula, 1800–1914

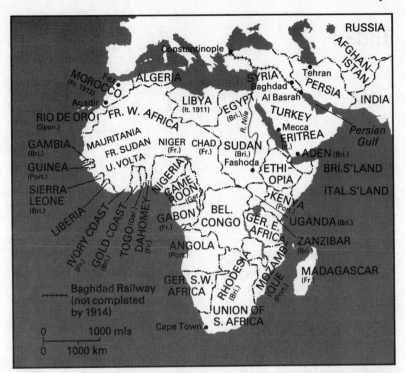

Map 7 Africa and the Middle East in 1914

Index